Advancements in Artificial Intelligence and Machine Learning

Edited by

Asif Khan

Department of Computer Application, Integral University, Kursi Rd, Lucknow, India

Mohammad Kamrul Hasan

Department of Computer Science and Engineering, University Kebangsaan Malaysia (UKM), Selangor, Malaysia

Naushad Varish

Department of Computer Science and Engineering, GITAM University, Hyderabad, India

&

Mohammed Aslam Husain

Department of Electrical Engineering, Rajkiya Engineering College, Ambedkar Nagar, Akbarpur, India

Advancements in Artificial Intelligence and Machine Learning

Editors: Asif Khan, Mohammad Kamrul Hasan, Naushad Varish & Mohammed Aslam Husain

ISBN (Online): 978-981-5322-58-3

ISBN (Print): 978-981-5322-59-0

ISBN (Paperback): 978-981-5322-60-6

need for a court order if at any point you breach any terms of this License Agreement. In no event will any delay or failure by Bentham Science Publishers in enforcing your compliance with this License Agreement constitute a waiver of any of its rights.

3. You acknowledge that you have read this License Agreement, and agree to be bound by its terms and conditions. To the extent that any other terms and conditions presented on any website of Bentham Science Publishers conflict with, or are inconsistent with, the terms and conditions set out in this License Agreement, you acknowledge that the terms and conditions set out in this License Agreement shall prevail.

Bentham Science Publishers Pte. Ltd.
80 Robinson Road #02-00
Singapore 068898
Singapore
Email: subscriptions@benthamscience.net

BENTHAM SCIENCE

CONTENTS

PREFACE

Artificial Intelligence (AI) and Machine learning (ML) are big fields and their algorithms have been employed in various domains for the last decade to solve complex problems. John McCarthy defined AI in 1956 as "AI involves machines that can perform tasks that are characteristics of human intelligence". In this book, the authors cover the basics of AI, and ML and the applicability of these fields to many real-life applications. Arthur Samuel defined Machine Learning (ML) in 1959 as a "Machine Learning: Field of study that gives computers the ability to learn without being explicitly programmed".

The presented book will consist of twelve full chapters which cover the use of AI and ML tools in a number of practical applications such as the analysis of power transformer oil, awareness and prevention of crimes against women, next-gen mechatronics, social media, digital forensics, cyber security, sentiment analysis, image processing, pattern recognition, medical device network system, business sectors, tumor detection, classification, cloud services, automation in drone robotics and human detection systems.

The landscape has shifted significantly since those early days, with the emergence of advanced AI and ML tools and the exponential increase in computing power. These advancements have enabled the analysis of vast quantities of data on a monumental scale. AI now relies heavily on Big Data and Machine Learning to expand its capabilities. Machine learning involves the training of algorithms, enabling them to learn from extensive datasets and enhance their performance over time. Deep Learning, a subset of Machine Learning, draws inspiration from the intricate workings of complex datasets and functionality.

This book gives a brief overview of Machine Learning and lists various ML techniques such as decision tree learning, Hidden Markov Models, reinforcement learning, and Bayesian networks, as well as covering some aspects of Deep Learning and how this relates to AI. It will help you achieve an understanding of some of the advances in the field of AI and Machine Learning, and at the same time, giving you an idea of the specific skills so that you can apply advanced techniques if you wish to work as a Machine Learning expert.

The authors stand behind the assurance that this book will serve as a valuable asset and a wellspring of inspiration for all those captivated by the advancements in AI and ML. As you delve into its pages, you are invited to embark on a journey into the enthralling realm of intelligent solutions. Let us together envision the limitless possibilities that await us with these transformative technologies, and enthusiastically embrace the opportunity to shape the future.

Asif Khan
Department of Computer Application
Integral University, Kursi Rd
Lucknow, India

Mohammad Kamrul Hasan
Department of Computer Science and Engineering
University Kebangsaan Malaysia (UKM)
Selangor, Malaysia

Naushad Varish
Department of Computer Science and Engineering
GITAM University, Hyderabad, India

&

Mohammed Aslam Husain
Department of Electrical Engineering
Rajkiya Engineering College, Ambedkar Nagar
Akbarpur, India

List of Contributors

A.K.M. Ahasan Habib	Faculty of Information Science and Technology, Universiti Kebangsaan Malaysia (UKM), 43600 Bangi, Selangor, Malaysia
A.B. Pradeep Kumar	CSE, GITAM (deemed to be) University, Hyderabad, India
Ahmed F. El Sayed	Department of Mechanical Power Engineering, Zagazig University, Zagazig 2, Egypt
Ahmad Neyaz Khan	Department of Computer Science and Engineering, Koneru Lakshmaiah Education Foundation, Vaddeswaram, Andhra Pradesh 522502, India
Arvind Mewada	SCSET, Bennett University, Greater Noida, U.P., India
Aasim Zafar	Department of Computer Science, Aligarh Muslim University, Aligarh, India
B. Pruthviraj Goud	IT Department, Anurag University, Hyderabad, India
Fadzai Ethel Muchina	Department of Computer Science and Engineering, SRM University, AP-Andhra Pradesh, India
Illa Mahesh Kumar Swamy	Department of IT, Anurag University, Hyderabad, India
Kiran Kumar	Department of Mechanical Engineering, GITAM School of Technology, Hyderabad, India
Khalid Anwar	SCSET, Bennett University, Greater Noida, U.P., India
Kalangi Praveen Kumar	Department of IT, Anurag University, Hyderabad, India
Mohd Faizan	Department of Computer Application, Integral University, Lucknow, India
Mohd Faisal	Department of Computer Application, Integral University, Lucknow, India
Malik Shahzad Ahmad Iqbal	Department of Computer Science & Engineering, Acharya University, Karakul, Uzbekistan
Mohammad Ishrat	Department of Computer Science and Engineering, Koneru Lakshmaiah Education Foundation, Vaddeswaram, Andhra Pradesh 522502, India
Md Akhtar Khan	Department of Aerospace Engineering, GITAM School of Technology, Hyderabad, India
Md Muzakkir Hussain	Department of Computer Science and Engineering, SRM University, AP-Andhra Pradesh, India
Mohammad Kamrul Hasan	Faculty of Information Science and Technology, Universiti Kebangsaan Malaysia (UKM), 43600 Bangi, Selangor, Malaysia
Mohammad Aslam Ansari	Department of Electrical Engineering, I.E.T.M.J.P. Rohilkhand University, Bareilly, India
Mohd. Aquib Ansari	SCSET, Bennett University, Greater Noida, U.P., India
Masood Ahmad	Department of Computer Application, Integral University, Lucknow, India

Mohd Haleem	Department of Computer Science, Era University, Lucknow, Uttar Pradesh 226003, India
Mohd Waris Khan	Department of Computer Application, Integral University, Lucknow, India
Mohammad Islam	Department of Computer Science, Era University, Lucknow, Uttar Pradesh 226003, India
Mohd Khursheed	Department of Electrical Engineering, Integral University, Lucknow, India
M. Sarfraz	Department of Electrical Engineering, AMU, Aligarh, India
Nafees Akhter Farooqui	Department of CSE, Koneru Lakshmaiah Education Foundation, Vaddeswaram, Andhra Pradesh 522502, India
Nadiya Parveen	Department of Computer Application, Faculty of Engineering, Integral University, Lucknow, India
Naresh Tangudu	Department of IT, Aditya Institute of Technology and Management, Tekkali, Andhra Pradesh, India
Niranjan Panigrahi	Parala Maharaja Engineering College, Berhampur, Odisha, India
Prakash Babu Yandrapati	CSE, GITAM (deemed to be) University, Hyderabad, India
P. Nagamani	Department of IT, Anurag University, Hyderabad, India
Priyanka Singh	Department of Computer Science and Engineering, SRM University, AP-Andhra Pradesh, India
Raees Ahmad Khan	Department of Information Technology Babasaheb Bhimrao Ambedkar University, Lucknow, India
Rafeeq Ahmed	Department of CSE, Government Engineering College, West Champaran, Kumarbagh, Bihar, India
Shadab Siddiqui	Department of Computer Science and Engineering, Koneru Lakshmaiah Education Foundation, Hyderabad-500075, Telangana, India
Sarosh Patel	School of Engineering, University of Bridgeport, Bridgeport, CT 06604, USA
S. Vijaykumar	IT Department, Anurag University, Hyderabad, India
Santoshachandra Rao Karanam	Department of CSE, GITAM (deemed to be) University, Hyderabad, India
Shayla Islam	Institute of Computer Science and Digital Innovation, UCSI University, Federal Territory of Kuala Lumpur, Malaysia
Shamsul Haque Ansari	Department of CSE, Koneru Lakshmaiah Education Foundation, Vaddeswaram, Andhra Pradesh 522502, India
Satish Kumar	Department of Computer Application, Integral University, Lucknow, India
T.N.S. Padma	Department of CSE-DS, Sreenidhi Institute of Science and Technology, Hyderabad, India

Vendra Durga Ratna Kumar   Department of Computer Science and Engineering, SRM University, AP-Andhra Pradesh, India

Zulfikar Ali Ansari   Department of Computer Science and Engineering, Koneru Lakshmaiah Education Foundation, Vaddeswaram, Andhra Pradesh 522502, India

CHAPTER 1

Next-Gen Mechatronics: The Role of Artificial Intelligence

Nafees Akhter Farooqui[1], Zulfikar Ali Ansari[1,*], Rafeeq Ahmed[2], Ahmad Neyaz Khan[1], Shadab Siddiqui[3], Mohammad Ishrat[1], Mohd Haleem[4] and **Sarosh Patel[5]**

[1] *Department of Computer Science and Engineering, Koneru Lakshmaiah Education Foundation, Vaddeswaram, Andhra Pradesh 522502, India*

[2] *Department of CSE, Government Engineering College, West Champaran, Kumarbagh, Bihar, India*

[3] *Department of Computer Science and Engineering, Koneru Lakshmaiah Education Foundation, Hyderabad-500075, Telangana, India.*

[4] *Department of Computer Science, Era University, Lucknow, Uttar Pradesh 226003, India*

[5] *School of Engineering, University of Bridgeport, Bridgeport, CT 06604, USA*

Abstract: The incorporation of artificial intelligence (AI) into healthcare systems has demonstrated significant potential to transform patient care, diagnosis, and treatment. Nevertheless, the implementation of artificial intelligence (AI) in the healthcare sector presents difficulties concerning transparency, interpretability, and trust, especially when there are new possibilities for automated decision-making and enhanced efficiency in many different areas, thanks to the combination of artificial intelligence and mechatronics. Automation and robotics are improving as mechatronics integrates AI. Grand View Research expects the global mechatronics and robotics course market to reach $3.21 billion by 2028, expanding 13.7% from 2021 to 2028. This chapter aims to give a general outline of mechatronics-related artificial intelligence (AI), including its applications, advantages, and challenges. The field focuses on developing intelligent machines with the ability to learn, understand data, and react accordingly. Machine learning and deep learning are two forms of artificial intelligence that have enabled robots and autonomous vehicles to detect their environment, traverse complicated scenarios, and make smart decisions using the data they collect. Artificial intelligence (AI) improves mechatronic systems by expanding their capabilities, which boosts their performance, output, and reliability. Nevertheless, ethical considerations and implementation challenges need to be resolved before the full potential of AI in mechatronics can be realized.

---

* **Corresponding author Zulfikar Ali Ansari:** Department of Computer Science and Engineering, Koneru Lakshmaiah Education Foundation, Vaddeswaram, Andhra Pradesh 522502, India; E-mail: zulfi78692@gmail.com

Keywords: Artificial Intelligence, Deep learning, Machine learning, Mechatronic, Robots.

INTRODUCTION

The primary objective of mechatronics is to build intelligent systems through the integration of several disciplines, including electronics, control engineering, computer science, mechanical engineering, and mechanical engineering. It is a young and expanding area that has already made a big splash in many sectors, including robotics, manufacturing, aerospace, healthcare, and automobiles. In the development of cutting-edge technology and novel approaches to difficult challenges, mechatronics is an indispensable tool. The Japanese invented the word "mechatronics" in the late 1960s, fusing the mechanical "mecha" with the electrical "tronics" [1].

It arose in reaction to the growing need for systems and products to incorporate both mechanical and electronic parts. Intelligent machines that are precise, efficient, and adaptable in their work are the goal of mechatronics.

The remarkable adaptability and versatility of mechatronic systems are attributed to their capacity to perceive and react to their surroundings. To accomplish complicated tasks independently or with little to no human involvement, these systems are programmed to communicate with one another, with other machines, and with the real environment. They can detect, analyze, and respond to data because of the sensors, actuators, microcontrollers, and algorithms built into their software.

Everything from basic home appliances and cell phones to advanced industrial robots and driverless cars falls under the umbrella of mechatronics. When it comes to making sure these systems work, are reliable, and are safe to use, mechatronic engineers are the ones to call. The capacity of mechatronics to unite several branches of engineering is one of its main strengths. More efficient, dependable, and cost-effective systems can be created by mechatronics engineers by integrating mechanical, electrical, and computer engineering principles [2]. By bringing together experts from different fields, we can improve performance and functionality by integrating hardware and software components seamlessly.

Innovation and technological progress are propelled by mechatronics. It makes possible the creation of state-of-the-art technology including smart systems, automation, robotics, and artificial intelligence. In addition to enhancing productivity, security, and quality of life, these technologies may cause a revolution in several different industries [3].

Hence, mechatronics is an interdisciplinary discipline that integrates electrical engineering, control engineering, computer science, and mechanical engineering to develop intelligent systems. Because it facilitates the creation of cutting-edge technology and novel solutions, it has grown into an important field in many different sectors. When it comes to developing flexible and versatile systems, mechatronics experts are crucial in combining software and hardware components [4]. I am confident that mechatronics will revolutionize engineering and our daily lives thanks to its capacity to spur innovation and technical progress.

OVERVIEW OF ARTIFICIAL INTELLIGENCE

The field of Artificial Intelligence (AI) is ever-evolving as scientists work tirelessly to develop increasingly intelligent and powerful machines. Over the past few years, advancements in artificial intelligence (AI) have completely altered our daily lives and the way we accomplish collective goals. An extensive review of AI, including its background, current uses, difficulties, and possible future advancements, will be presented in this essay [5]. Artificial intelligence has been around for a long time; in fact, machines that look like humans first appeared in ancient tales and folklore. In contrast, computer scientists began investigating the possibility of developing computers with intelligence comparable to that of humans in the 1950s, marking the beginning of the contemporary era of AI development. The inaugural use of the term "artificial intelligence" was during the 1956 Dartmouth Symposium, when researchers deliberated on developing intelligent robots [6]. Fig. (**1**) shows just an overview of Artificial Intelligence.

Creating expert systems and rule-based systems that could simulate human decision-making was the primary goal of early artificial intelligence research. Unfortunately, data shortages and insufficient computer capacity caused progress to be slow. A lot of data was available and machine learning techniques came out in the 1990s, but AI didn't take off until then [7]. The term "artificial intelligence" describes computers that can learn, reason, and make judgments just like a person. Two main schools of thought exist within the field of artificial intelligence: narrow AI and general AI. Narrow AI is purpose-built to excel in a small subset of general AI activities. However, the goal of general AI is to make machines as smart as humans are in a variety of contexts. The widespread use of AI is revolutionizing many different industries and bringing about significant gains in productivity. The healthcare industry is seeing a surge in the use of artificial intelligence. Medical data can be analysed by machine learning algorithms to aid in drug discovery, forecast patient outcomes, and identify disorders. The use of AI-powered robots in surgery has also been found to increase accuracy and decrease the likelihood of human mistakes [8].

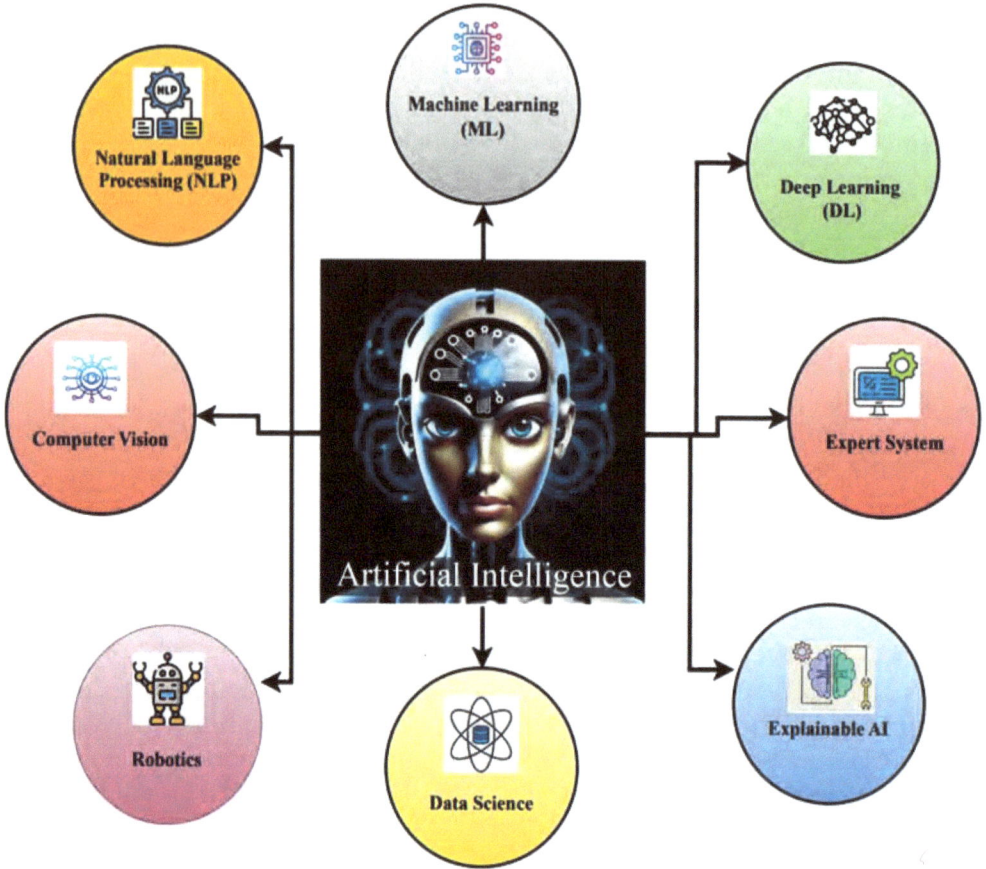

Fig. (1). Overview of artificial intelligence.

Autonomous vehicles are being reshaped by artificial intelligence in the transportation industry. To assess their surroundings, make decisions, and makeovers safely, self-driving cars employ artificial intelligence algorithms. Better and more environmentally friendly transportation may be possible with the help of this technology if it can lessen traffic jams, accidents, and carbon emissions. The banking sector is another area where AI is creating a splash. Financial fraud can be detected, market trends can be predicted, and individualized financial advice can be provided by algorithms that analyse massive volumes of data. Artificial intelligence (AI) chatbots are revolutionizing customer care by offering instant and efficient assistance.

Although AI has tremendous promise, it also raises serious concerns about ethics and presents a number of obstacles. Concerns about job loss are significant. Some worry that AI may make people unemployed since it takes over jobs that people have been doing for a long time. Experts, however, contend that AI will open up new employment options, necessitating that people acquire new skills and adjust to a different way of working. The issue of AI systems' impartiality and prejudice is another obstacle. If the data used to train machine learning algorithms is biased, then those biases will likely be amplified and perpetuated by the algorithms themselves [9]. Questions of equity and prejudice in hiring and loan approval procedures arise from this. The goal of current AI research is to create systems that are open, and comprehensible.

An enormous amount of potential lies in AI's future. Artificial intelligence is being expanded by recent developments in robotics, deep learning, and natural language processing. In the fight against climate change, for more affordable healthcare, and for the end of poverty, artificial intelligence is anticipated to be an indispensable tool. Machines that can do a broad variety of tasks at a human level are the goal of continuing artificial general intelligence (AGI) research. Although artificial general intelligence is still a way off, progress toward it might cause us to reevaluate our understanding of consciousness and the ethics of machines.

Machine Learning (ML)

The goal of machine learning, a branch of artificial intelligence, is to create algorithms that let computers analyse, interpret, and forecast data in order to make judgments. It encompasses methods such as deep learning, reinforcement learning, unsupervised learning, and supervised learning [10].

Deep Learning (DL)

A branch of machine learning, deep learning mimics the way the human brain's neural networks are organised and operate. It entails feeding massive volumes of data into artificial neural networks in order to teach them to spot patterns and make judgements automatically [11].

Natural Language Processing (NLP)

A subfield of Artificial Intelligence, natural language processing (NLP) focuses on how computers and humans communicate using everyday language. Applications like language translation, sentiment analysis, chatbots, and more are made possible by machines' ability to comprehend, interpret, and produce human language [12].

Computer Vision

The area of artificial intelligence known as computer vision focuses on teaching computers to recognize and understand visual data found in the physical world, including photos and films. Image generating, object tracking, object classification, and object identification are all part of it [13].

Robotics

Robotics is the integration of artificial intelligence and engineering to create, construct, and control robots. Artificial intelligence empowers robots to observe their surroundings, make choices, and carry out activities independently or with a certain level of autonomy. Applications encompass a wide spectrum, including industrial automation, household robotics, and autonomous vehicles [14].

Expert Systems

Expert systems are AI programs that are made to make decisions like a person expert in a certain field. These systems look at data, make choices, and offer suggestions or answers by using rules and knowledge bases [15].

Data Science

The goal of data science is to discover new insights and information by integrating several disciplines, such as statistics, machine learning, data visualisation, and domain knowledge. It includes a variety of approaches that try to explain complicated events, forecast their future occurrence, and guide people in making decisions [16].

Explainable AI

The term "explainable artificial intelligence" (XAI) refers to the development of artificial intelligence (AI) systems and algorithms that can provide meaningful explanations for their decisions or outputs. This is especially important in high-stakes or critical applications where transparency and interpretability are necessary [17].

So, to sum up, AI has come a long way from its humble beginnings, and its impact on society is still growing. As a result of AI, many sectors are undergoing radical changes and becoming more efficient, including healthcare, transportation, and finance [18]. To make sure that an AI-powered future is fair and inclusive, though, problems like bias and job loss must be solved. Future AI research and development bode well for this technology, which could alter our daily lives and the way we do business.

APPLICATIONS OF AI IN MECHATRONICS

AI has found extensive applications in mechatronics, enabling the development of intelligent systems that can perform complex tasks with high precision and efficiency as shown in Fig. (**2**). Some of the key applications of AI in mechatronics include:

Robotics

AI-driven robots can execute a diverse array of activities, spanning from industrial automation to healthcare support. They possess the ability to traverse intricate surroundings, identify items, and engage with individuals, rendering them highly advantageous assets across several sectors as shown in (Fig. **3**). The swift progress in AI technology has facilitated the development of robotics powered by AI. Advancements in machine learning algorithms, deep learning networks, and natural language processing techniques have led to increased sophistication in robots' ability to learn, adapt, and engage with their surroundings [19].

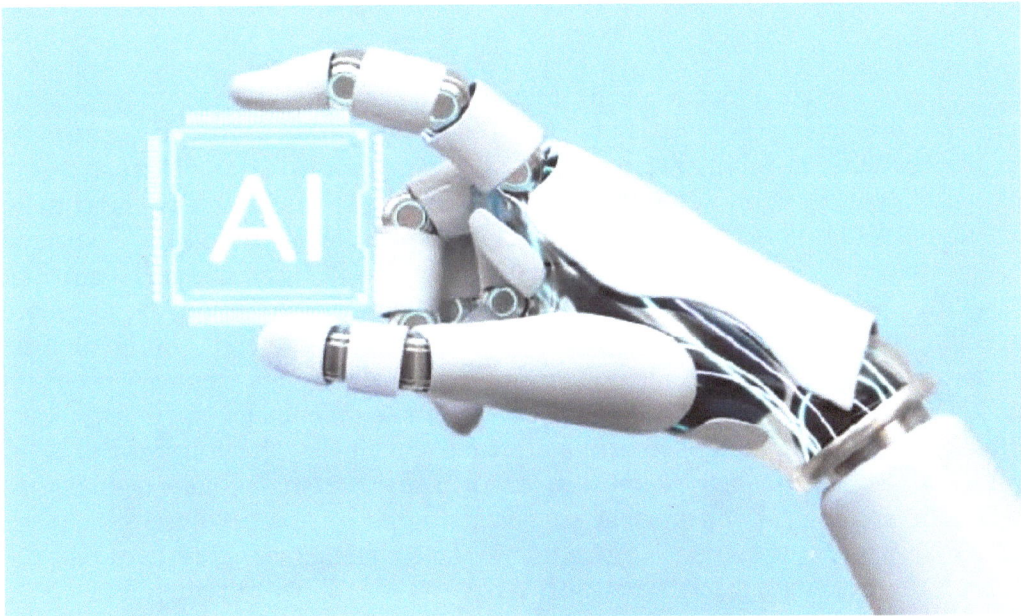

Fig. (2). AI mechatronics (https://www.themechatronicsblog.com).

These technological developments have enabled robots to carry out jobs that were previously considered unattainable. Artificial intelligence (AI) driven robots have been utilized in numerous sectors. Within the industrial industry, robots that are equipped with artificial intelligence algorithms have the capability to carry out repetitive activities with a high level of accuracy and efficiency. This results in a decrease in human errors and an increase in overall productivity [20].

Fig. (3). AI in robotics (https://medium.com/vsinghbisen/ai-in-robotics).

AI-powered robotic devices in healthcare aid surgeons in executing intricate surgery with enhanced precision and less invasiveness. Moreover, artificial intelligence-driven robots are currently employed in the fields of logistics and transportation, agriculture, and even space exploration. The use of artificial intelligence algorithms in robotic systems has numerous advantages. AI-powered robots have the ability to work constantly without experiencing weariness, resulting in enhanced production and efficiency [21]. Additionally, they are capable of carrying out operations in dangerous settings, thereby mitigating the potential harm to human beings. Furthermore, AI algorithms empower robots to acquire knowledge from their past encounters and enhance their efficiency gradually, rendering them increasingly flexible and clever. The utilization of AI in robotics has significant possibilities, but it also necessitates the resolution of problems and ethical concerns. A significant apprehension revolves around the potential ramifications on employment since businesses may witness the substitution of human workers for AI-powered robots. Furthermore, it is imperative to thoroughly analyse ethical ramifications of AI decision-making to guarantee that robots behave in a responsible and secure manner [22].

The prospects for AI-powered robotics in the future are highly encouraging. With the ongoing progress of AI algorithms, robots will further enhance their capabilities and intelligence. Anticipate witnessing robots executing intricate jobs throughout diverse areas, encompassing household chores, eldercare, and education. Nevertheless, it is imperative to guarantee that the advancement of AI-driven robotics is directed by ethical principles and that suitable legislation is implemented to tackle any threats.

Self-driving Vehicles

Self-driving cars, also known as autonomous vehicles, are an innovative form of technology that has the potential to significantly transform our transportation methods. These self-driving vehicles are capable of operating and moving without human intervention due to their integration of advanced sensors, artificial intelligence, and machine-learning algorithms [23]. The emergence of autonomous vehicles has generated substantial interest and controversy among legislators, industry moguls, and the general populace. This essay seeks to examine the diverse facets of autonomous vehicles, encompassing their advantages, obstacles, and future ramifications on society. AI algorithms are essential in facilitating the safe and efficient navigation of autonomous cars. These algorithms analyze sensor data, make instantaneous choices, and guarantee the vehicle's adherence to traffic norms and regulations.

The main advantages of autonomous vehicles lie in their capacity to enhance road safety. Human error is a primary contributor to accidents, and autonomous cars have the capacity to eradicate this variable. Self-driving cars, equipped with sophisticated sensors and algorithms, possess the ability to respond swiftly and make precise judgments, hence minimizing the probability of accidents [24]. In addition, autonomous vehicles have the capability to establish communication among themselves, facilitating synchronized movements and reducing the likelihood of accidents [25]. Autonomous vehicles offer a notable benefit in terms of enhanced mobility and accessibility. Autonomous vehicles offer transportation alternatives for persons who lack the ability to operate a vehicle independently, such as the elderly or those with disabilities. Furthermore, self-driving vehicles possess the capability to enhance traffic movement and alleviate congestion by effectively exchanging information and collaborating with one another to minimize delays and maximize effectiveness. Moreover, self-driving vehicles possess the capacity to diminish fuel consumption and pollutants. Self-driving cars possess the capability to optimize routes and driving patterns, so minimizing superfluous idling and mitigating traffic congestion. Consequently, this leads to less fuel consumption and emissions. This can aid in global endeavors to alleviate climate change and enhance air quality.

Given the technology constraints and dependability issues of autonomous vehicles, it is imperative to address several obstacles and concerns. Notwithstanding notable progress, autonomous cars remain susceptible to errors and malfunctions. Securing the safety and dependability of self-driving vehicles is vital in order to establish public confidence and approval. Another issue of worry is the potential effect on employment. The emergence of autonomous vehicles presents a potential risk of job displacement for persons employed in the transportation sector, including truck drivers and taxi drivers. It is imperative to take into account the social and economic ramifications of this technological transition and formulate solutions to alleviate any adverse effects. Moreover, driverless vehicles raise ethical and legal concerns. Who should bear liability in the event of an accident involving an autonomous vehicle? Assessing responsibility and creating legal structures to tackle moral quandaries is an intricate undertaking that necessitates meticulous deliberation and cooperation among policymakers, industry participants, and legal scholars.

Smart Manufacturing

The manufacturing sector has experienced a substantial overhaul in recent years because of technological improvements. An example of such a revolution is the rise of smart manufacturing, which combines advanced technology to enhance production processes and increase overall efficiency. The integration of automation, data analytics, and artificial intelligence has brought about a significant transformation in traditional manufacturing, known as smart manufacturing [26]. Smart manufacturing encompasses multiple facets, including its advantages, difficulties, and potential ramifications for the future of the manufacturing sector. The integration of AI technology into mechatronic systems has revolutionized conventional manufacturing procedures by facilitating proactive maintenance, enhancing production planning, and elevating the standards of quality control.

Smart manufacturing is a transformative change in the manufacturing sector that utilizes cutting-edge technologies to enhance production processes and increase overall efficiency. The amalgamation of automation, data analytics, IoT, and AI holds the capacity to transform conventional production techniques and yield a multitude of advantages, such as heightened efficiency, improved quality control, cost reduction, adaptability, and enhanced safety [27]. Nevertheless, to fully exploit the possibilities of smart manufacturing, it is imperative to tackle obstacles such as the upfront capital required, the shift in workforce, the safeguarding of data, and the compatibility between different systems. The future of smart manufacturing appears hopeful due to ongoing technological breakthroughs, which will enhance efficiency and competitiveness in the field of manufacturing.

Healthcare

The implementation of mechatronics has led to tremendous progress in healthcare in recent years. Healthcare services and advancements have been radically altered by mechatronics. Intelligent medical technologies, such as prosthetic limbs, and robotic surgical systems, have been made possible by AI, which has completely changed the healthcare industry. Better patient outcomes are the result of these gadgets' ability to increase the accuracy and efficiency of medical processes. Modern surgery has been revolutionized by robotic surgical technologies like the da Vinci Surgical System. Surgeons can use these technologies with more accuracy, control, and dexterity, which leads to less invasive procedures, faster recoveries, and better patient outcomes. Not only have surgical techniques been enhanced with the integration of mechatronics, but the spectrum of minimally invasive operations has also been broadened [28].

Remote monitoring systems and telemedicine have both benefited greatly from mechatronics. By combining sensors, actuators, and communication technology, medical personnel may track patients' vital signs from afar, gather data, and give immediate feedback. Early diagnosis of health problems, prevention of complications, and reduction in hospitalizations have all resulted from this, in addition to better access to healthcare services, particularly in distant locations. The advancement of prosthetics and rehabilitation devices is an area where mechatronics has played a crucial role. The use of prosthetic limbs that are fitted with actuators and sensors enables amputees to restore their mobility and carry out intricate activities. Additionally, exoskeletons and other mechatronic rehabilitation devices aid patients in recovering motor capabilities. People with impairments now have a lot better quality of life thanks to these innovations.

One area where mechatronics has been quite useful is medical imaging. Mechatronic devices are crucial to advanced imaging methods like ultrasound, CT, and MRI because they provide precise and high-resolution images [29]. Medical picture interpretation and abnormality detection are both improved by computer-aided diagnosis systems, which have their roots in mechatronics. The field of mechatronics has undoubtedly improved healthcare, but it still faces a variety of obstacles. We must overcome obstacles such as the exorbitant price of mechatronic systems, the lack of availability in underdeveloped nations, and worries about patient confidentiality and safety. Further promising in enhancing healthcare outcomes is the merging of mechatronics with artificial intelligence and machine learning.

With mechatronics, the healthcare industry has enormous potential for the future. Some of the fascinating future possibilities include the creation of autonomous decision-making intelligent surgical robots, the improvement of wearable mechatronic devices for continuous health monitoring, and the combination of nanotechnology and mechatronics for targeted drug delivery. In addition, mechatronics has the potential to automate hospital logistics and build smart healthcare facilities, both of which would enhance healthcare infrastructure.

With its revolutionary impact on surgical operations, rehabilitation, telemedicine, and medical imaging, AI-based Mechatronics has become a major player in the healthcare industry. As technology continues to improve and new opportunities arise, mechatronics will play an increasingly important role in healthcare delivery in the years to come, providing novel approaches to long-standing medical problems. A better and healthier future for everyone depends on healthcare providers, engineers, and lawmakers working together and investing in mechatronic system research and deployment.

CHALLENGES IN AI-MECHATRONICS INTEGRATION

The creation of sophisticated robotic systems that are capable of carrying out difficult tasks has been made possible by the fusion of artificial intelligence (AI) and mechatronics, which has transformed a number of industries [30]. However, having accessibility using diverse and high-quality datasets is critical to the successful application of AI in mechatronics. It examines the difficulties in obtaining data for AI-mechatronics integration and talks about possible ways to get beyond these obstacles. Despite the significant advancements in AI and mechatronics, there are several challenges that researchers and engineers face when integrating AI into mechatronic systems as shown in Fig. (4). Some of these challenges include:

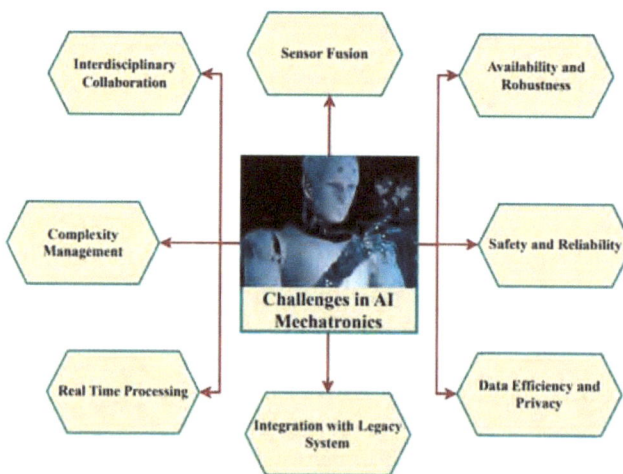

Fig. (4). Challenges in AI Mechatronics.

Multidisciplinary Coordination

The integration of AI with mechatronics necessitates cooperation between specialists in computer science, mechanical engineering, electrical engineering, and artificial intelligence [31]. It can be difficult to close the knowledge gap across various fields and promote productive teamwork.

Handling Complexity

Control systems, actuators, sensors, and mechanical parts make mechatronic systems intrinsically complex. The integration of AI introduces an additional level of complexity, necessitating the use of advanced algorithms for perception, control, and decision-making [32]. It is quite difficult to manage this complexity while maintaining the efficiency, safety, and dependability of the system.

Real-time Processing

For prompt decision-making and control, real-time processing is essential in many mechatronic applications, including robotics and autonomous cars [33]. Deep learning models, which are AI algorithms, can be computationally demanding, making real-time implementation on embedded devices with limited resources difficult.

Sensor Fusion

To sense their surroundings and obtain input for control, mechatronic systems use a variety of sensors, including encoders, cameras, LiDAR, and ultrasonic sensors [34]. It can be difficult to integrate data from several sensors and combine them to produce accurate and trustworthy information, particularly in unpredictable and dynamic environments.

Robustness and Adaptability

Mechatronic systems frequently work in a variety of dynamic contexts with unpredictable or hostile conditions [35]. To guarantee dependable performance in real-world scenarios, artificial intelligence systems must be flexible and resilient to changes in the surroundings, sensor noise, disturbances, and uncertainties.

Safety and Reliability

To avoid mishaps and injuries, safety-critical mechatronic systems, such as industrial robots and driverless cars, must always function properly. Additional safety problems that arise from integrating AI include the dependability of AI decision-making, resilience to hostile attacks, and capacity to deal with unforeseen circumstances [36].

Data Efficiency and Privacy

A significant amount of labelled data must be obtained for artificial intelligence algorithms to be trained. This can be expensive and time-consuming, particularly for mechatronic applications that include physical systems [37]. Furthermore, it is essential to maintain data security and privacy when gathering and utilizing sensor data, especially for applications that involve private or sensitive data.

Integration with Legacy Systems

AI integration was not a primary consideration in the design of many current mechatronic systems. It can be difficult to retrofit AI capabilities into historical systems while preserving reliability, performance, and reliability; this may call for major improvements or alterations [38].

Data Availability

The absence of an extensive and varied dataset is one of the main obstacles to AI-mechatronics integration. It is essential to have access to massive amounts of data that faithfully portray the real-world situations in which artificial intelligence algorithms and robotic systems are intended to function to train them [39]. Privacy issues, private data, and restricted access to certain locations are just a few of the reasons why collecting such datasets might be difficult. Verifying the accuracy and trustworthiness of the data that is accessible is another formidable obstacle. Mechatronic systems aren't as good as they could be when AI models are based on biased or partial datasets. If we want our data to be a true reflection of the world as it actually is, we need to make sure that our data collection techniques are foolproof. Furthermore, in order to accommodate ever-changing situations and settings, the data should be updated on a frequent basis. Integrating AI with mechatronics is difficult because of data privacy and security issues. When dealing with private or proprietary information, the collection and exchange of massive amounts of sensitive data might give rise to ethical and legal questions [40]. Gaining public trust and complying with legislation requires comprehensive security measures and the assurance of data privacy. Finding a happy medium between data availability and data privacy, however, isn't always easy.

Working together, businesses, universities, and governments can conquer the obstacles posed by restricted dataset access. The development of large and varied datasets suitable for training artificial intelligence models for mechatronic systems can be facilitated by the promotion of data-sharing programs and the formation of partnerships.

The available data can be made more diverse by artificially increasing the dataset using techniques like picture scaling, rotation, or noise addition. In addition, a wider variety of training data can be produced using synthetic data creation methods to build simulated datasets that reflect real-world situations. One way to make integration easier is to standardize data annotation techniques. To make sure that diverse datasets are consistent and comparable, it is helpful to develop standards and best practices for data annotation and labelling. As a result, AI models in mechatronic systems would be able to make better use of combined datasets from various sources.

Data anonymization and differential privacy are two privacy-preserving approaches that can help with data security and privacy problems. To advance AI and mechatronics integration without jeopardizing privacy, it is necessary to secure private or personal information while permitting access to pertinent data.

An easier way to harmonize and integrate disparate datasets is to establish data integration platforms and tools. To alleviate compatibility issues related to AI-mechatronics integration, these platforms can supply standardized protocols and interfaces that allow for the seamless integration of data from various sources.

For AI systems to learn and make decisions, they need copious quantities of high-quality data. It can be difficult to obtain such information, particularly in fields wherein data collecting is few or costly [41].

Safety and Reliability

The design of AI-powered mechatronic devices needs to prioritize dependability and safety. The successful operation of these systems without endangering people or the environment is an important concern. Lack of explainability in AI algorithms is a major obstacle to AI-mechatronics integration. Understanding and explaining how AI systems make decisions gets more challenging as their complexity increases. People are worried about the security and dependability of these systems because of how opaque they are. Having a solid grasp of decision-making processes is vital in mission-critical applications like autonomous vehicles or medical devices.

Machine learning algorithms that can learn and adapt to new environments are commonly used in AI-mechatronics integration [42]. Uncertainty is a byproduct of adaptation, which is otherwise a desirable trait. Artificial intelligence systems pose a threat to human safety because their behavior can become unpredictable in the face of new situations. The enormous difficulty lies in making sure these systems can deal with unexpected situations without endangering safety.

New dangers to cybersecurity are introduced by the integration of mechatronics and AI. Cyberattacks are becoming more common as these systems are becoming increasingly linked. Apocalyptic outcomes are possible if bad actors take advantage of flaws in AI algorithms or mechatronic parts. Strong cybersecurity measures are necessary to guarantee the dependability and security of AI-mechatronics systems [43]. Any problem or breakdown in one part of the system might affect the whole, making it difficult to coordinate the interactions between the many subsystems. Comprehensive testing, fault tolerance measures, and redundancy are necessary to guarantee the dependability of such intricate systems.

Data is crucial for AI systems to learn from their experiences and make judgments. Nevertheless, trustworthy performance relies on data that is both high-quality and intact. Artificial intelligence (AI) mechatronics systems are vulnerable to biased or inaccurate data since it can cause them to make incorrect conclusions. To address this difficulty, it is crucial to have strong data validation and verification procedures in place [21].

There is a risk of reliability difficulties due to aging or degradation of mechatronic components over time. Though it adds another layer of complexity, AI integration can aid in detecting and compensating for such degradation. To guarantee the long-term dependability of AI-mechatronics systems, it is critical to develop prediction maintenance procedures that use artificial intelligence (AI) algorithms to track and fix part deterioration.

Ethical Considerations

There must be extensive education and dialogue on the ethical concerns and difficulties of integrating AI and mechatronics. To make sure these technologies are built and used in a way that doesn't conflict with society's ideals, people need to be aware of them and get involved. To encourage well-informed debates and public participation in decision-making, programs of education and communication should be launched [44]. The integration of AI with mechatronics is happening at a faster rate than there have been thorough ethical frameworks developed. The specific ethical problems presented by these systems necessitate the formulation of rules and regulations. Building strong frameworks requires teamwork amongst professionals in fields as diverse as ethics, law, and technology. While AI-mechatronics systems are built to make judgments on their own, it often takes judgment from humans to make ethical decisions [45]. It is quite challenging to develop AI systems that can take ethical factors into account and conform to community values. Integrating the ability of AI systems to make ethical decisions ought to be the primary goal of research and development initiatives. Ethical concerns around the usage of AI in mechatronics are growing in significance as the technology spreads throughout the industry. Responsible and ethical deployment of AI in mechatronics requires addressing issues like privacy, bias, and accountability.

FUTURE PROSPECTS

Future developments in mechatronics could be greatly aided by the incorporation of AI. Industrial automation is anticipated to be significantly impacted by AI-based mechatronics. Mechatronic systems that use AI algorithms enable machines to learn from and adapt to their surroundings, hence maximizing their efficiency and performance. As a result, there will be more output, less downtime, and better quality control. AI-based mechatronics can also facilitate predictive maintenance, in which devices can anticipate malfunctions and organize maintenance tasks appropriately, limiting unscheduled downtime and cutting expenses for enterprises. Some of the areas that researchers are actively exploring include:

Explainable AI

The goal of explainable AI is to make AI decisions more understandable to humans. This area of artificial intelligence focuses on creating models and methods that can accurately predict outcomes while also providing clear explanations for those outcomes. Artificial intelligence (AI) has the potential to revolutionize many industries by making it easier for people to comprehend and have faith in AI technology.

In artificial intelligence, there are various ways to make things more understandable. Decision trees and rule-based systems are examples of interpretable models that often give explanations or rules for their predictions. These models are more suited to fields where openness is paramount because they are simpler to comprehend and apply.

Another strategy involves developing post-hoc explainability algorithms that can deduce the reasoning behind the judgments made by advanced AI models like deep neural networks [46]. These techniques provide justifications by drawing attention to the salient characteristics or patterns that the AI considered when making its conclusion. Methods that aid in understanding how AI models make decisions include saliency maps, attention processes, and feature importance scores.

Not only does explainable AI help consumers, but it is also crucial for businesses to stay in compliance with regulations. Explainable Artificial Intelligence (XAI) can bring the required openness to industries like healthcare and finance, where actions need to be explainable to regulatory agencies [47]. For example, in the medical field, an AI system that suggests a certain treatment can justify its choice by pointing out the pertinent patient characteristics and scientific literature on which it depended. Because of this openness, medical experts may verify and put their faith in the system's suggestions.

In addition, detecting and reducing biases in AI systems relies heavily on explainability. Inaccurate or biased results may result from biases introduced by the training data or the algorithms themselves. By offering explanations, XAI may aid in identifying these biases and implementing corrective measures, guaranteeing that AI systems are fair and accountable.

To sum up, explainable AI is an important field of study since it seeks to solve the problem of AI systems not being transparent or interpretable. The use of XAI improves responsibility, trust, and compliance with regulations by offering explanations that humans can understand. It is also useful for finding biases and making sure AI decisions are fair. Still, it's not easy to get explainability without sacrificing performance. In order to shape the appropriate and ethical use of AI technology, the discipline of XAI will be crucial as AI evolves further. To be able to foster trust and enable human-AI collaboration, it is essential to develop AI systems that can offer clear justifications for their choices.

Cognitive Mechatronics

AI and cognitive science together could result in mechatronic systems with human-like perception, reasoning, and learning capabilities. Human-machine interactions may become more interactive and intuitive as a result. Systems that use cognitive mechatronics are able to learn from their experiences and modify their behavior as necessary [48]. This skill makes performance optimization and ongoing improvement possible, which results in more productive and successful operations.

A new subject called "cognitive mechatronics" combines the ideas of mechatronics and cognitive science to create intelligent systems that can see, reason, and act in dynamic environments [49]. This multidisciplinary field has enormous potential to transform a number of sectors, including entertainment, industry, healthcare, and transportation.

The integration of cognitive skills into mechatronic systems—robotic systems that combine computer, electrical, and mechanical engineering principles—is known as cognitive mechatronics. These intelligent systems can efficiently interact with humans and other machines, learn from experiences, and adapt to changing surroundings by integrating cognitive abilities like sensing, learning, decision-making, and interaction. Robots with cognitive mechatronics are able to observe and comprehend their environment, make defensible decisions, and work in tandem with human operators to improve production processes [50]. Productivity gains, enhanced worker safety, and better quality control are all possible outcomes of this integration. Autonomous vehicles can be revolutionized by cognitive mechatronics. These vehicles will be able to sense their environment, make decisions based on that information, and interact with pedestrians and other vehicles thanks to the integration of cognitive skills, which will result in safer and more effective transportation networks.

To sum up, cognitive mechatronics is a major development in the robotics and intelligent systems fields. We can create intelligent machines that can perceive, reason, and act in dynamic surroundings by incorporating cognitive capacities into mechatronic systems. Cognitive mechatronics has a wide range of applications, from transportation and entertainment to manufacturing and healthcare. Cognitive mechatronics is a promising topic for future research and innovation because of the possible advantages, which include enhanced efficiency, safety, personalization, and learning.

Swarm Robotics

Swarm robotics is a subfield of robotics that studies how social insects like ants, bees, and termites carry out complicated tasks by coordinating the actions of small robots in a group [51]. The foundational principle is that a group of weakly equipped robots can accomplish more than a single strong robot could on its own. The goal of swarm robotics is to create control systems and algorithms that allow a group of robots to work together more efficiently through improved communication, coordination, and collaboration [52]. Algorithms like these might use ideas from AI, optimization, and even biology.

Multiple robots can be programmed to work together towards a shared objective by using AI algorithms to coordinate their actions. Many areas could be profoundly affected by this, including environmental monitoring and search and rescue activities.

CONCLUSION

Mechatronics has been revolutionized by AI, which has made it possible to create smart systems capable of efficiently and accurately carrying out complicated tasks. Robotics, autonomous vehicles, smart manufacturing, and healthcare have all benefited from mechatronics' incorporation of artificial intelligence. To use AI in mechatronics in a responsible and ethical manner, however, issues including data availability, safety, and ethics must be resolved. Research on cognitive mechatronics, explainable AI, and swarm robots is continuing, which bodes well for the future of AI in mechatronics.

By incorporating AI technologies like neural networks, machine learning, and natural language processing, mechatronic systems can now learn from data, adapt to changing surroundings, and make smart judgments. Thanks to this cooperation, several sectors have achieved new heights, including production, transportation, medicine, and more. Advanced medical robotics, predictive maintenance, and autonomous driving capabilities are just a few examples of how AI-driven mechatronic devices are changing the game in healthcare. Despite the many benefits, mechatronics' effective use of AI has not been without its share of complicated obstacles. It is critical to thoroughly test, validate, and think about ethics while designing AI-driven mechatronic systems to ensure their dependability and safety. Responsible navigation of this emerging landscape requires interdisciplinary collaboration among mechatronics, AI, ethics, and regulation professionals as these systems become more advanced.

REFERENCES

[1]   R. H. Bishop, and M. K. Ramasubramanian, "What is mechatronics", *The Mechatronics Handbook.,* CRC Press, pp. 2012-1229, 2012.

[2]   F. Gauthier, Y. Chinniah, G. Abdul-Nour, S. Jocelyn, B. Aucourt, G. Bordeleau, and A. Ben Mosbah, "Practices and needs of machinery designers and manufacturers in safety of machinery: An exploratory study in the province of Quebec, Canada", *Saf. Sci.,* vol. 133, p. 105011, 2021. [http://dx.doi.org/10.1016/j.ssci.2020.105011]

[3]   A. Adamik, M. Nowicki, and A. Puksas, "Energy Oriented Concepts and Other SMART WORLD Trends as Game Changers of Co-Production—Reality or Future?", *Energies,* vol. 15, no. 11, p. 4112, 2022. [http://dx.doi.org/10.3390/en15114112]

[4]   C. Bordin, A. Håkansson, and S. Mishra, "Smart Energy and power systems modelling: an IoT and Cyber-Physical Systems perspective, in the context of Energy Informatics", *Procedia Comput. Sci.,* vol. 176, pp. 2254-2263, 2020. [http://dx.doi.org/10.1016/j.procs.2020.09.275]

[5]   Z. Jan, "Artificial intelligence for industry 4.0: Systematic review of applications, challenges, and opportunities", *Expert Syst. Appl.,* vol. 216, p. 119456, 2022.

[6]   S.L. Wamba-Taguimdje, S. Fosso Wamba, J.R. Kala Kamdjoug, and C.E. Tchatchouang Wanko, "Influence of artificial intelligence (AI) on firm performance: the business value of AI-based transformation projects", *Bus. Process. Manag. J.,* vol. 26, no. 7, pp. 1893-1924, 2020. [http://dx.doi.org/10.1108/BPMJ-10-2019-0411]

[7]   A. Panesar, *Machine learning and AI for healthcare.* Springer, 2019. [http://dx.doi.org/10.1007/978-1-4842-3799-1]

[8]   M.Y. Shaheen, "Applications of Artificial Intelligence (AI) in healthcare: A review", *ScienceOpen Preprints,* 2021. [http://dx.doi.org/10.14293/S2199-1006.1.SOR-.PPVRY8K.v1]

[9]   N.A. Farooqui, "A study on early prevention and detection of breast cancer using three-machine

learning techniques", *Education (Chula Vista),* vol. 2020, 2020.

[10] J. Alzubi, A. Nayyar, A. Kumar, J. Alzubi, A. Nayyar, and A. Kumar, "Machine Learning from Theory to Algorithms: An Overview", *J. Phys. Conf. Ser.,* vol. 1142, no. 1, p. 012012, 2018. [http://dx.doi.org/10.1088/1742-6596/1142/1/012012]

[11] H. Kim, "Deep Learning", *Artif. Intell.,* vol. 6G, pp. 247-303, 2022. [http://dx.doi.org/10.1007/978-3-030-95041-5_6]

[12] S.C. Fanni, M. Febi, G. Aghakhanyan, and E. Neri, Natural Language Processing. In: Klontzas, M.E., Fanni, S.C., Neri, E. (eds) Introduction to Artificial Intelligence. Imaging Informatics for Healthcare Professionals. Springer, Cham, 2023, pp. 87-99. [http://dx.doi.org/10.1007/978-3-031-25928-9_5]

[13] K. Bayoudh, "A survey on deep multimodal learning for computer vision: advances, trends, applications, and datasets", *The Visual Computer,* vol. 38, no. 8, pp. 2939-2970, 2021. [http://dx.doi.org/10.1007/s00371-021-02166-7]

[14] C. Russo, *Knowledge design and conceptualization in autonomous robotics.* 2024. Available from: https://theses.hal.science/tel-03542455

[15] R.R. Hoffman, *Modeling Human Expertise in Expert Systems,* no. Feb, pp. 29-60, 2014. [http://dx.doi.org/10.4324/9781315806105-5]

[16] I. Martinez, E. Viles, and I.G. Olaizola, "Data Science Methodologies: Current Challenges and Future Approaches", *Big Data Research,* vol. 24, p. 100183, 2021. [http://dx.doi.org/10.1016/j.bdr.2020.100183]

[17] D. Minh, H. X. Wang, Y. F. Li, and T. N. Nguyen, "Explainable artificial intelligence: a comprehensive review", *Artificial Intelligence Review,* vol. 55, no. 5, pp. 3503-3568, 2021. [http://dx.doi.org/10.1007/s10462-021-10088-y]

[18] N.A. Farooqui, R. Mehra, and S.B. Faridi, An Intellectual Analysis of Structural Healthcare Systems in India Using Intelligence-Based Techniques.*Security Implementation in Internet of Medical Things.* CRC Press, 2023, pp. 37-58. [http://dx.doi.org/10.1201/9781003269168-3]

[19] M. Islam, N. Farooqui, M. Haleem, and S.A. Zaidi, "An Efficient Framework For Software Maintenance Cost Estimation Using Genetic Hybrid Algorithm: OOPs Prospective", *International Journal of Computing and Digital Systems,* vol. 14, no. 1, pp. 933-943, 2023. [http://dx.doi.org/10.12785/ijcds/140172]

[20] N.A. Farooqui, A.K. Mishra, and R. Mehra, "Concatenated deep features with modified LSTM for enhanced crop disease classification", *Int. J. Intell. Robot. Appl.,* vol. 3, pp. 510-34, 2022.

[21] M. Zhang, C. Li, Y. Shang, H. Huang, W. Zhu, and Y. Liu, "A task scheduling model integrating micro-breaks for optimisation of job-cycle time in human-robot collaborative assembly cells", *Int. J. Prod. Res.,* vol. 60, no. 15, pp. 4766-4777, 2022. [http://dx.doi.org/10.1080/00207543.2021.1937746]

[22] J.P. Boada, B.R. Maestre, and C.T. Genís, "The ethical issues of social assistive robotics: A critical literature review", *Technol. Soc.,* vol. 67, p. 101726, 2021. [http://dx.doi.org/10.1016/j.techsoc.2021.101726]

[23] W. Khan, M. Ishrat, M. Haleem, A.N. Khan, M.K. Hasan, and N.A. Farooqui, An Extensive Study and Review on Dark Web Threats and Detection Techniques.*Advances in Cyberology and the Advent of the Next-Gen Information Revolution.* IGI Global, 2023, pp. 202-219. [http://dx.doi.org/10.4018/978-1-6684-8133-2.ch011]

[24] B. Woodward, and T. Kliestik, "Intelligent transportation applications, autonomous vehicle perception sensor data, and decision-making self-driving car control algorithms in smart sustainable urban mobility systems", *Contemp. Read. Law Soc. Justice,* vol. 13, no. 2, pp. 51-64, 2021. [http://dx.doi.org/10.22381/CRLSJ13220214]

[25]   M.A. Khoury, and F.A. Hussein, "Efficiency and Safety: The Impact of Autonomous Controls on Transportation", *International Journal of Information and Cybersecurity,* vol. 7, no. 1, pp. 13-39, 2023.

[26]   D.R. Sjödin, V. Parida, M. Leksell, and A. Petrovic, "Smart Factory Implementation and Process Innovation: A Preliminary Maturity Model for Leveraging Digitalization in Manufacturing Moving to smart factories presents specific challenges that can be addressed through a structured approach focused on people, processes, and technologies", *Res. Technol. Manag.,* vol. 61, no. 5, pp. 22-31, 2018.
[http://dx.doi.org/10.1080/08956308.2018.1471277]

[27]   U. Tariq, R. Joy, S-H. Wu, M.A. Mahmood, A.W. Malik, and F. Liou, *A state-of-the-art digital factory integrating digital twin for laser additive and subtractive manufacturing processes.* Rapid Prototyp J, 2023.
[http://dx.doi.org/10.1108/RPJ-03-2023-0113]

[28]   N.A. Farooqui, and R. Mehra, "A Novel Ensemble Machine Learning Models for Classification of Brain Tumors from MRI", *Neuroquantology,* vol. 20, no. 14, pp. 823-828, 2022.

[29]   J. Cornejo, *Anatomical Engineering and 3D printing for surgery and medical devices: International review and future exponential innovations.* vol. Vol. 2022. Biomed Res Int, 2022.

[30]   M. Haleem, M.F. Farooqui, and M. Faisal, "Tackling requirements uncertainty in software projects: a cognitive approach", *International Journal of Cognitive Computing in Engineering,* vol. 2, pp. 180-190, 2021.
[http://dx.doi.org/10.1016/j.ijcce.2021.10.003]

[31]   O.V. Nass, S.S. Bekenova, A.S. Bekenova, and Zh.S. Mutalova, "Combination of mechatronic engineering and artificial intelligence technology", 2023. Available from: http://rep.wkau.kz/handle/123456789/2689

[32]   M. Andronie, G. Lăzăroiu, M. Iatagan, C. Uță, R. Ştefănescu, and M. Cocoşatu, "Artificial Intelligence-Based Decision-Making Algorithms, Internet of Things Sensing Networks, and Deep Learning-Assisted Smart Process Management in Cyber-Physical Production Systems", *Electronics,* vol. 10, no. 20, p. 2497, 2021.
[http://dx.doi.org/10.3390/electronics10202497]

[33]   G. Joshi, and A. Professor, "Real-Time Image Processing and Computer Vision Techniques in Mechatronic Systems", *Mathematical Statistician and Engineering Applications,* vol. 70, no. 1, pp. 401-408, 2021.
[http://dx.doi.org/10.17762/msea.v70i1.2490]

[34]   "Sensors for Mechatronics - Paul P.L. Regtien, Edwin Dertien - Google Books", 2024. Availabe from: https://books.google.co.in/books?hl=en&lr=&id=OX9XDwAAQBAJ&oi=fnd&pg=PP1&dq=To+sens e+their+surroundings+and+obtain+input+for+control,+mechatronic+systems+use+a+variety+of+sens ors,+including+encoders,+cameras,+LiDAR,+and+ultrasonic+sensors&ots=KSEGimBgsO&sig=oEB mOItdWNTDBcveET6S7wBi6sM&redir_esc=y#v=onepage&q&f=false

[35]   M. Schranz, G.A. Di Caro, T. Schmickl, W. Elmenreich, F. Arvin, A. Şekercioğlu, and M. Sende, "Swarm Intelligence and cyber-physical systems: Concepts, challenges and future trends", *Swarm Evol. Comput.,* vol. 60, p. 100762, 2021.
[http://dx.doi.org/10.1016/j.swevo.2020.100762]

[36]   H. He, J. Gray, A. Cangelosi, Q. Meng, T.M. McGinnity, and J. Mehnen, "The Challenges and Opportunities of Artificial Intelligence for Trustworthy Robots and Autonomous Systems", *IRCE 2020 - 2020 3rd International Conference on Intelligent Robotics and Control Engineering,* pp. 68-74, 2020.
[http://dx.doi.org/10.1109/IRCE50905.2020.9199244]

[37]   K. Pietrusewicz, "Metamodelling for Design of Mechatronic and Cyber-Physical Systems", *Applied Sciences,* vol. 9, no. 3, p. 376, 2019.

[http://dx.doi.org/10.3390/app9030376]

[38]   A. Nüßgen, R. Degen, M. Irmer, F. Richter, C. Boström, and M. Ruschitzka, "Leveraging Robust Artificial Intelligence for Mechatronic Product Development—A Literature Review", *Int. J. Intell. Sci.,* vol. 14, no. 1, pp. 1-21, 2024.
[http://dx.doi.org/10.4236/ijis.2024.141001]

[39]   B. Zhao, D. Yang, H.R. Karimi, B. Zhou, S. Feng, and G. Li, "Filter-wrapper combined feature selection and adaboost-weighted broad learning system for transformer fault diagnosis under imbalanced samples", *Neurocomputing,* vol. 560, p. 126803, 2023.
[http://dx.doi.org/10.1016/j.neucom.2023.126803]

[40]   L.G. Guntrum, S. Schwartz, and C. Reuter, "Dual-Use Technologies in the Context of Autonomous Driving: An Empirical Case Study From Germany", *Zeitschrift für Außen- und Sicherheitspolitik,* vol. 16, no. 1, pp. 53-77, 2023.
[http://dx.doi.org/10.1007/s12399-022-00935-3]

[41]   H. Hassani, and E. S. Silva, "The role of ChatGPT in data science: how ai-assisted conversational interfaces are revolutionizing the field", *Big data and cognitive computing,* vol. 7, no. 2, p. 62, 2023.
[http://dx.doi.org/10.3390/bdcc7020062]

[42]   A.F. Vermeulen, *Industrial Machine Learning: Using Artificial Intelligence as a Transformational Disruptor.* Apress, 2019.

[43]   R. Abd Shukor, and W. K. Mooi, "Assessing the Economic Impact of COVID-19 on the Implications of the Internet of Things Adoption on Small and Medium Enterprise Business's Sustainability", *Emerging Technologies for Combatting Pandemics: AI, IoMT, and Analytics,* 2022.
[http://dx.doi.org/10.1201/9781003324447-3]

[44]   L. Edwards, *Understanding public relations: Theory, culture and society.* Understanding Public Relations, 2018, pp. 1-288.
[http://dx.doi.org/10.4135/9781473983571]

[45]   S. Schwartz, L.G. Guntrum, and C. Reuter, "Vision or Threat—Awareness for Dual-Use in the Development of Autonomous Driving", *IEEE Trans. Technol. Soc.,* vol. 3, no. 3, pp. 163-174, 2022.
[http://dx.doi.org/10.1109/TTS.2022.3182310]

[46]   N.A. Farooqui, A.K. Mishra, and R. Mehra, "Automatic crop disease recognition by improved abnormality segmentation along with heuristic-based concatenated deep learning model", *Intell. Decision Technol.,* vol. 16, no. 2, pp. 407-429, 2022.
[http://dx.doi.org/10.3233/IDT-210182]

[47]   P. Weber, K.V. Carl, and O. Hinz, *Applications of Explainable Artificial Intelligence in Finance—a systematic review of Finance, Information Systems, and Computer Science literature.* Management Review Quarterly, 2023, pp. 1-41.

[48]   J.P.A. Joel, R.J.S. Raj, and N. Muthukumaran, "Cognitive and Cybernetics based Human Adaptive Mechatronics System in Gait Rehabilitation Therapy", *2021 Third International Conference on Intelligent Communication Technologies and Virtual Mobile Networks (ICICV),* IEEE, pp. 516-521, 2021.
[http://dx.doi.org/10.1109/ICICV50876.2021.9388423]

[49]   A. Cangelosi, and M. Asada, *Cognitive robotics.* MIT Press, 2022.
[http://dx.doi.org/10.7551/mitpress/13780.001.0001]

[50]   H. Oliff, Y. Liu, M. Kumar, and M. Williams, "A framework of integrating knowledge of human factors to facilitate HMI and collaboration in intelligent manufacturing", *Procedia CIRP,* vol. 72, pp. 135-140, 2018.
[http://dx.doi.org/10.1016/j.procir.2018.03.047]

[51]   E. Bonabeau, "Swarm intelligence", In: *A Primer on Multiple Intelligences*, 2003, p. 211.

[52]   S.J. Chung, A.A. Paranjape, P. Dames, S. Shen, and V. Kumar, "A survey on aerial swarm robotics", *IEEE Trans. Robot.,* vol. 34, no. 4, pp. 837-855, 2018.
[http://dx.doi.org/10.1109/TRO.2018.2857475]

CHAPTER 2

Advancements and Applications of Artificial Intelligence and Machine Learning: A Comprehensive Review

Santoshachandra Rao Karanam[1,*], **A.B. Pradeep Kumar**[1], **Prakash Babu Yandrapati**[1], **B. Pruthviraj Goud**[2], **S. Vijaykumar**[2] and **Illa Mahesh Kumar Swamy**[2]

[1] *CSE, GITAM (deemed to be) University, Hyderabad, India*

[2] *IT Department, Anurag University, Hyderabad, India*

Abstract: Rapid advances in machine learning, deep learning, and AI are changing business and society. The history of these technologies reveals their transformative impact on a variety of industries. Convolutional, Deep, and Recurrent Neural Network studies show their evolution. Deep learning has facilitated the development of novel applications in several industries and stimulated technological progress. Reinforcement learning, a core component of artificial intelligence, has made notable progress, particularly in the realm of autonomous systems. This paper discusses the latest algorithms and their applications, stressing reinforcement learning's impact on robotics and automated decision-making. The study of natural language processing is crucial. Through language modelling, sentiment analysis, and translation, it shows banking, healthcare, and customer service applications. After that, the paper examines real-world AI applications. These technologies help doctors detect, treat, and forecast medical disorders. Fraud detection, risk management, and algorithmic trading benefit financial institutions. Industry 4.0 combines AI-driven autonomous vehicle navigation, control, and ethical decision-making with intelligent manufacturing and predictive maintenance.

KEYWORDS: Artificial intelligence (AI), Computer vision(CV), Deep learning(DL), Industry 4.0, Machine learning (ML), Natural language processing (NLP), Reinforcement learning.

INTRODUCTION

AI and ML are powerful technologies that can profoundly change several aspects of human existence. In recent decades, notable progress in AI and ML algorithms,

* **Corresponding author Santoshachandra Rao Karanam:** CSE, GITAM (deemed to be) University, Hyderabad, India; E-mail: kschandra.rao@gmail.com

Asif Khan, Mohammad Kamrul Hasan, Naushad Varish & Mohammed Aslam Husain (Eds.)

together with the rapid expansion in computer power and data accessibility, have driven these disciplines into widespread use. This review article attempts to examine the development, fundamental principles, current progress, and many uses of AI and ML [1, 2]. It seeks to provide a deeper understanding of their influence, difficulties, and prospects.

BACKGROUND

The notion of artificial intelligence originated in the mid-20th century, aiming to develop robots that can replicate human intellect. Initial AI systems were based on a set of rules and had limited skills, but they provided the groundwork for further investigation and advancement. Machine learning emerged in the late 20th century, representing a significant change in approach. It enabled machines to learn from data and improve performance without programming.

OBJECTIVES

This article's primary goal is to provide a comprehensive analysis of the developments and applications of ML and AI technology. This paper examines the history of AI, key ideas, and new findings in an effort to provide light on the basic principles behind the rapidly progressing fields of ML and AI, particularly deep learning. Additionally, it looks at the many applications of AI and ML in various industries, including healthcare, entertainment, banking, transportation and more [3, 4].

STRUCTURE OF THE PAPER

The paper is divided into many parts, each dedicated to various areas of AI and ML. The "Evolution of Artificial Intelligence" section offers a chronological account of the development of AI, charting its origins from early symbolic systems to the transformative deep learning revolution. The section titled "Key Concepts and Techniques" explores the basic principles and methodologies that form the basis of AI and ML algorithms. It covers topics such as supervised, unsupervised, reinforcement learning, and neural networks.

The next sections examine current progress in AI and ML, including transfer learning, federated learning, and explainable AI, emphasizing their possible uses and consequences. This work explores the use of AI and ML in many fields such as healthcare, banking, transportation, and entertainment, highlighting their significant influence and discussing the related problems and ethical concerns.

Ultimately, the article ends by examining probable future paths and possibilities in the fields of AI and ML, highlighting the need to tackle significant obstacles like bias, privacy, and accountability. This is crucial to fully use the capabilities of these technologies for the sake of society.

EVOLUTION OF ARTIFICIAL INTELLIGENCE

AI has seen a significant transformation since its beginning, propelled by improvements in computational capacity, innovative algorithms, and the amassing of extensive data. This section offers a chronological account of the development of AI shown in Fig. (**1**), mapping its advancement from the first symbolic systems to the transformative era of deep learning [5].

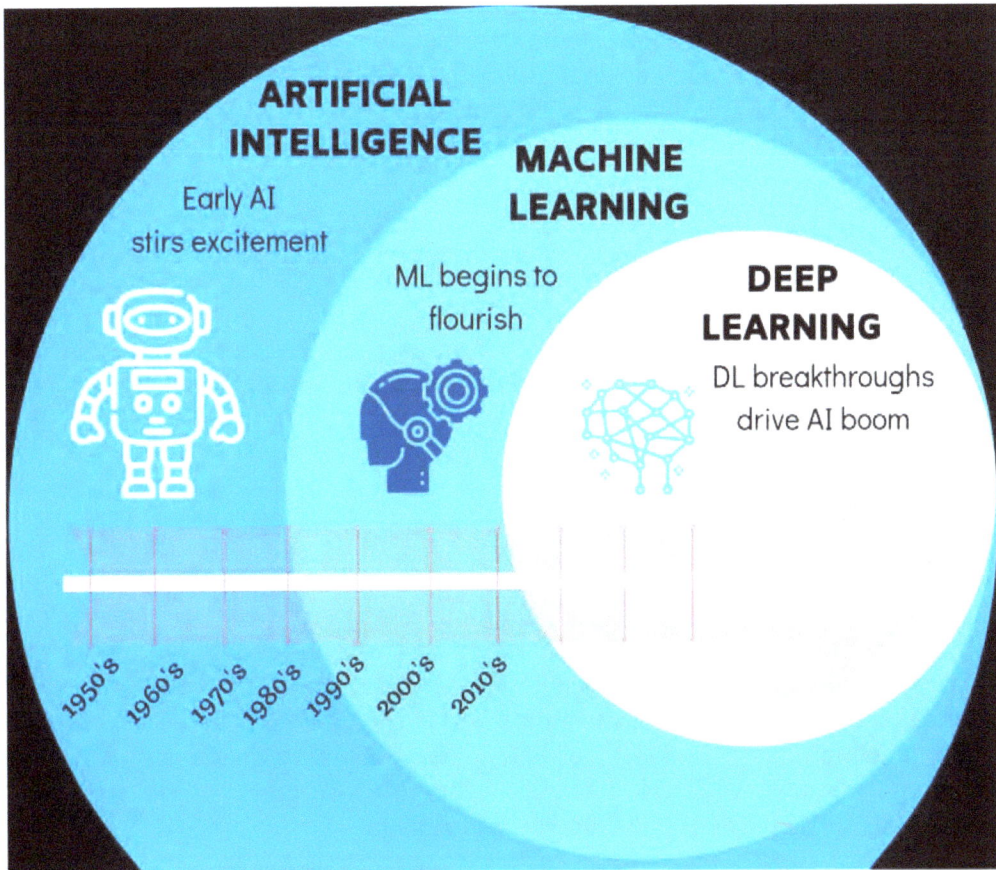

Fig. (1). Evolution of Artificial Intelligence.

Early Developments

Myths and legends about artificial beings with human-like intelligence may have inspired AI. Yet, it was not until the mid-20th century that the contemporary age of artificial intelligence (AI) began, thanks to the ground breaking efforts of academics like Alan Turing. Turing introduced the Turing Test as a means to evaluate machine intelligence. During the 1950s and 1960s, the area of AI saw significant expansion, driven by a sense of optimism and eagerness to develop intelligent robots. Initially, artificial intelligence (AI) systems relied on symbolic thinking and logic. Researchers focused on creating expert systems that could carry out certain tasks by using rule-based algorithms. Nevertheless, these systems had restricted capacities and had difficulties in managing uncertainty and complexity [6, 7].

Emergence of Machine Learning

The late 20th century saw a notable transformation in the area of AI with the birth of machine learning. Machine learning allows systems to learn from data and improve over time without explicit programming or rules. A significant contribution to this field was the creation of the perceptron by Frank Rosenblatt in 1957, which established the basis for further research on neural networks.

In the 1980s and 1990s, academics achieved substantial advancements in the domain of machine learning by creating algorithms such as decision trees, support vector machines, and Bayesian networks. These techniques empowered computers to address a diverse array of tasks, including pattern recognition, classification, and regression and found applications in domains such as image processing, NLP, and data mining [6, 7].

Deep Learning Revolution

Deep learning, which used neural networks with several layers of connected nodes, changed artificial intelligence in the 20th century. CNNs and RNNs, deep learning algorithms, thrive in image, audio, and language translation. Significant advancements in deep learning, such as the creation of deep belief networks by Geoffrey Hinton and the triumph of AlexNet in the ImageNet competition, accelerated the progress of the discipline and garnered considerable interest from both academia and business. Currently, deep learning has emerged as the prevailing framework in AI research, propelling progress in fields such as autonomous cars, robotics, healthcare, and finance.

To summarize, the development of AI has been marked by a transition from the first symbolic systems to the rise of machine learning and the following revolution of deep learning. The continual research and technical innovation in AI are fuelling its progress, leading to its increasing potential to disrupt society and modernize numerous sectors [6, 7].

PRINCIPLE CONCEPTS IN ARTIFICIAL INTELLIGENCE

The fundamental principles and methodologies serve as the underlying structure on which AI and ML algorithms function. Comprehending these notions is crucial for comprehending the principles behind AI systems and their applications. This section delves into the underlying principles and methodologies in the fields of AI (Fig. **2**) [8, 9].

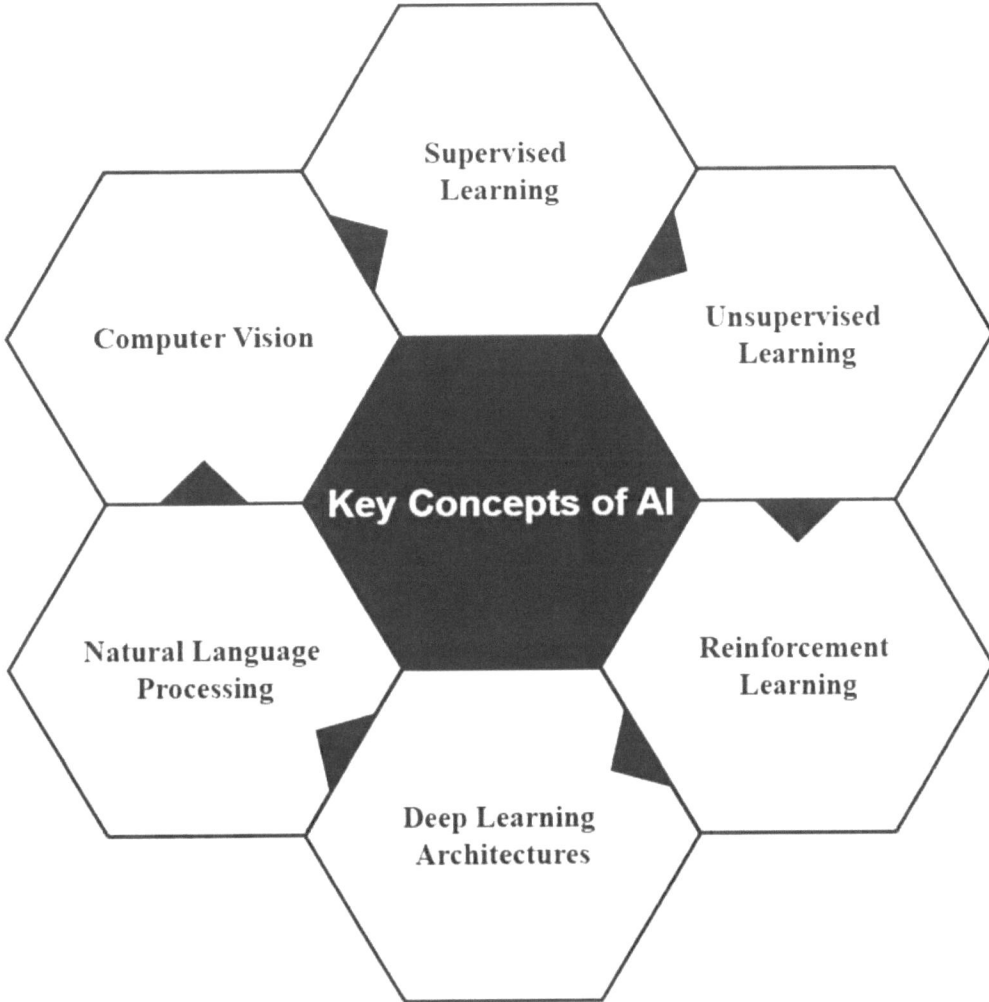

Fig. (2). Essential Principles Concepts of Artificial Intelligence.

Supervised Learning

Supervised learning, a fundamental machine learning approach, trains models using labeled datasets containing inputs and outputs. Supervised learning aims to create a predictive function that consistently maps inputs to outputs, allowing accurate predictions on unseen data. Linear regression, logistic regression, decision trees, and support vector machines are common supervised learning techniques. Using the labeled dataset during training, supervised learning helps models identify patterns and correlations in the data, allowing them to generalize and predict new occurrences. Finance, healthcare, natural language processing, and computer vision use this method to construct intelligent systems that make data-driven judgments and insights [10, 11].

Unsupervised Learning

Unsupervised machine learning trains models using unlabeled data to find latent patterns or structures. Unsupervised learning requires models to independently describe input in a cohesive and understandable way without output labels. K-means and hierarchical clustering algorithms for unsupervised learning group comparable data points by inherent similarity. With unsupervised learning, models may reveal data structures, making data exploration, dimensionality reduction, and anomaly identification easier. This method is used in customer segmentation, picture segmentation, and anomaly detection to get insights from unlabeled information and augment machine learning [12-14].

Reinforcement Learning

The dynamic machine learning algorithm reinforcement learning is based on behavioural psychology. In this paradigm, an agent learns to make decisions by interacting with an environment and getting rewards or penalties. Reinforcement learning aims to maximize cumulative rewards by finding the best approach. Q-learning, Deep Q Networks (DQN), and policy gradient approaches are reinforcement learning methods. These methods allow agents to learn from their mistakes and optimise their decision-making strategies to maximise rewards in complicated contexts. Reinforcement learning can educate agents to independently perform a variety of tasks, from game playing and robotic control to resource management and recommendation systems, by replicating biological learning principles [15].

Deep Learning Architectures

Neural networks, inspired by the human brain, are important computer models with layers of neurons. Input signals are processed mathematically by each neuron using weights and biases to create output signals. Deep neural networks, with several layers of linked neurons, have revolutionized artificial intelligence, performing well in image recognition, natural language processing, and reinforcement learning. CNNs, RNNs, and transformer models have advanced the area by extracting complex patterns and representations from raw data. CNNs thrive at spatial data like photos, whereas RNNs excel at sequential data like text or time series. Deep learning has transformed artificial intelligence in natural language processing and generation, as shown by transformer models like BERT and GPT [16].

Natural Language Processing

Natural Language Processing (NLP) has improved greatly in recent decades. After rule-based systems in the mid-20th century, NLP developed probabilistic models for machine translation and part-of-speech tagging using enormous datasets in the 1990s and 2000s. The year 2010 saw deep learning transform the field. Neural networks and transformer topologies enhanced NLP, allowing pre-trained language models to perform cutting-edge tasks *via* transfer learning and attention. This invention has extensive commercial use in healthcare, finance, and ethics. NLP technology increases privacy, discrimination, justice, and misuse issues. Researchers and practitioners must address these ethical issues to establish responsible AI systems that prioritize transparency, accountability, and inclusion in NLP technology implementation. NLP's advancement might transform natural language data used in many fields, notwithstanding its hurdles. NLP-enabled business chatbots personalize service. Chatbots automate troubleshooting, appointment scheduling, and order tracking by responding to natural language client inquiries. NLP helps doctors examine massive medical records, research papers, and patient data. NLP-powered systems may help physicians diagnose, record, and design drugs, increasing patient outcomes.

NLP enables sentiment analysis to assess product, corporate, and social problem opinions. NLP algorithms can categorize sentiments as good, negative, or neutral from huge amounts of text data from social media, customer reviews, and news articles, giving organizations client preferences insights. NLP is used for financial news summaries, sentiment analysis, and fraud detection. NLP systems can analyse financial data, news articles, and social media to assist investors in predicting market trends, identifying fraud, and minimizing risks and maximizing returns [16].

Computer Vision

AI changed when computer vision transformed robots' visual perception and interpretation. Advanced technology and algorithms replaced simple picture processing. Early edge detection and image segmentation enabled more complex tasks. Deep learning improved computer vision by allowing computers to directly generate hierarchical representations from raw pixels. CNN architecture dominated object recognition, image classification, and semantic segmentation. It trains and evaluates models faster using large labeled datasets like ImageNet. Combining computer vision with natural language processing and robotics enabled photo captioning and autonomous automobiles. Computer vision changes healthcare, agriculture, surveillance, and entertainment visual interactions and interpretation. Computer vision is enhancing business and life in many fields. Computer vision aids in medical image analysis in cancer detection, organ segmentation, and sickness diagnosis. Computer algorithms can properly interpret complex medical images like X-rays, MRIs, and CT scans, letting clinicians make quick and informed patient care decisions. Remote patient monitoring and virtual consultations need computer vision in telemedicine, particularly in places with limited healthcare access. New retail solutions using computer vision enhance customer experiences, operations, and security. Cashier-less companies bill customers when they depart using computer vision technologies. Amazon Go streamlines shopping by eliminating checkout. Image-based computer vision-powered recommendation systems analyse user behaviour and preferences for personalized product recommendations and targeted marketing. Real-time monitoring, face recognition, and anomaly detection using computer vision improve urban public safety and crime prevention in video surveillance and security systems.

These fundamental principles and methodologies serve as the foundation for creating artificial intelligence in many fields of application. By using these concepts, researchers and practitioners may create algorithms that acquire knowledge from data, adjust to dynamic contexts, and make intelligent judgments independently [17].

RECENT ADVANCEMENTS IN AI AND ML

AI and ML have advanced significantly in recent years. The quantity of data, computing power, and algorithms have driven these advances. Fig. (**3**) shows current advances in AI and ML that have improved these systems.

Transfer Learning: Transfer learning is a strategy that utilizes information from pre-trained models to enhance the performance of models on new tasks or domains with little data. It has shown to be a strong approach to machine learning. Transfer learning is a technique that speeds up training and enhances generalization by fine-tuning pre-trained models or employing them as feature extractors, instead of starting the training process from scratch. Transfer learning is effective in many fields such as computer vision, natural language processing, and healthcare [18].

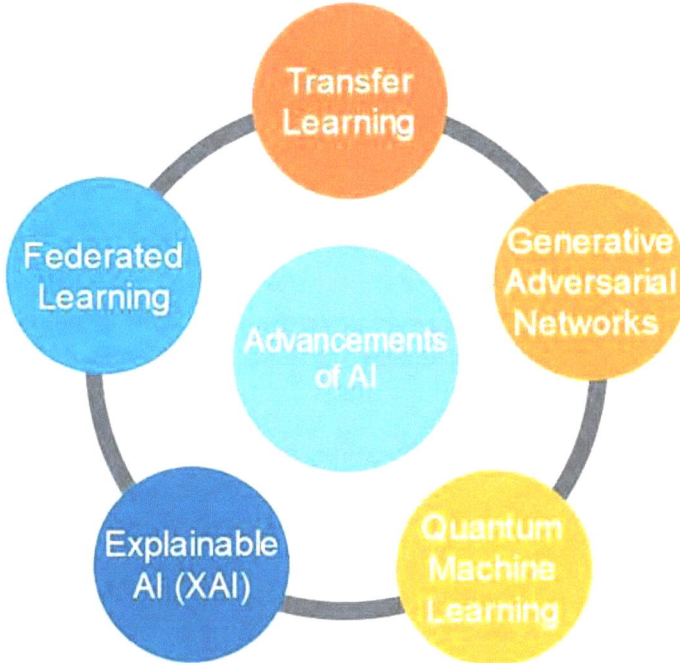

Fig. (3). Recent Advancements in AI and ML.

Federated Learning: Federated learning is a method of training machine learning models that are decentralized and involves training across several devices or servers while keeping the data local. Federated learning enables collaborative training of models using device or server data, where only model changes are aggregated and shared centrally, instead of transmitting raw data to a central server. This facilitates the use of machine learning techniques that protect privacy by ensuring that sensitive data stays stored on the device or server, hence minimizing the likelihood of data breaches and safeguarding user privacy. Federated learning is applicable in several sectors, including healthcare, finance, and edge computing [19].

Generative Adversarial Networks (GANs): GANs have transformed the area of generative modelling by allowing the creation of authentic data samples, such as pictures, audio, and text, from random noise. GANs include a pair of neural networks, namely a generator and a discriminator, which are trained in an adversarial manner to produce authentic samples while distinguishing between genuine and counterfeit samples. Recent progress in Generative Adversarial

Networks (GANs) has resulted in enhancements in the quality, stability, and variety of generated samples. These gains have found applications in several fields such as picture production, style transfer, and data augmentation [20].

Explainable AI (XAI): Explainable AI (XAI) is becoming more significant as AI systems are used in crucial fields that need transparency and interpretability. Explainable Artificial Intelligence (XAI) strategies have the objective of offering a deeper understanding of the internal mechanisms of AI models, allowing users to comprehend the decision-making process and its rationale. Techniques such as feature significance, saliency maps, and model-agnostic explanations aid users in comprehending and having confidence in AI predictions. This, in turn, promotes cooperation between humans and AI and improves accountability. Explainable Artificial Intelligence (XAI) is used in several fields such as healthcare, finance, and autonomous systems, where the capacity to understand and explain the AI's decisions is essential for making informed choices [21].

Quantum Machine Learning: Quantum machine learning, which combines quantum computers with machine learning, will revolutionize many applications. Quantum algorithms like quantum support vector machines and quantum neural networks use quantum states to compute, improving optimization, pattern recognition, and cryptography. Quantum machine learning, however young, might transform artificial intelligence and machine learning by solving problems beyond conventional computers. Quantum computing might accelerate and solve machine learning activities, altering AI and solving intractable challenges. Research in quantum machine learning is expected to spur innovation and extraordinary computing capabilities across several domains.

These recent developments only constitute a small portion of the continuous research and innovation in the domain of AI and ML. The rapid advancement of technology and ongoing discoveries have unlocked endless possibilities for AI and ML to tackle intricate problems and propel social advancement [22].

RECENT ADVANCEMENTS IN NLP AND COMPUTER VISION

Progress in Natural Language Processing (NLP) and Computer Vision has been propelled by significant developments in deep learning, namely in the creation of increasingly complex structures and training methods. Within the field of natural language processing (NLP), significant progress is the ongoing development of transformer-based models. Transformers, like BERT and GPT, have significantly transformed NLP workloads by collecting contextual information more efficiently than earlier systems. Recent iterations such as GPT-3 have shown exceptional proficiency in comprehending and producing language, attaining the highest level of performance in several language-related assignments. Furthermore, there has been an increasing focus on multimodal models that include both textual and visual data, allowing computers to comprehend and produce content that integrates information from both text and images. As a result, there have been advancements in tasks like as generating descriptions for images, answering questions based on visual content, and analyzing sentiment using several modes of data. Models like CLIP have shown a remarkable ability to comprehend information across many modalities. The progress in Computer Vision has been propelled by the emergence of increasingly potent convolutional neural network (CNN) structures and the growing accessibility of extensive labeled datasets. EfficientNet and Vision Transformers (ViTs) have advanced the limits of picture categorization accuracy by attaining improved performance with fewer parameters. Furthermore, there has been notable advancement in the fields of semantic segmentation and object identification. Models such as U-Net and Mask R-CNN have shown the ability to provide accurate predictions at the pixel level and instance level, respectively. Moreover, the advent of self-supervised and semi-supervised learning methods has facilitated the more effective usage of unlabeled data, hence enhancing performance on diverse computer vision tasks [23]. The fusion of computer vision and reinforcement learning methodologies has resulted in notable progress in the field of robotics and autonomous systems, empowering machines to perceive and interact with their surroundings in a more intelligent and independent manner.

APPLICATIONS OF ML IN AI

It is possible to see the substantial and intricate impact that Artificial Intelligence had on several domains, such asthe healthcare industry, the financial sector, transportation and autonomous systems, as well as the entertainment and gaming industries as shown in Fig. (**4**).

APPLICATIONS OF AI IN HEALTHCARE

AI is a revolutionary technology in healthcare that provides innovative solutions to increase patient outcomes, improve clinical decision-making, and optimize healthcare delivery. This section examines several uses of AI and ML in the healthcare field. These applications include illness diagnosis and prediction, drug discovery and development, customized treatment, and health monitoring and management [24].

Disease Diagnosis and Prediction: AI and ML algorithms have shown the potential to assist with the identification and forecasting of many illnesses, such as cancer, cardiovascular ailments, and neurological conditions. AI models may use medical imaging data, including X-rays, MRI scans, and histopathology slides, to discover early indications of illness, detect anomalies, and aid radiologists in making precise diagnoses. Moreover, machine learning algorithms can examine electronic health records (EHRs), genetic data, and physiological signals to forecast the likelihood of developing a disease, its course, and the response to therapy. This allows for preemptive interventions and the creation of tailored healthcare plans [24].

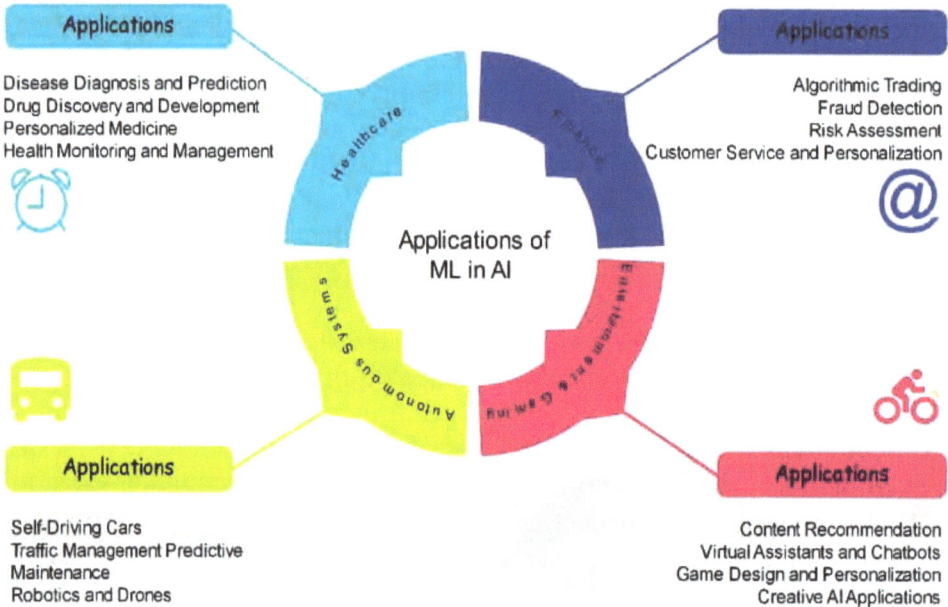

Fig. (4). Major Applications of ML in AI.

Drug Discovery and Development: The process of drug discovery and development is intricate, lengthy, and expensive, with a significant failure rate. AI and ML methods provide possibilities to expedite and enhance many phases of the drug development process, ranging from identifying potential targets and refining lead compounds to designing clinical trials and repurposing drugs. Artificial intelligence algorithms can examine extensive biological and chemical datasets to discover new targets for drugs, forecast interactions between drugs and proteins, and enhance the effectiveness and safety of potential drugs. Moreover, machine learning models can examine real-world data obtained from clinical trials and electronic health records. This analysis enables the identification of specific groups of patients, the categorization of treatment responses, and the facilitation of precision medicine techniques [24].

Personalized Medicine: Personalized medicine is a field that seeks to customize medical treatments and interventions for individual patients by taking into account their specific genetic composition, clinical attributes, and lifestyle variables. AI and ML technologies are essential in facilitating customized treatment *via* the analysis of complex data from many sources and producing patient-specific insights. ML algorithms may use genomic data to detect genetic variations linked to illness susceptibility and response to therapy, aiding in the choice of specific medicines and dosage plans. AI models may combine clinical, behavioural, and environmental data to create customized treatment plans, forecast the progression of diseases, and enhance patient results [24].

Health Monitoring and Management: Systems for proactive intervention, early detection of health issues, and continuous remote monitoring are made possible by AI and ML-powered health monitoring and management systems. Wearable technology, smart sensors, and AI-powered mobile health applications may collect and evaluate real-time health data such as vital signs, activity levels, and sleep patterns to monitor patients' health and spot any deviations from the norm. Machine learning models may examine longitudinal health data to detect trends that suggest the development of diseases, adherence to medicine, and occurrence of adverse events. This allows for prompt interventions and individualized treatments [24].

To summarize, AI and ML technologies have immense potential to transform healthcare by aiding in the early diagnosis of diseases, expediting the process of discovering new drugs, facilitating individualized treatment methods, and allowing patients to actively engage in their own care. The continuous advancement and maturation of these technologies are anticipated to have a significant and rapid effect on healthcare delivery and patient outcomes. This will stimulate innovation and bring about change across the whole healthcare ecosystem.

AI IN FINANCE

Artificial intelligence (AI) has become an essential element of the banking sector, providing robust tools for analysing data, managing risks, devising trading strategies, delivering customer support, and detecting fraud. This section examines the primary uses of AI and ML in finance, such as algorithmic trading, fraud detection, risk assessment, and personalized customer care [25].

Algorithmic Trading: Algorithmic trading utilizes AI and ML algorithms to carry out frequent transactions in financial markets. Machine learning algorithms use historical market data, news feeds, and social media sentiment to detect and discern patterns, trends, and potential trading opportunities. These algorithms have the ability to rapidly execute trades, taking advantage of market inefficiencies and arbitrage possibilities in order to create alpha. Furthermore, trading systems driven by artificial intelligence have the ability to adjust to dynamic market circumstances in real-time, enhancing trading tactics and reducing risk [25].

Fraud Detection: AI and ML approaches play a major role in identifying and stopping fraudulent behaviour in the financial sector, such as identity theft, credit card fraud, and money laundering. Machine learning models use transactional data, user activity patterns, and network connections to detect abnormal behaviours and questionable transactions. Financial institutions may identify potentially fraudulent transactions and reduce financial losses by using sophisticated anomaly detection techniques, including clustering, classification, and outlier identification [25].

Risk Assessment: Risk assessment is an essential component of making financial decisions. It involves evaluating credit risk, market risk, operational risk, and compliance risk. AI and ML algorithms enhance the ability of financial institutions to evaluate and measure different categories of risks with more accuracy and efficiency compared to conventional approaches. Machine learning algorithms use historical data, market patterns, and macroeconomic variables to forecast credit defaults, market volatility, and regulatory compliance breaches. Financial institutions may enhance their decision-making processes, improve capital allocation, and reduce risk exposure by using AI-powered risk assessment tools [25].

Customer Service and Personalization: AI and ML technologies are revolutionizing customer service and customization in the banking sector. These technologies empower financial institutions to provide customized experiences, predictive insights, and proactive support to their consumers. NLP techniques enable virtual assistants and chatbots to engage with clients, respond to queries, and provide tailored suggestions. In addition, machine learning algorithms examine consumer data, transaction histories, and behavioural patterns to predict client requirements, recognize possibilities for cross-selling, and customize product offers based on individual preferences [25].

AI and ML technologies are significantly impacting the finance sector by driving innovation and change. These technologies are transforming the operations, decision-making processes, and consumer interactions of financial institutions. Financial institutions may optimize efficiency, reduce risk, ensure compliance, and provide exceptional client experiences by harnessing the capabilities of AI and ML in a challenging and competitive environment.

TRANSPORTATION AND AUTONOMOUS SYSTEMS

Artificial intelligence is crucial in revolutionizing transportation and facilitating the creation of autonomous systems, such as self-driving automobiles, traffic management systems, predictive maintenance solutions, and robotics applications. This section examines the primary uses of AI and ML in transportation and autonomous systems.

Self-Driving Cars: Self-driving cars, or autonomous vehicles (AVs), are a popular example of how AI and ML are used in transportation. Artificial intelligence methods, such as deep learning models, computer vision systems, and reinforcement learning approaches, allow autonomous vehicles (AVs) to understand their environment, analyze road signs, identify impediments, and make immediate driving choices. Machine learning algorithms use data from various sensors such as cameras, LiDAR, radar, and GPS to effectively traverse intricate surroundings, predict traffic patterns, and guarantee secure and efficient transit. Waymo, Tesla, and Uber are now engaged in the active development and testing of autonomous vehicle technology, which has the potential to significantly transform transportation and decrease the occurrence of accidents and traffic congestion [26].

Traffic Management: The use of AI and ML technologies is transforming traffic management and urban mobility systems, allowing cities to enhance traffic flow, minimize congestion, and enhance transportation efficiency. Machine learning algorithms use data collected from sensors, cameras, and mobile devices to assess real-time traffic information. Their purpose is to forecast traffic patterns, detect areas of congestion, and enhance the timing of traffic signals for optimal efficiency. In addition, traffic management systems driven by artificial intelligence can adapt traffic signals, redirect cars, and give priority to emergency vehicles in order to reduce delays and enhance the overall flow of traffic. Through the use of AI and ML, cities have the ability to improve their transportation infrastructure and create urban settings that are both sustainable and conducive to a high quality of life [26].

Predictive Maintenance: Predictive maintenance is a crucial use of AI and ML in the transportation industry. It empowers operators to actively monitor and upkeep vehicles, infrastructure, and equipment to avoid failures and minimize periods of inactivity. Machine learning models use sensor data, telemetry information, and historical maintenance records to recognize first indications of mechanical malfunctions, ascertain maintenance requirements, and arrange for repairs or replacements before the breakdown of crucial components. Transportation businesses may enhance asset usage, prolong asset lifetime, and save maintenance expenses by adopting predictive maintenance solutions, all while enhancing safety and dependability [26].

Robotics and Drones: The progress of robotics and drones is being propelled by AI and ML technologies, which allow for independent navigation, identification of objects, and automation of tasks in many transportation-related uses. Autonomous drones, which are equipped with computer vision systems and machine learning algorithms, can carry out activities such as conducting aerial surveys, delivering packages, and inspecting infrastructure with great accuracy and effectiveness. Furthermore, warehouses, ports, and logistics hubs are using AI-powered robots to automate tasks such as material handling, inventory management, and order fulfillment. The use of AI and ML in robots and drones is revolutionizing transportation and logistics operations, resulting in increased productivity and improved operational effectiveness [26].

To summarize, AI and ML technologies are transforming transportation and facilitating the creation of autonomous systems that provide the potential to enhance safety, efficiency, and sustainability in mobility. AI-driven advancements are transforming the future of transportation and urban mobility. These breakthroughs include self-driving vehicles, traffic management systems, predictive maintenance solutions, and robotics applications. They are revolutionizing the transportation ecosystem, making it more connected, efficient, and sustainable.

AI IN ENTERTAINMENT AND GAMING

The entertainment and gaming industries are being transformed by the advancements in AI and ML technology. These technologies are improving the generation of content, customization, and user experiences. This section examines the primary uses of AI and ML in entertainment and gaming, such as content recommendation, virtual assistants and chatbots, game creation, and creative AI applications [14, 19, 25].

Content Recommendation: AI and ML algorithms are being used to create tailored content recommendation systems for different entertainment platforms, such as streaming services, music platforms, and social networking platforms. Machine learning algorithms use user preferences, watching behaviors, and interaction patterns to provide customized suggestions for movies, TV programs, music, articles, and social media postings. Recommendation systems may enhance user satisfaction, retention, and engagement by using collaborative filtering, content-based filtering, and reinforcement learning approaches to present pertinent and captivating material [26].

Virtual Assistants and Chatbots: Virtual assistants and chatbots, which use artificial intelligence (AI) and machine learning (ML) technology, are revolutionizing user interactions and customer support experiences in the entertainment business. Natural language processing (NLP) algorithms facilitate the comprehension of user questions by virtual assistants and chatbots. They also allow the provision of pertinent information and assistance with activities such as ticket reservations, event scheduling, and content discovery. Through the integration of machine learning models, virtual assistants can acquire knowledge from user interactions, tailor their replies to individual users, and enhance their conversational skills progressively, hence augmenting user engagement and happiness [26].

Game Design and Personalization: The use of AI and ML approaches in game design and development is on the rise, enabling the creation of captivating, ever-changing, and tailored gaming experiences. Machine learning algorithms use player behaviour, preferences, and performance data to adaptively modify the game difficulty, tempo, and material to align with players' skill levels and interests. In addition, the use of AI-driven generative content generation methods empowers game creators to create limitless iterations of game levels, locations, and characters, hence augmenting the potential for replayability and increasing player involvement. Through the use of AI and ML in the field of game design, developers can create gaming experiences that are more captivating, tailored to individual preferences, and deeply engaging [26].

Creative AI Applications: AI and ML technologies are used to amplify and enrich the creative process in the entertainment business, empowering artists, musicians, and filmmakers to delve into novel creative opportunities and expand the limits of artistic expression. Generative AI approaches, such as style transfer, deep dreaming, and neural art, allow artists to create unique and visually impressive artworks by training machine learning models on extensive collections of photos, videos, and music. In addition, artists are supported by AI-driven tools for music composition, video editing, and narrative, which aid in the generation, editing, and improvement of their creative works. This enables experimentation and creativity in the creative process [26].

To summarize, AI and ML technologies are fueling innovation and revolutionizing the entertainment and gaming sectors by facilitating tailored content suggestions, immersive user experiences, dynamic game development, and creative expression. Through the use of AI and ML, entertainment firms and game developers have the ability to provide highly captivating, customized, and groundbreaking experiences that deeply connect with audiences and enhance user involvement and contentment.

CHALLENGES AND ETHICAL CONSIDERATIONS

The incorporation of AI and ML technology offers considerable advantages to several industries, such as entertainment and gaming. However, it also poses notable obstacles and ethical concerns that need attention. This section examines the primary obstacles and moral deliberations linked to the use of AI and ML in the fields of entertainment and gaming [27].

Bias and Fairness: A significant obstacle in AI and ML systems is the existence of bias, which may result in unjust or discriminating results, especially in content recommendation algorithms and virtual assistants. Bias might stem from skewed training data, algorithmic design decisions, or the subjective assessment of fairness indicators. To achieve fairness and reduce prejudice, it is crucial to carefully choose the dataset, make the algorithm transparent, and apply strategies that prioritize fairness to provide equal results for all users [27].

Privacy and Security: The extensive use of AI and ML technologies in entertainment and gaming gives rise to apprehensions over privacy and data security, specifically about the gathering, retention, and examination of user data. Personalized content recommendation systems and virtual assistants depend on user data to provide customized suggestions and replies, which raises issues regarding the gathering, monitoring, and profiling of data. Moreover, machine learning models that are trained using sensitive user data might be susceptible to security risks, including data breaches, illegal entry, and adversarial assaults. This emphasizes the need to implement strong security measures and privacy-preserving approaches to protect user privacy and ensure the integrity of the data [27].

Accountability and Transparency: The intricate and obscure nature of AI and ML algorithms provides obstacles to ensuring accountability and transparency. This makes it challenging to comprehend, analyze, and clarify their choices and behavior. Within the realm of entertainment and games, individuals may have difficulties comprehending the rationale behind the recommendations of certain material or the decision-making process used by virtual assistants. Insufficient openness in AI systems may erode user trust and confidence, giving rise to worries about accountability, responsibility, and possible biases. Promoting accountability and developing trust with users requires the use of approaches such as interpretable ML models, explainable AI (XAI) procedures, and algorithmic audits to enhance algorithmic transparency and explainability [27].

Impact on Employment: The use of AI and ML technologies in entertainment and gaming might result in job displacement or alterations in work responsibilities and skill requirements, thereby affecting employment. The use of automated processes for content curation, customer support, and creative jobs might potentially decrease the need for certain kinds of labor, while simultaneously generating fresh prospects for AI professionals, data scientists, and content producers. To ensure a seamless shift to a workforce that incorporates AI technology, it is necessary to take proactive steps. These include implementing efforts to train employees in new skills and enhance their existing skills, establishing programs to improve the workforce, and implementing regulations that encourage employment growth and economic inclusion [27].

To tackle these difficulties and address ethical concerns, it is essential to foster collaboration and cooperation among many stakeholders, such as technology developers, legislators, regulators, and end-users. The entertainment and gaming industries can optimize the benefits of AI and ML systems while reducing risks and ensuring societal well-being by implementing principles of fairness, transparency, privacy, and accountability. This can be achieved by integrating ethical considerations into the design, deployment, and governance of these systems.

FUTURE DIRECTIONS AND OPPORTUNITIES

The potential for innovation, creativity, and immersive experiences in the entertainment and gaming industry is great when it comes to AI and ML. This section examines the significant prospects and possibilities for AI and ML in the entertainment and gaming sectors [27].

Advancements in AI Hardware: With the increasing complexity and computational demands of AI and ML algorithms, there is a rising need for progress in AI hardware, including processors, accelerators, and memory architectures. Specialized hardware accelerators, such as GPUs, TPUs, and neuromorphic circuits, are being created to fulfill the requirements of AI workloads, facilitating quicker training, inference, and deployment of AI models. Anticipated progress in AI hardware is projected to lead to significant improvements in performance, energy efficiency, and scalability, hence enabling novel opportunities for AI-driven entertainment and gaming encounters.

Integration with IoT and Edge Computing: The integration of AI and ML with IoT and edge computing technologies enables the development of intelligent, responsive, and context-aware entertainment and gaming experiences. Through the use of Internet of Things (IoT) sensors, wearable technology, and intelligent gadgets, artificial intelligence (AI) systems may gather up-to-the-minute information on user actions, preferences, and surrounding circumstances. This allows for the delivery of tailored content, adaptable gaming, and captivating narrative experiences. Edge computing infrastructure offers fast processing and real-time analytics capabilities at the network edge. This allows AI-powered apps to swiftly react to user inputs and provide smooth experiences, even in contexts with limited resources.

AI Ethics and Regulation: With the ongoing advancement and widespread use of AI and ML technologies in entertainment and gaming, there is an increasing acknowledgment of the need for ethical norms and regulatory frameworks to guarantee responsible and accountable AI research and implementation. The design, deployment, and governance of AI systems are becoming increasingly influenced by ethical issues, including bias, justice, privacy, and transparency. Efforts are underway to create regulations and standards that tackle these issues and encourage ethical behaviours in the field of AI. These projects focus on values like as fairness, transparency, accountability, and designing AI systems that prioritize human needs. By following ethical norms and legal criteria, stakeholders may establish trust with consumers, reduce risks, and promote a culture of responsible AI innovation in the entertainment and gaming industry.

Human-AI Collaboration: The future of AI and ML in entertainment and gaming relies on the smooth integration of human creativity, intuition, and knowledge with AI-powered technology to provide really revolutionary experiences. Platforms, tools, and interfaces are being created to facilitate cooperation between humans and AI. These tools aim to allow creators, developers, and users to connect with AI systems in a manner that is easy to understand and feels natural. Through the provision of tools that enable users to collaborate in content creation, tailor their experiences, and interact with AI-driven assistants and characters, entertainment and gaming firms may access hitherto untapped realms of ingenuity, individualization, and absorption, therefore erasing the distinctions between actuality and virtual environments.

Overall, the future of AI and ML in the entertainment and gaming industry is marked by progress in AI hardware, incorporation with the Internet of Things (IoT) and edge computing, adherence to ethical AI principles and regulations, and cooperation between humans and AI. By adopting these upcoming trends and possibilities, those involved may use the revolutionary capabilities of AI to provide engaging, customized, and ethically conscious entertainment and gaming experiences that capture viewers and enhance the quality of life.

CONCLUSION

This study illuminates the profound impact of AI, ML, NLP, and computer vision across diverse fields. Through meticulous examination of recent advancements and applications, it is evident that these technologies have ushered in a new era of innovation, transforming industries and revolutionizing human-machine interactions. From healthcare and finance to entertainment and gaming, AI and ML, bolstered by breakthroughs in NLP and computer vision, have enabled unprecedented capabilities, ranging from predictive analytics and personalized recommendations to autonomous vehicles and intelligent virtual assistants. The synergistic integration of these disciplines has not only enhanced efficiency and productivity but has also paved the way for novel solutions to complex challenges, fostering a more connected, intelligent, and responsive world.

Looking ahead, the trajectory of AI, ML, NLP, and computer vision promises continued advancement and ever-expanding applications. As researchers and practitioners push the boundaries of what is possible, the pursuit of responsible and ethical development remains paramount. Addressing issues such as bias and fairness, privacy and security, and societal impact requires a concerted effort to ensure that the benefits of these technologies are equitably distributed and aligned with human values and interests. By leveraging the transformative potential of AI, ML, NLP, and computer vision while upholding principles of transparency, accountability, and inclusivity, we can navigate the complexities of the digital age and harness these tools to create a brighter, more sustainable future for all.

REFERENCES

[1]   N. Anantrasirichai, and D. Bull, "Artificial intelligence in the creative industries: a review", *Artif. Intell. Rev.,* vol. 55, no. 1, pp. 589-656, 2022.
[http://dx.doi.org/10.1007/s10462-021-10039-7]

[2]   M. Bertolini, D. Mezzogori, M. Neroni, and F. Zammori, "Machine Learning for industrial applications: A comprehensive literature review", *Expert Systems with Applications,* p. 175, 2021.
[http://dx.doi.org/10.1016/j.eswa.2021.114820]

[3]   D. Ueda, T. Kakinuma, S. Fujita, K. Kamagata, Y. Fushimi, R. Ito, Y. Matsui, T. Nozaki, T. Nakaura, N. Fujima, F. Tatsugami, M. Yanagawa, K. Hirata, A. Yamada, T. Tsuboyama, M. Kawamura, T. Fujioka, and S. Naganawa, "Fairness of artificial intelligence in healthcare: review and recommendations", *Jpn. J. Radiol.,* vol. 42, no. 1, pp. 3-15, 2024.
[http://dx.doi.org/10.1007/s11604-023-01474-3] [PMID: 37540463]

[4]   S. Bahoo, M. Cucculelli, X. Goga, and J. Mondolo, "Artificial intelligence in Finance: a comprehensive review through bibliometric and content analysis", *SN Bus. Econ.,* vol. 4, no. 2, p. 23, 2024.
[http://dx.doi.org/10.1007/s43546-023-00618-x]

[5]   J. Bajwa, U. Munir, A. Nori, and B. Williams, "Artificial intelligence in healthcare: transforming the practice of medicine", *Future Healthc. J.,* vol. 8, no. 2, pp. e188-e194, 2021.
[http://dx.doi.org/10.7861/fhj.2021-0095] [PMID: 34286183]

[6]   S. Cohen, "Chapter 1 - The evolution of machine learning: past, present, and future", In: *Artificial Intelligence and Deep Learning in Pathology* Editor(s): Stanley Cohen, Elsevier, 2021, pp. 1-12.
[http://dx.doi.org/10.1016/B978-0-323-67538-3.00001-4]

[7]   L. Alexander, "History of Machine Learning", *IFAC-PapersOnLine,* vol. 53, no. 2, pp. 1385-1390, 2020.
[http://dx.doi.org/10.1016/j.ifacol.2020.12.1888]

[8]   D. Kim, S.H. Kim, T. Kim, B.B. Kang, M. Lee, W. Park, S. Ku, D. Kim, J. Kwon, H. Lee, J. Bae, Y.L.

Park, K.J. Cho, and S. Jo, "Review of machine learning methods in soft robotics", *PLoS One,* vol. 16, no. 2, p. e0246102, 2021.
[http://dx.doi.org/10.1371/journal.pone.0246102] [PMID: 33600496]

[9]   R. Pugliese, S. Regondi, and R. Marini, "Machine learning-based approach: global trends, research directions, and regulatory standpoints", *Data Science and Management,* vol. 4, pp. 19-29, 2021.
[http://dx.doi.org/10.1016/j.dsm.2021.12.002]

[10]   C. Elendu, D.C. Amaechi, T.C. Elendu, K.A. Jingwa, O.K. Okoye, M. John Okah, J.A. Ladele, A.H. Farah, and H.A. Alimi, "Ethical implications of AI and robotics in healthcare: A review", *Medicine (Baltimore),* vol. 102, no. 50, p. e36671, 2023.
[http://dx.doi.org/10.1097/MD.0000000000036671] [PMID: 38115340]

[11]   S. Polevikov, "Advancing AI in healthcare: A comprehensive review of best practices", *Clin. Chim. Acta,* vol. 548, p. 117519, 2023.
[http://dx.doi.org/10.1016/j.cca.2023.117519] [PMID: 37595864]

[12]   N. Nazareth, and V.R.R. Yeruva, "Financial applications of machine learning: A literature review", *Expert Systems with Applications,* vol. 219, 2023.
[http://dx.doi.org/10.1016/j.eswa.2023.119640]

[13]   W. Lakhchini, R. Wahabi, and M. Kabbouri, "Artificial Intelligence & Machine Learning in Finance: A literature review", *International Journal of Accounting, Finance, Auditing, Management and Economics,* vol. 3, no. 6-1, pp. 437-455, 2022.
[http://dx.doi.org/10.5281/zenodo.7454232]

[14]   S. Ahmed, M.M. Alshater, A. El Ammari, and H. Hammami, "Artificial intelligence and machine learning in finance: A bibliometric review", *Research in International Business and Finance,* vol. 61, p. 101646, 2022.
[http://dx.doi.org/10.1016/j.ribaf.2022.101646]

[15]   M. Giannakos, I. Voulgari, S. Papavlasopoulou, Z. Papamitsiou, and G. Yannakakis, "Games for Artificial Intelligence and Machine Learning Education: Review and Perspectives", *Lecture Notes in Educational Technology,* pp. 117-133, 2020.
[http://dx.doi.org/10.1007/978-981-15-6747-6_7]

[16]   S. Khastgir, J. Vreeswijk, S. Shladover, R. Kulmala, T. Alkim, A. Wijbenga, S. Maerivoet, I. Kotilainen, H. Kawashima, and P. Jennings, "Distributed ODD Awareness for Connected and Automated Driving", *Transp. Res. Procedia,* vol. 72, pp. 3118-3125, 2023.
[http://dx.doi.org/10.1016/j.trpro.2023.11.874]

[17]   S. Grigorescu, "A Survey of Deep Learning Techniques for Autonomous Driving", *arXiv preprint.* Journal of Field Robotics, arXiv:1910.07738v2.

[18]   M. Badawy, N. Ramadan, and H.A. Hefny, "Healthcare predictive analytics using machine learning and deep learning techniques: a survey", *J. Electr. Syst. Inf. Technol.,* vol. 10, no. 1, p. 40, 2023.
[http://dx.doi.org/10.1186/s43067-023-00108-y]

[19]   M. Abdullahi, Y. Baashar, H. Alhussian, A. Alwadain, N. Aziz, L.F. Capretz, and S.J. Abdulkadir, "Detecting Cybersecurity Attacks in Internet of Things Using Artificial Intelligence Methods: A Systematic Literature Review", *Electronics (Basel),* vol. 11, no. 2, p. 198, 2022.
[http://dx.doi.org/10.3390/electronics11020198]

[20]   Y. Ghasemi, H. Jeong, S.H. Choi, K.B. Park, and J.Y. Lee, "Deep learning-based object detection in augmented reality: A systematic review", *Comput. Ind.,* vol. 139, p. 103661, 2022.
[http://dx.doi.org/10.1016/j.compind.2022.103661]

[21]   Z. Liu, W. Zhang, and F. Zhao, "Impact, challenges and prospect of software-defined vehicles", *Automot. Innov.,* vol. 5, no. 2, pp. 180-194, 2022.
[http://dx.doi.org/10.1007/s42154-022-00179-z]

[22]   R.I. Mukhamediev, Y. Popova, Y. Kuchin, E. Zaitseva, A. Kalimoldayev, A. Symagulov, V.

Levashenko, F. Abdoldina, V. Gopejenko, K. Yakunin, E. Muhamedijeva, and M. Yelis, "Review of Artificial Intelligence and Machine Learning Technologies: Classification, Restrictions, Opportunities and Challenges", *Mathematics,* vol. 10, no. 15, p. 2552, 2022.
[http://dx.doi.org/10.3390/math10152552]

[23]   U. Bordoloi, S. Chakraborty, M. Jochim, P. Joshi, A. Raghuraman, and S. Ramesh, ""Autonomy-driven Emerging Directions in Software-defined Vehicles," in 2023 Design", *Automation & Test in Europe Conference & Exhibition,* no. Apr, pp. 1-6, 2023. [DATE].

[24]   M. Jeyaraman, S. Balaji, N. Jeyaraman, and S. Yadav, "Unraveling the Ethical Enigma: Artificial Intelligence in Healthcare", *Cureus,* vol. 15, no. 8, p. e43262, 2023.
[http://dx.doi.org/10.7759/cureus.43262] [PMID: 37692617]

[25]   W. John, "Artificial intelligence and machine learning in finance: Identifying foundations, themes, and research clusters from bibliometric analysis", *Journal of Behavioral and Experimental Finance,* vol. 32, 2021.
[http://dx.doi.org/10.1016/j.jbef.2021.100577]

[26]   A. Khakpour, and R. Colomo-Palacios, "Convergence of Gamification and Machine Learning: A Systematic Literature Review", *Technology, Knowledge and Learning,* vol. 26, no. 3, pp. 597-636, 2021.
[http://dx.doi.org/10.1007/s10758-020-09456-4]

[27]   G. Rong, Arnaldo M., Elie B.A., Bo Z., Mohamad S., "Artificial Intelligence in Healthcare: Review and Prediction Case Studies", *Engineering,* vol. 6, no. 3, pp. 291-301, 2020.
[http://dx.doi.org/10.1016/j.eng.2019.08.015]

CHAPTER 3

AI-based Aging Analysis of Power Transformer Oil

Mohammad Aslam Ansari[1], **Mohd Khursheed**[2,*] and **M. Sarfraz**[3]

[1] *Department of Electrical Engineering, I.E.T.M.J.P. Rohilkhand University, Bareilly, India*

[2] *Department of Electrical Engineering, Integral University, Lucknow, India*

[3] *Department of Electrical Engineering, AMU, Aligarh, India*

Abstract: The power transformer stands as a critical and costly component within electrical networks. Transformer oil serves the dual purpose of cooling and insulation within these systems. Its insulating efficacy and overall health are reflected in its physical, electrical, and chemical attributes, which inevitably deteriorate over the transformer's operational lifespan. The properties of transformer oil, such as volume resistivity, viscosity, breakdown voltage, and dissipation factor, undergo alterations over time. Consequently, regular monitoring of the oil condition is necessary to judge the aging effect. Six properties, including moisture content, resistivity, tan delta, interfacial tension, and flash point, have been examined. Data pertaining to these properties across varying ages (in days) have been collected from ten operational power transformers ranging from 16 to 20 MVA. In this paper, Artificial Neural Network (ANN) and Adaptive Neuro-Fuzzy Inference System (ANFIS) based models are presented for predicting the age of transformer oil samples in service. The ANN model employs a multi-layer feedforward network with the backpropagation algorithm, while the ANFIS model is based on the Sugeno model. A comparative examination of the two models indicates that the ANFIS model demonstrates superior performance over the ANN model, producing better outcomes.

Keywords: ANN, ANFIS, Insulation, Prediction, Transformer oil.

INTRODUCTION

In today's modern industrial landscape, electrical power plays a critical role. To prevent significant power disruptions, utility companies must maintain continuous oversight of the key components within the power system. Liquid-filled electrical power transformers represent an indispensable element within the power system. They constitute a vital asset upon which everyone depends [1, 2]. Within these transformers, insulating oils serve a dual purpose: functioning both as a coolant and as a dielectric fluid [3, 4]. During operational use, the oil experiences gradual

* **Corresponding author Mohd Khursheed:** Department of Electrical Engineering, Integral University, Lucknow, India; E-mail: khursheed20@gmail.com

Asif Khan, Mohammad Kamrul Hasan, Naushad Varish & Mohammed Aslam Husain (Eds.)

degradation characterized by aging, elevated temperatures, and chemical processes like oxidation [5]. Therefore, it is essential to conduct regular monitoring of the oil condition. This practice aids in predicting, whenever feasible, the operational lifespan or remaining service life of the transformer oil at various intervals [6]. Typically, power transformers exhibit high reliability, designed for a lifespan ranging from 20 to 35 years. However, with proper maintenance, transformers can often operate for as long as 60 years in practical scenarios [7, 8].

Organizations strive to accurately predict the lifespan of critical assets within various sections of the grid, such as transformers. This foresight enables preemptive measures to be implemented before significant faults arise in the power grid, consequently enhancing network reliability. Moreover, identifying potential transformer faults aids in mitigating aging effects. In essence, the significance of estimating the lifespan of transformers can be encapsulated as follows:

- Enhancing the system reliability
- Developing a maintenance schedule for transformers to ensure optimal functioning and longevity.
- Creating a structured timetable for the replacement of new transformers.

In recent years, various approaches have emerged for estimating the lifespan of transformers. While accelerated thermal aging of solid insulation remains the primary cause of early degradation, moisture also significantly influences the severity of faults [9]. Partial discharge (PD) [10] and dissolved gas analysis (DGA) are two techniques utilized to assess the insulation condition of transformers and ascertain the DP value [12]. An intelligent method for classifying faults in power transformers using dissolved gas analysis (DGA) is introduced in a study [11]. The experimental findings demonstrate that employing the SVM approach notably enhances the accuracy of diagnosing faults in power transformers. Novel methodologies are introduced for Health Index (HI), leveraging machine learning algorithms tailored for comprehensive big data analysis, owing to advancements in computer science and data processing [13, 14]. In another study [15], the analysis explores the impact of data uncertainty on the reliability and precision of lifetime estimation. The primary source of uncertainty stems from insufficient existing data. Another investigation [16] involved a sensitivity analysis of the Health Index (HI) on a transformer, employing a self-adaptive neuro-fuzzy inference system (ANFIS) with parameter tuning accomplished through a partial swarm optimizer (PSO) algorithm. In another study [17, 24], a method is presented that evaluates the effectiveness of various artificial intelligence (AI) techniques in identifying the health index of transformers. In a study [18], a novel AI-driven technique was introduced for categorizing transformer conditions into four distinct classes: 1. good, 2. fair, 3. poor, and 4. very poor. While existing literature has addressed AI-based methodologies for estimating transformer lifespan, there remains a need to enhance the accuracy of these approaches due to data unavailability and uncertainty. Nevertheless, the exploration and examination of AI-based lifetime models in managing data uncertainty have not been thoroughly investigated with established implementation probability.

Understanding the process of transformer aging is intricate and multifaceted. The degradation and aging of transformers result from a combination of factors including electric field intensity, temperature, humidity, oxygen with impurities, water content, and various other elements [19]. Importantly, these factors influencing the aging process of transformers are interconnected and not independent of one another. Discussions on aging are prevalent across various equipment types by researchers. Typically, the lifespan of equipment is influenced by electrical, thermal, and environmental factors. The aging of transformers significantly affects various factors including power outages, environmental impact, and operations of electricity companies. Factors such as excessive transformer loading and harsh environmental conditions are primary contributors to damage to transformer insulation, consequently accelerating the aging process. Additionally, failure to detect equipment defects and faults in a timely manner, coupled with inadequate maintenance practices, further exacerbates transformer aging. Damaged insulation leads to malfunctions and undesirable changes in physical parameters. For instance, the deterioration of paper and oil insulations leads to moisture production, thereby accelerating the aging of transformers. As a transformer reaches the end of its service life, maintenance costs can escalate significantly. The lifespan of the equipment serves as one of the key indicators for determining when a transformer should be replaced [20, 21]. Factors such as alterations in the polymerization coefficient, load variations, and harmonics within the network play pivotal roles in the aging process of transformers. Additionally, external factors including radiation intensity, ambient temperature, and wind conditions contribute to the rate of transformer aging [22, 23].

Motivation: Given the aforementioned points, there are various reasons driving the pursuit of this research, as detailed below:

- Numerous AI-driven techniques have been proposed for predicting the lifespan of power transformers. Nevertheless, their precision remains inadequate and they may not be deemed reliable.

- None of the current estimation methods can be deemed reliable yet, as their precision heavily relies on data, thus leading to unreliable results due to data uncertainty.

PROPERTIES OF TRANSFORMER OIL

Transformer oil possesses exceptional electrical insulating properties and maintains stability even when exposed to high temperatures. It plays multiple critical roles *i.e.* serving as insulation, preventing arcing and corona discharge, and dissipating heat, essentially functioning as a coolant.

Moreover, transformer oil helps preserve the transformer's core and windings, as they are fully submerged within it. Another vital attribute of transformer oil lies in its capacity to stave off the oxidation process that affects cellulose-based paper insulation. By serving as a shield against atmospheric oxygen, transformer oil effectively inhibits direct contact with cellulose, thus reducing the risk of oxidation. To assess its fitness for service, attention must be paid to several distinctive properties inherent in insulating oil. 1. Electrical Properties: 2. Chemical Properties, and 3. Physical Properties:

Electrical Properties

Electrical Breakdown Voltage (BDV)

The dielectric strength of transformer oil, often referred to as the breakdown voltage (BDV), is determined by observing the voltage at which sparking occurs between two electrodes submerged in the oil, with a specified gap between them. A lower BDV value suggests the presence of moisture content and conducting substances within the oil. BDV testing is a vital and widely used method for assessing transformer oil health, as it offers a primary indicator of the oil's condition, testing for breakdown voltage can be conveniently conducted on-site. The acceptable breakdown voltage for transformer oil is typically around 30 KV/cm.

Resistivity

Another critical property of transformer oil is its resistivity or specific resistance, which is expressed in ohm-cm at a specific temperature. Notably, the specific resistance of oil decreases rapidly with an increase in temperature.

Following the charging of a transformer after a prolonged shutdown, the oil temperature remains at ambient levels. Nevertheless, under full load operation, the temperature can rise significantly, reaching 90°C during overload conditions. Consequently, the resistivity of the insulating oil should ideally remain high at room temperature and exhibit good values even at elevated temperatures. Hence, it is crucial to gauge the specific resistance or resistivity of transformer oil at both 27°C and 90°C. The mandated minimum specific resistance of transformer oil at 90°C stands at 35×10^{12} ohm-cm, whereas at 27°C, it should not fall below 1500×10^{12} ohm-cm.

Dielectric Dissipation Factor (Tan Delta)

The dielectric dissipation factor, also referred to as the loss factor or tan delta of transformer oil, is a crucial property to consider. When an insulating material is placed between the live and grounded components of an electrical device, it can lead to the occurrence of a leakage current. Ideally, within a purely dielectric material, the current through the insulation would lead the voltage by 90 degrees. However, in reality, no insulating material is a perfect dielectric. As a result, the current passing through the insulator leads the voltage by an angle slightly below 90 degrees. The tangent of this angle, indicating the deviation from 90 degrees, is referred to as the dielectric dissipation factor or tan delta of transformer oil. To simplify, the current leakage through insulation consists of two elements: one capacitive or reactive and the other resistive or active. A high resistive insulation is desirable for effective insulation. Therefore, it is advantageous to minimize the loss angle, also known as tan delta, as much as possible. Elevated values of tan delta suggest the presence of contaminants in transformer oil. Hence, keeping the tan delta value low is essential for maintaining optimal insulation properties.

Physical Properties

Water Content

Excessive water content within the oil poses a detrimental impact on the transformer's core and winding insulation. The inherent hygroscopic properties of paper lead to substantial water absorption from the oil, thereby undermining insulation effectiveness and accelerating degradation, consequently reducing the lifespan of oil. Under loading conditions, the solubility of oil further increases, causing the paper to release water and further raise the water content in the oil. Thus, the oil temperature during sampling for testing is crucial. Throughout the oxidation process, acids form in the oil, which increases water solubility. These acids, in conjunction with water, expedite the decomposition of the oil, resulting in an increased degradation rate. As per the recommendation outlined in IS–335(1993), the permissible water content in oil stands at up to 50 ppm.

Interfacial Tension

The interfacial tension **(IFT)** at the boundary between water and oil is a measure of the molecular attraction between the two substances, usually expressed in Dyne/cm or milli-Newton/meter. This characteristic proves particularly valuable for identifying polar impurities and degradation by-products within the oil. High-quality fresh oil typically shows a higher interfacial tension, while contaminants from oil oxidation tend to lower this value. Fresh oil samples typically have a high IFT, around 0.04 N/m (at 29.5°C).

Flash Point

The flash point of transformer oil signifies the temperature threshold at which the oil releases enough vapors to create a combustible blend with air. When subjected to a flame under standard conditions, this blend can briefly ignite. This parameter holds significance as it indicates the potential fire hazard associated with the transformer. Therefore, it is preferable for transformer oil to possess a very high flash point, typically exceeding 140°C.

Viscosity

The viscosity of the oil is defined as resistance to flow under standard conditions. When transformer oil exhibits high viscosity, it obstructs the convection circulation within the transformer. Ideally, good-quality oil should possess low viscosity, minimizing resistance to conventional oil flow and ensuring efficient cooling of the transformer. Maintaining low viscosity in transformer oil is crucial. However, it is equally important to ensure that viscosity does not increase significantly as temperature decreases. This is because, like any liquid, transformer oil becomes more viscous as the temperature drops. Therefore, it is essential to minimize the rise in viscosity with decreasing temperature. Transformer oil should possess low viscosity to facilitate efficient heat transfer from the core to the radiators for dissipation. The prescribed viscosity value is approximately 22 kg/m3 at 20°C.

Pour Point

The pour point (PP) of transformer oil represents the minimum temperature at which the oil initiates flow under standardized test conditions. This property holds significant relevance, particularly in regions with icy climates. If the oil temperature drops below the PP, the convection flow of oil halts, impeding cooling within the transformer. Paraffin-based oil typically exhibits a higher pour point compared to Naphtha-based oil. However, in countries like India with warmer climate conditions, the use of Paraffin oil remains unaffected. The PP of transformer oil primarily hinges on the wax present in the oil. As Paraffin-based oil contains a higher wax content, it tends to have a higher pour point. A low pour point is desirable for transformer oil, enabling it to flow even at low temperatures, typically starting at -6°C.

Chemical Properties

Neutralization Value

Acidity in transformer oil poses a substantial risk. When oil turns acidic, the solubility of water content in the oil increases. This acidity adversely affects the insulation properties of the paper insulation within the windings. Furthermore, It accelerates the oxidation process within the oil, leading to further degradation. The presence of acidity also plays a significant role in accelerating the corrosion of iron components when exposed to moisture. To assess the acidic constituents of contaminants in transformer oil, an acidity test can be performed. The acidity of the oil is quantified in terms of the milligrams of potassium hydroxide (KOH) required to neutralize the acid present in one gram of oil. This measurement is commonly referred to as the neutralization number.

Corrosive Sulphur

The occurrence of corrosive sulfur, which originates from crude petroleum, can lead to the formation of pitting and dark deposits on copper surfaces. These deposits hinder the effective dissipation of heat. Therefore, it is essential to eliminate sulfur compounds during the refining process to uphold the integrity of transformer oil.

BASICS OF "ANN" AND "ANFIS" METHODS

Traditional models typically necessitate linear data for processing. Nonetheless, modern methodologies such as Artificial Neural Networks (ANN) and Adaptive Neuro-Fuzzy Inference Systems (ANFIS), which are rooted in soft computing principles, play a pivotal role in tackling non-linear challenges [24, 25]. Soft computing diverges from traditional (hard) computing due to its capacity to accommodate imprecision, uncertainty, partial truth, and approximation. Neural networks boast numerous advantageous traits, including their ability to map data, associate patterns, generalize findings, exhibit robustness, tolerate faults, and execute parallel processing at high speeds. These networks learn from examples and can undergo training using known instances of a problem to develop expertise. Once suitably trained, they can proficiently resolve unfamiliar or untrained instances of the problem.

The ANN model, employing a multilayer feed-forward network, relies on the backpropagation (BP) learning algorithm [26]. Backpropagation extends the Widrow Hoff learning rule that is extended to multiple-layer networks with non-linear differentiable transfer functions. Through the utilization of input and target vectors, the network undergoes training until it can accurately approximate a function. Networks equipped with biases, a sigmoid layer, and a linear layer can approximate any function with a finite number of discontinuities. Backpropagation demonstrates excellent generalization capabilities, producing accurate outputs even when presented with previously unseen inputs. This characteristic enables training the network on a given set of input-target pairs to yield good outputs.

Using a provided input/output dataset, the ANFIS toolbox function constructs a fuzzy inference system (FIS). This FIS's membership function (MB) parameters are adjusted using either a back-propagation algorithm alone or in combination with a least squares type of method [27]. These techniques enable the fuzzy systems to learn from the data they model. This approach provides a means for the fuzzy modeling procedure to glean information from a dataset, allowing it to compute the MF parameters that best enable the associated FIS to track the given input/output data. Similar to neural networks, this learning method facilitates the adaptation of the FIS to the specific dataset. The Fuzzy Logic Toolbox function responsible for adjusting the MB parameters is called ANFIS.

DEVELOPMENT OF ANN MODEL FOR AGE PREDICTION OF OIL

Numerous parameters are employed to assess the present condition of oil, broadly classified into physical, chemical, and electrical characteristics. These parameters encompass viscosity, specific gravity, flash point, oxidation stability, total acid number, breakdown voltage, dissipation factor, volume resistivity, and dielectric constant. Some oil properties exhibit correlation and undergo changes over time [28]. These temporal variations in oil properties have been leveraged to develop two models, as previously mentioned.

For the proposed study, training data have been sourced from literature, analysing ten operational transformers with capacities ranging from 16 to 20 MVA and operating at 66/11 KV in various substations across Punjab, India. Six key properties of transformer oil—breakdown voltage (BDV), moisture content, resistivity, tangent delta, interfacial tension, and flash point—are taken into account as input parameters, while the age of the transformers is the focal variable. The dataset comprises test results obtained from generator transformers with a capacity of 250 MVA, operating at 15.75kV/400kV, located in the Anpara Thermal Power.

The suggested ANN model employs the "Levenburg-Marquardt (trainlm)" algorithm, which is not reliant on a fixed learning rate. Thus, by adjusting the number of neurons in the hidden layer, it becomes possible to minimize both training and testing errors. A dataset consisting of 700 entries from [25] was compiled into a tabular format and utilized for training the neural network. The model is designed with a straightforward two-layer architecture, featuring one hidden layer and one output layer. The input layer encompasses six neurons, each corresponding to an input variable, while the output layer consists of a single neuron, representing the age of the oil sample.

After experimentation, it was determined that a network architecture employing 20 neurons in the hidden layer achieved optimal performance, exhibiting a regression coefficient of 0.999 and a mean square error (MSE) of 83.0. It is worth noting that since the data is non-normalized, the error might appear relatively large. The training process spanned 184 iterations, utilizing the logsig function in the hidden layer and the purelin function in the output layer. A regression value of 0.9999, nearing unity, suggests a close alignment between the target and output, indicating successful training.

Fig. (**1**) illustrates the performance plots, including the training plot (in blue), testing plot (in red), and validation plot (in green). It is apparent from this visual representation that the performance has been commendable, as the plots closely align with each other, and the mean square error steadily decreases until reaching its peak performance at epoch 178, where the MSE stands at 175.8955.

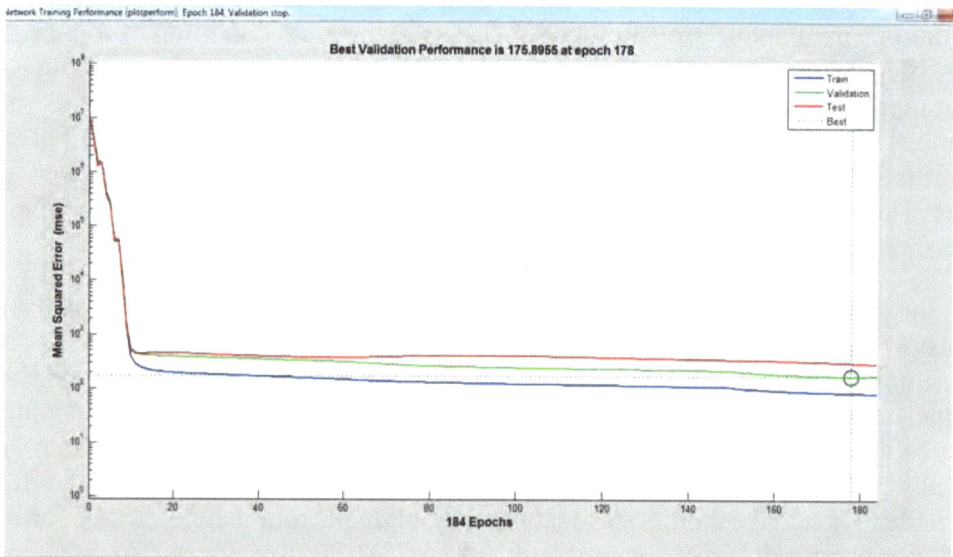

Fig. (1). Performance Plots.

This model is utilized with data acquired from the Anpara Thermal Power Project in India. The dataset has been presented in Table **1**.

Table 1. Data of different parameters.

S. No.	BDV (KV/cm.)	Flash Point (⁰C)	Resistivity (Ω-cm)x10¹²	Tan δ (at 90⁰C)	Moisture (ppm)	IFT (N/m) (at 27⁰C)	Age (days)
1.	56.8	152	1.25	0.026	16.7	0.03	604
2.	64.8	147	3.4	0.0058	16	0.031	1153
3.	51.6	145	4.08	0.0065	17.4	0.031	1933
4.	50.2	144	1.2	0.021	20	0.029	1934
5.	48.2	146	0.88	0.025	19	0.026	2258
6.	48.8	142	3.2	0.007	20	0.03	2306
7.	47.8	145	0.88	0.026	19.6	0.026	2407
8.	59.2	145	0.86	0.0317	16.6	0.027	2406

Simulation Results of "ANN Model

The comparison between the predicted age by the model and the actual age of the oil samples is conducted using error indices such as error, percentage error, and mean absolute percentage error. These indices are calculated using the following formulas:

1. Error = Output by ANN – Actual Output
2. Percentage Error = (Error / Actual Output) x 100
3. Mean Absolute Percentage Error (MAPE) = Σ |% Error| / No. of samples

The actual values, network output, and error indices are given in Table **2**, while graphs illustrating the relationship between actual age and age predicted by the network are presented in Fig. (**2**).

Table 2. Actual age and predicted age by ANN.

S. No.	Actual Age (in days)	Age Predicted by ANN (in days)	Error	% Error
1.	604	741.87	-137.87	-22.83
2.	1153	1175.82	-22.82	-1.98
3.	1933	1659.28	273.72	14.16
4.	1934	2104.46	-170.46	-8.81

(Table 2) cont.....

S. No.	Actual Age (in days)	Age Predicted by ANN (in days)	Error	% Error
5.	2258	2382.22	-124.22	-5.50
6.	2306	2186.38	119.62	5.19
7.	2407	2436.94	-29.94	-1.24
8.	2406	3122.65	-716.65	-29.78
Mean Absolute Percentage Error (MAPE)= 11.18				

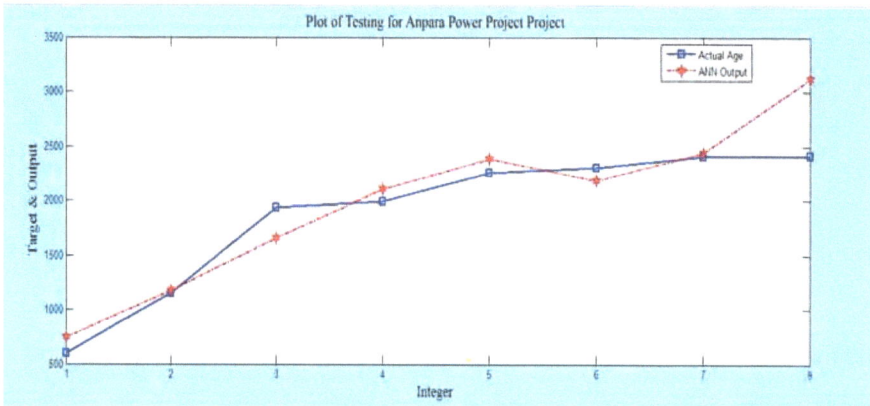

Fig. (2). Plot of Actual Age *Vs*. Age Predicted by ANN.

Table 2 shows that the age predicted by the developed model has a comparatively larger error, especially for transformer oil samples no. 1, 3, and 8, for others, the errors are tolerable. The value of mean absolute percentage error (MAPE) is also large and equals 11.18.

It is evident from Fig. (2) that oil samples 3 and 8 have a larger deviation from the actual values, while samples 2 and 7 are very close to the actual value, and the remaining three lie in the medium range of error.

DEVELOPMENT OF "ANFIS" MODEL FOR AGE PREDICTION OF OIL

An Adaptive Neuro-Fuzzy Inference System (ANFIS) model, which integrates Artificial Neural Network (ANN) and Fuzzy Logic techniques, is employed to enhance the performance of the previous ANN model. In the Fuzzy Toolbox of MATLAB, the ANFIS model utilizes the Sugeno model. Initially, a new Fuzzy Inference System (FIS) is created in the FIS editor window with six input variables and one output variable, and the same FIS configuration is employed for training.

The data is partitioned into separate sets for training and testing purposes. Subsequently, the data for the ANFIS model is loaded from variable sheets stored in Excel worksheets. Initially, 700 training data pairs are loaded to train the FIS. The FIS is generated using grid partitioning, and subsequently, adjustments are made to modify the number and types of membership functions assigned to each input and output variable. Specifically, two membership functions of the "gaussmf" type are assigned to each input variable, while a "linear" type membership function is assigned to the output variable.

Once the number and types of membership functions have been assigned to each input and output variable, they can be modified too. A membership function editor offers this facility. The general shape and number of MFs are also visible in the Membership Function Editor window. Now after the FIS has been generated and MFs are defined, the ANFIS model structure has been created as shown in Fig. (**3**).

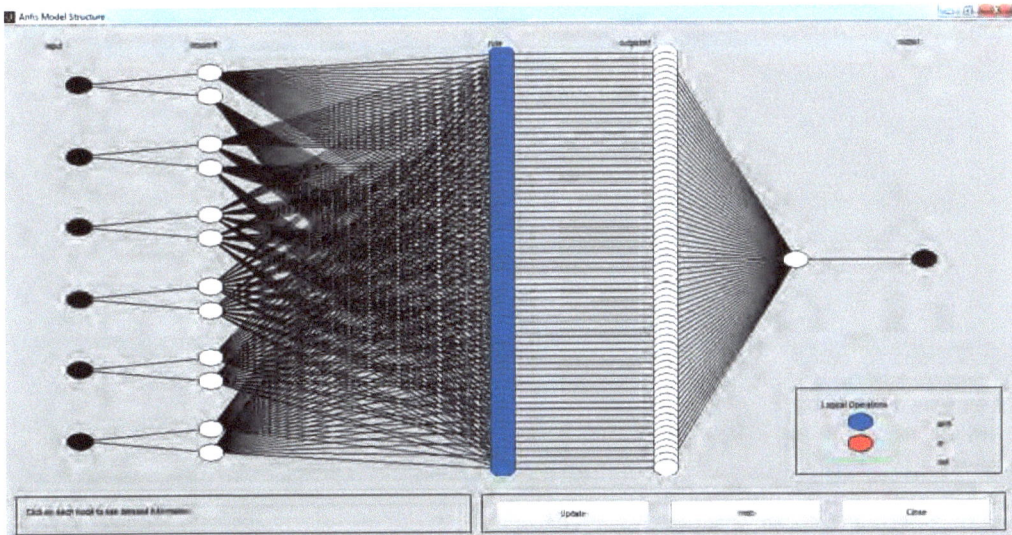

Fig. (3). Proposed ANFIS Structure.

The rule base shows 64 rules in the given structure. The logical operations applied to these rules include AND, OR, and NOT. The output obtained from these rules is initially in fuzzified form, which is subsequently defuzzified to yield a single crisp output value.

Following the generation of the Fuzzy Inference System (FIS), it undergoes training using a hybrid optimization method. Initially, the number of epochs is set to 10; however, training concludes within just two epochs, resulting in 64 fuzzy rules and an error of 10.0586. Detailed information regarding the training process is displayed in the command window of MATLAB upon completion, as illustrated in Fig. (**4**).

ANFIS info:

Number of nodes: 161

Number of linear parameters: 448

Number of nonlinear parameters: 24

Total number of parameters: 472

Number of training data pairs: 700

Number of checking data pairs: 0

Number of fuzzy rules: 64

Start training ANFIS ...

1   10.0586

2   12.5353

Designated epoch number reached --> ANFIS training completed at epoch 2.

Fig. (4). Command Window of MATLAB showing Information About ANFIS data.

Fig. (**4**) reveals that the training of the proposed ANFIS model utilized a total of 472 parameters, comprising 448 linear and 24 nonlinear parameters. With 700 training data pairs, the model required 161 nodes, and 64 fuzzy rules were activated. Subsequently, following the development of the proposed model, it was simulated using the unknown test data pertinent to this study.

Simulation Results of "ANFIS" Model

The age predicted by the ANFIS model was compared with the actual age of the oil samples, assessing error indices such as error, percentage error, and mean absolute percentage error. The tabulation of actual values, network output, and error indices is presented in Table **3**, while graphs depicting the relationship between actual age and age predicted by the network are plotted in Fig. (**5**) using MATLAB software.

Table 3. Comparison table for Actual age and age predicted by ANFIS model.

S. No.	Actual Age (in days)	Predicted Age (in days)	% Error
1.	604	680.73	-12.70
2.	1153	1203.77	-4.10
3.	1933	1743.46	9.81
4.	1934	2017.30	-4.30
5.	2258	2327.75	-3.08
6.	2306	2329.06	1.00
7.	2407	2468.50	-2.55
8.	2406	2853.65	-18.60

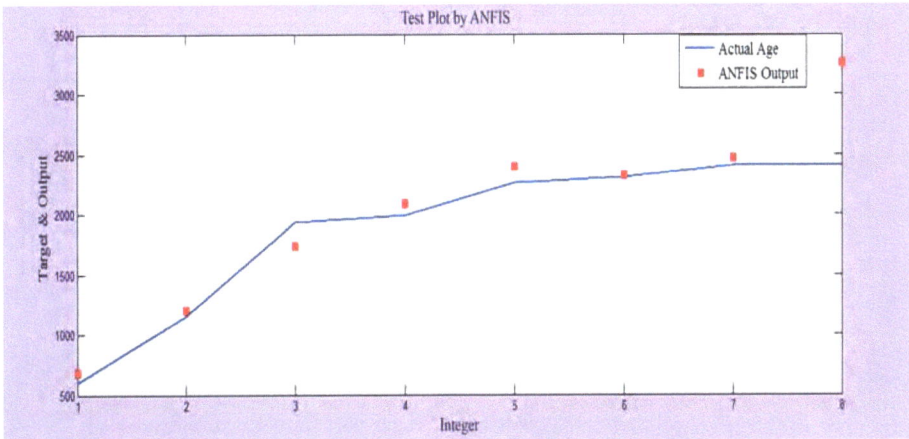

Fig. (5). Comparing plot for both actual age as well as age predicted by the ANFIS model.

Table **3** shows that a maximum error of 18.6% for sample 8 and a minimum error of 1% for sample 6 have been observed. The value of mean absolute percentage error (MAPE) is found to be 7.01, which indicates an overall improvement in the performance because its value for the ANN model was 11.18.

Fig. (**5**) illustrates that the age predicted by the ANFIS model generally exhibits insignificant errors for the majority of results. However, for samples 1, 3, and 8, the errors are comparatively high. Nonetheless, there is a noticeable enhancement in the output values predicted by the ANFIS model when compared to the previous ANN model.

COMPARISON OF "ANN" AND "ANFIS" MODEL

Now, a comparison between the performances of the two models has been made and the outcomes of this comparison have been presented in Table **4**.

Table 4. Comparison table for results obtained from ANN and ANFIS method.

Oil Sample	Actual Age (in days)	Predicted Age by ANN (in days)	Predicted age by ANFIS (in days)	% Error (by ANN)	% Error (by ANFIS)
1.	604	741.87	680.73	-22.83	-12.70
2.	1153	1175.82	1203.77	-1.98	-4.10
3.	1933	1659.28	1743.46	14.16	9.81
4.	1934	2104.46	2017.30	-8.81	-4.30
5.	2258	2382.22	2327.75	-5.50	-3.08
6.	2306	2186.38	2329.06	5.19	1.00
7.	2407	2436.94	2468.50	-1.24	-2.55
8.	2406	3122.65	2853.65	-29.78	-18.60
MAPE of ANN: 11.18 MAPE of ANFIS: 7.01					

The comparison results between the two methods are plotted in Fig. (**6**) as depicted below:

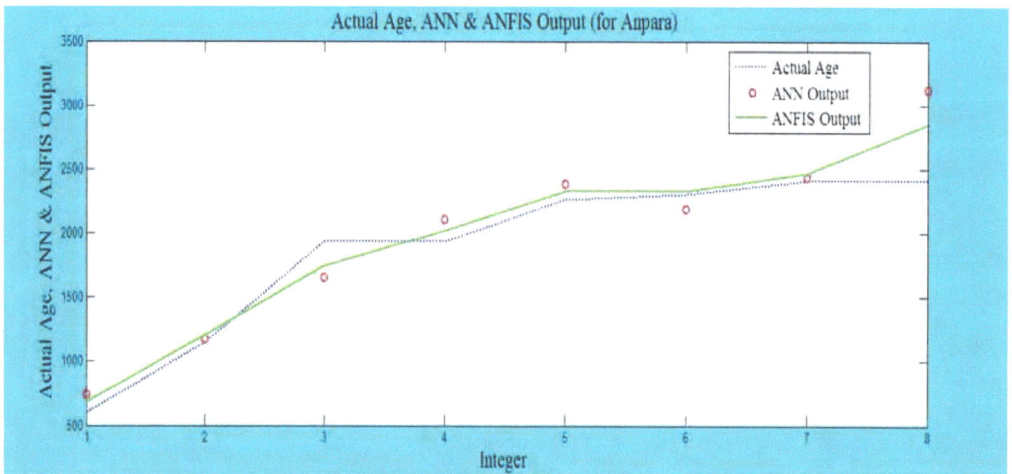

Fig. (6). Actual Age and Age Predicted by ANN and ANFIS.

CONCLUSION

The paper presents a novel method employing two AI models to predict the remaining lifespan of transformer oil insulation. These models leverage essential input parameters such as breakdown voltage (BDV), interfacial tension (IFT), tan delta, resistivity, flash point (FP), and moisture content for diagnostic purposes.

ANN and ANFIS models were constructed using the "nntool" and "fuzzy tool" functionalities within the MATLAB software. The methodology includes a phase of training and testing the models to attain optimal configurations, particularly concerning the number of neurons in the hidden layer, thus enhancing prediction accuracy. These models underwent testing with unknown data, and the simulation results were gathered, including predicted age, error, percentage error (%error), and mean absolute percentage error (MAPE).

To validate the neural network (NN) models, pre-tested samples are employed, ensuring their applicability in real-world scenarios. A comparative analysis was conducted between the two developed models, revealing a notable enhancement in the output values of the ANFIS model compared to the ANN model. Specifically, the mean absolute percentage error (MAPE) decreased from 11.18 to 7.01, indicating an improvement of 4.17 points. Additionally, the regression score improved from 0.93 to 0.97, signifying a reduction in errors in the predicted values by the ANFIS model.

Through this comparative analysis, a thorough evaluation of the model's performance is conducted, revealing their potential as a dependable method for estimating the remaining useful life of transformer insulation. The error percentage closely aligns with the mathematical model, exhibiting minimal discrepancies in predicted insulation life.

Expanding these models to different types of oil samples is feasible, as long as the training dataset is sufficiently extensive to cover diverse operating conditions. The flexibility of the proposed models in handling nonlinear systems suggests their applicability to solving nonlinear problems. The valuable outcomes of this study could be utilized to design an effective and economical mechanism for monitoring the health and aging of any insulation system.

REFERENCES

[1]   S. Wu, H. Zhang, Y. Wang, Y. Luo, J. He, X. Yu, Y. Zhang, J. Liu, and F. Shuang, "Concentration prediction of polymer insulation aging indicator – alcohols in oil based on genetic algorithm – optimized support vector machines", *Polymers (Basel)*, vol. 14, no. 7, p. 1449, 2022. [http://dx.doi.org/10.3390/polym14071449] [PMID: 35406322]

[2]   X. Ma, H. Hu, and Y.Z. Shang, "A new method for transformer fault prediction based on multifeatured enhancement and refined long short-term memory", *IEEE Trans. Instrum. Meas.*, vol. 70, pp. 1-11, 2021.

[3]   A. Krontiris, *"Fuzzy systems for condition assessment of equipment in electric power systems"*, Ph.D. Thesis, Darmstadt University of Technology, Darmstadt, Germany, 2012.

[4]   S. Boudraa, L. Mokhnache, and I. Fofana, "Artificial neural networks for predicting the gassing tendency under electrical discharge in insulating oil for extended time", *J. Electr. Eng.,* vol. 14, pp. 45-52, 2014.

[5]   M.R. Meshkatodd, "Aging Study and Lifetime Estimation of Transformer Mineral Oil", *Am. J. Eng. Appl. Sci.,* vol. 1, no. 4, pp. 384-388, 2008.
[http://dx.doi.org/10.3844/ajeassp.2008.384.388]

[6]   J. Liu, X. Fan, C. Zhang, C.S. Lai, Y. Zhang, H. Zheng, L.L. Lai, and E. Zhang, "Moisture diagnosis of transformer oil-immersed insulation with intelligent technique and frequency-domain spectroscopy", *IEEE Trans. Industr. Inform.,* vol. 17, no. 7, pp. 4624-4634, 2021.
[http://dx.doi.org/10.1109/TII.2020.3014224]

[7]   C. Zhou, B. Li, and L. Shu, *Estimation of Remaining Lifetime of Power Transformer Oil: A Review.* Authors Energies, 2019.

[8]   M.M. Islam, G. Lee, and S.N. Hettiwatte, "A review of condition monitoring techniques and diagnostic tests for lifetime estimation of power transformers", *Electr. Eng.,* vol. 100, no. 2, pp. 581-605, 2018.
[http://dx.doi.org/10.1007/s00202-017-0532-4]

[9]   B. García, D. Urquiza, and J.C. Burgos, "Investigating the influence of moisture on the 2FAL generation rate of transformers: A new model to estimate the DP of cellulosic insulation", *Electr. Power Syst. Res.,* vol. 140, pp. 87-94, 2016.
[http://dx.doi.org/10.1016/j.epsr.2016.06.036]

[10]   G.C. Montanari, "Aging and life models for insulation systems based on PD detection", *IEEE Trans. Dielectr. Electr. Insul.,* vol. 2, no. 4, pp. 667-675, 1995.
[http://dx.doi.org/10.1109/94.407031]

[11]   "Mineral oil-impregnated electrical equipment in service guide to the interpretation of dissolved and free gases analysis", *IEC Stand.,* vol. 44, p. 60599, 2013.

[12]   M.K. Pradhan, and T.S. Ramu, "On the estimation of elapsed life of oil-immersed power transformers", *IEEE Trans. Power Deliv.,* vol. 20, no. 3, pp. 1962-1969, 2005.
[http://dx.doi.org/10.1109/TPWRD.2005.848663]

[13]   R. Behkam, A. Moradzadeh, H. Karimi, M. S. Nadery, B. Mohammadi Ivatloo, G.B. Gharehpetian, and S. Tenbohlen, "Mechanical fault types detection in transformer windings uing interpretation of frequency responses *via* multilayer perceptron", *J. Oper. Autom. power Eng.,* vol. 11, no. 1, pp. 11-21, 2022.

[14]   N. Eskandari, and S. Jalilzadeh, "Electrical load manageability factor analyses by artificial neural network training", *J. Oper. Autom. power Eng.,* vol. 7, no. 2, pp. 187-195, 2019.

[15]   "Condition Assessment of Power Transformers", *CIGRE,* 2019.

[16]   K. Ibrahim, R.M. Sharkawy, H.K. Temraz, and M.M.A. Salama, "Transformer health index sensitivity analysis using neuro-fuzzy modelling", *in 2nd Int. Conf. Advanced TechNo. Appli. Sci. (ICaTAS),* 2017.

[17]   A. Alqudsi, and A. El-Hag, "Application of Machine Learning in Transformer Health Index Prediction", *Energies,* vol. 12, no. 14, p. 2694, 2019.
[http://dx.doi.org/10.3390/en12142694]

[18]   M.M. Islam, G. Lee, and S.N. Hettiwatte, "Application of a general regression neural network for health index calculation of power transformers", *Int. J. Electr. Power Energy Syst.,* vol. 93, pp. 308-315, 2017.
[http://dx.doi.org/10.1016/j.ijepes.2017.06.008]

[19]   M. Kohtoh, S. Kaneko, S. Okabe, and T. Amimoto, "Aging effect on electrical characteristics of insulating oil in field transformer", *IEEE Trans. Dielectr. Electr. Insul.,* vol. 16, no. 6, pp. 1698-1706,

2009.
[http://dx.doi.org/10.1109/TDEI.2009.5361592]

[20]   E. Fuchs, and M. Masoum, *Power quality in power systemsand electrical machines.* Elsevier Academic Press, 2008.

[21]   C.T. Dervos, C.D. Paraskevas, P.D. Skafidas, and N. Stefanou, "Dielectric spectroscopy and gas chromatography methods applied on high-voltage transformer oils", *IEEE Trans. Dielectr. Electr. Insul.,* vol. 13, no. 3, pp. 586-592, 2006.
[http://dx.doi.org/10.1109/TDEI.2006.1657972]

[22]   A. Elmoudi, M. Lehtonen, and H. Nordman, "Effect ofharmonics on transformers loss of life", *in Conf. Rec. IEEE Int. Symp. Elec. Insul.,* pp. 408-411, 2013.

[23]   P. Hari Mukti, F. Agung Pamuji, and B. Sofiarto Munir, "Implementation of artificial neural networks for determining power transfomer condition", *5th Int. Symp. Advanced Control of Indu. Processes (ADCONIP 2014),* pp. 4-8, 2014.

[24]   M.K. Asim Rahman Ansar, "Performance Assessment of Permanent Magnet Brushless DC Motors with Intelligent Controller", *2nd IEEE International Conference on Emerging Frontiers in Electrical and Electronic Technologies (ICEFEET- 2022) NIT Patna, India,* pp. 24-25, 2022.

[25]   Mohd Khursheed, Asim Rahman Ansari, Khadim Moin Siddiqui, Mohammad Sami, and Munish Kumar, "Intelligent Analysis of a Hybrid Energy System with Telecom Load", *in Intelligent Data Analytics for Power and Energy Systems, LNEE,* vol. 802, Springer, Singapore, no. 01, pp. 567-590, 2022.
[http://dx.doi.org/10.1007/978-981-16-6081-8_29]

[26]   S. Jashandeep, S.Y. Raj, and V. Piush, "The Influence of Service Aging on Transformer Insulating Oil Parameters", *Proc. ECOC'00,* vol. 19, pp. 421pp. 109-426, 2000.

[27]   M.A. Mohd Khursheed, "Performance Analysis of Closed loop Control of Diesel Generator Power Supply for Base Transceiver (BTS) Load", *International Journal of Innovative Technology and Exploring Engineering (IJTEE),* vol. 8, no. 9, pp. 2483-2495, 2019.

[28]   S. Rajasekaran, and G.A. Vijaylakshmi Pai, "Neural Networks, Fuzzy Logic, and Genetic Algorithm", *A text book of PHI Publications,* 2005.

CHAPTER 4

Artificial Intelligence and Social Media: Strength, Management and Responsibility

Nafees Akhter Farooqui[1,*], **Shamsul Haque Ansari**[1], **Mohd Haleem**[2,*], **Rafeeq Ahmed**[3] and **Mohammad Islam**[2]

[1] *Department of CSE, Koneru Lakshmaiah Education Foundation, Vaddeswaram, Andhra Pradesh 522502, India*

[2] *Department of Computer Science, Era University, Lucknow, Uttar Pradesh 226003, India*

[3] *Department of CSE, Government Engineering Collage, West Champaran, Kumarbagh, Bihar, India*

Abstract: The rapid development of new digital and online systems that are powered by artificial intelligence (AI), such as social media, targeted marketing, and personalized search engines, has resulted in the introduction of new ways to engage with individuals, collect information about them, and possibly influence the activities they take. Concerns have been expressed, however, regarding the possibility of manipulation brought about by such types of breakthroughs, they provide one-of-a-kind capabilities for targeting and exerting a significant amount of influence over individuals through the persistent application of automated tactics. When it comes to voting, electorates are likely to be influenced to vote for a particular entity. It is important to note that the strategies that involve targeting and profiling on social media platforms serve not just advertising reasons but also propaganda purposes. Through the monitoring of individuals' activity on the internet, social media algorithms can develop user profiles. These profiles are then leveraged to provide recommendations that are specifically customized to a certain audience segment. As a result, propaganda and incorrect information have a greater potential than ever before to influence the perspectives and decisions of voters, particularly in matters related to elections. This chapter provides a detailed survey of the existing literature on manipulation, with a particular focus on the impact of artificial intelligence and other technologies that are connected to manipulation. Furthermore, it considers the ethical imperatives and societal obligations of artificial intelligence developers, social media platforms, and regulatory agencies in the process of minimizing the adverse effects associated with the technology.

Keywords: Artificial Intelligence, Online system, Propaganda, Rapid development, Social media.

* **Corresponding author Nafees Akhter Farooqui:** Department of CSE, Koneru Lakshmaiah Education Foundation, Vaddeswaram, Andhra Pradesh 522502, India; E-mail: nafeesf@gmail.com

Asif Khan, Mohammad Kamrul Hasan, Naushad Varish & Mohammed Aslam Husain (Eds.)

INTRODUCTION

Social media has emerged as the predominant platform for interpersonal communication. Its widespread popularity for news dissemination, information sharing, and event participation is attributed to its ability to swiftly distribute information on a large scale. While this expansive capability fosters social trust and connectivity, it also facilitates the rampant spread of misinformation [1].

Misinformation spreads widely by taking advantage of people's trust and social relationships, spreading false information to stir hatred and hurt individuals or groups. It is widely acknowledged that disinformation poses a serious threat to democracy, justice, public trust, freedom of expression, journalism, and economic growth because it has reached previously unheard-of levels on social media. As a result, addressing the problem of digital disinformation is crucial and urgent [2]. Social media plays a crucial and multifaceted role in contemporary societies, impacting various aspects of communication, culture, politics, and social interactions. Its influence, whether positive or negative, is diverse and depends on factors like geographical location and demographics [3, 4]. The following are key aspects of how social media functions and its effects on societies:

Communication and Connectivity

Social media platforms enable immediate communication, connecting people globally and maintaining relationships despite geographical distances. On the other hand, excessive reliance on virtual communication may lead to a reduction in face-to-face interactions, potentially affecting relationship quality.

Information Dissemination

Social media offers a rapid and widespread means of sharing information, aiding in spreading awareness about social issues, emergencies, and significant events. On the other hand, the rapid dissemination of misinformation and fake news is a concern, leading to the spread of inaccurate or biased information with serious consequences.

Cultural Impact

Social media facilitates the exchange of cultural ideas, fostering a more interconnected global culture and providing a platform for cultural expression. On the other hand, cultural appropriation, stereotyping, and cultural homogenization may occur, potentially resulting in misunderstandings and conflicts.

Political Impact

Social media plays a crucial role in political activism and social movements, providing a platform for marginalized voices and aiding in the organization of protests and campaigns. On the other hand, it can contribute to political polarization, the formation of echo chambers, and the spread of extremist ideologies. Additionally, concerns arise about the manipulation of social media for political purposes.

Economic Influence

Social media platforms serve as effective marketing tools, allowing businesses to reach a global audience and engage with customers directly. On the other hand, ethical and privacy concerns arise due to issues such as online scams, the proliferation of counterfeit products, and the exploitation of user data for targeted advertising.

Mental Health

Social media provides support networks for individuals facing mental health challenges, creating communities of people with shared experiences. On the other hand, continuous exposure to curated and idealized representations on social media can contribute to feelings of inadequacy, anxiety, and depression. Cyberbullying is also a significant concern.

Privacy and Security

Social media allows individuals to control their online identities and connect with others based on shared interests and values. On the other hand, concerns about data privacy, identity theft, and cyberbullying can undermine trust in online platforms and have broader societal implications [5, 6, 7]. In a summarised way, social media has become an integral part of modern societies, influencing communication, culture, politics, and more. Recognizing both the positive and negative impacts is crucial for addressing challenges and maximizing the benefits of social media in a rapidly evolving digital landscape.

The word "manipulation" in common parlance describes the artful or cunning process of influencing or managing someone or something, usually with the goal of misleading or benefiting from it. Investigating this word's etymology offers fascinating perspectives on its meaning. The Latin word "manipulare," which means "to handle, control, or manipulate," is where the word first appeared. The term "manipulare" comes from the Latin word "manipulus," which means "a handful," "a sheaf," or "a troop." [8, 9, 10].

In modern-day society, the term "manipulation" is widely employed across different languages to characterize various behaviours associated with influence, control, and deceit. This usage underscores the ongoing significance and relevance of manipulation in today's world. Although the term itself is relatively recent, the underlying concept of manipulation has roots in historical discussions among philosophers, particularly within the realms of moral and political philosophy. Most people understand manipulation as a kind of power or control that includes exploited coercion, or deceit, which makes it immoral [11, 12].

The concept of manipulation has undergone significant evolution, especially in the context of modern clinical psychology. Specifically, narcissistic, borderline, and antisocial personality disorders are increasingly thought to be linked to manipulative tendencies. In the literature of clinical psychology, manipulation commonly denotes a series of actions aimed at controlling or influencing others in a self-centered, detrimental manner, often with little consideration for the well-being of the other person [13]. Such behaviours may encompass activities like dishonesty, guilt-tripping, gaslighting, or other tactics of emotional manipulation.

Modern psychology research has shown that manipulative behavior, in which one person tries to control or take advantage of another, is a major problem in interpersonal interactions. Isolation, low self-esteem, anxiety, and sadness are some of the negative outcomes that can stem from manipulation, which is often associated with power imbalances. Although manipulative behavior is not a strict diagnostic requirement for mental disorders, it can be an indicator of personality disorders and other mental health issues [14].

Ensuring a positive and constructive online atmosphere requires adhering to ethical and responsible practices on social media [15]. The following guidelines should be considered:

a. ***Authenticity and Honesty:*** Maintain truthfulness regarding your identity and online intentions. Steers clear of generating fake profiles or disseminating false information [16].
b. ***Privacy:*** Show respect for others' privacy by refraining from sharing personal information without explicit consent. Regularly review and modify your privacy settings to regulate access to your information.
c. ***Cyberbullying and Harassment:*** Refrain from participating in cyberbullying, harassment, or any form of online mistreatment. Take prompt action by reporting and blocking individuals engaging in harmful behaviour.
d. ***Content Accuracy:*** Prioritize the verification of information accuracy before sharing it online. Avoid the dissemination of rumours, misinformation, or unverified news.

THE ROLE OF SOCIAL MEDIA AND ITS IMPACT ON SOCIETIES

It is necessary to clarify the goals, workings, and legal status of the pertinent corporate entities in order to explain why the manipulation of society and politics is a special worry on social networks. Global interactive communication is made possible by platforms such as Facebook, Twitter, Instagram, YouTube, and TikTok, which also facilitate one-to-many or many-to-many interactions. In the era of Web 2.0, a vast and anonymous user base can easily express criticism and dissent at minimal cost through channels such as Twitter and Facebook [16].

It is a difficult endeavor to identify fake news and disinformation using computational techniques because of the many difficulties. First, there is a big data problem because misinformation and false information come in various subjects, styles, and media channels. Fake news often employs varied linguistic styles to distort truth, while simultaneously mimicking authentic news [17].

For example, false information got to a point during the 2020 Corona crisis that might have endangered the proper operation of democratic decision-making. Traditionally, crises have been marked by elevated feelings and worry, and this tendency seems to be exacerbated on social media. Both common people and self-described professionals disseminate unreliable COVID-19 advice on these sites. By combining facts with erroneous interpretations, they tried to find alleged offenders and create conspiracy theories. Sensational material spread increasingly unconventional beliefs, including concerns about vaccinations and the promotion of questionable, and sometimes dangerous, medical treatments [4].

In contemplating the causes and consequences of disinformation on social media, a hermeneutic process has been adopted to comprehend and interpret the ethical and societal implications. The anticipated outcome is a collection of ethically informed recommendations for actions that can be deliberated upon and put into effect by the proprietors of these platforms.

Therefore, it is not feasible to collect annotated data for fake news, and when labelled data is limited, integrating methods that are suited to specific data is inadequate for effective detection. Secondly, the dynamic nature of fake news and disinformation presents an ongoing challenge. Due to a lack of proof or assertions, current knowledge bases may not adequately verify developing, time-sensitive events, which is a hallmark of fake news [8].

Thirdly, the explanation problem appears while creating machine learning algorithms for disinformation detection. Many existing techniques function as opaque black boxes, offering minimal to no insight into the detection process. Establishing explainability is crucial to ensuring transparency and ethical responsibility in algorithms. Nevertheless, it is difficult to develop algorithmic explanations that are helpful to domain experts and to enhance explanations by adding previous expert information [9].

DIFFERENT WAYS THROUGH WHICH SOCIETIES CAN BE MANIPULATED

Societies can be influenced in various ways, both positively and negatively [10]. A few major ways have been highlighted in Fig. (**1**).

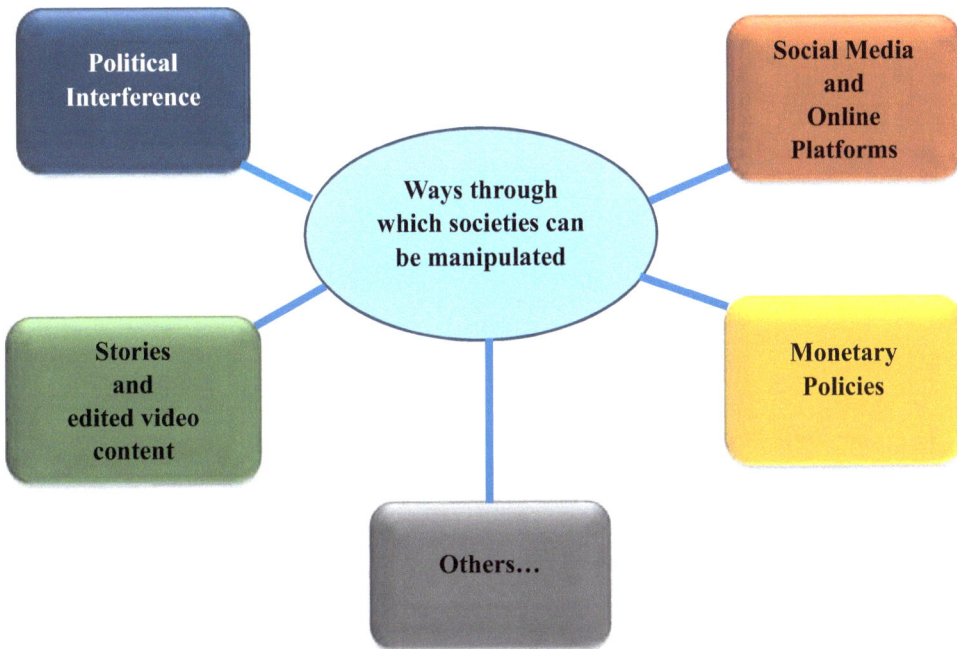

Fig. (1). Different ways through which societies can be manipulated.

Social Media and Online Platforms

Individuals disseminate information during tumultuous periods when they find it challenging to ascertain the truth or make decisions. Distinguishing between factual information and rumours/opinions becomes difficult, as human reactions tend to be intuitive rather than rational. Consequently, negative campaigns evoke heightened responses, and content that is personal and emotional tends to overshadow complexity. A more balanced majority stays silent as arguments get fierce and opposing viewpoints merge in the contemporary digital media convergence, which is functioning as "burning lenses" for an already unstable democracy. In a self-fulfilling prophecy, popular information gets even more prevalent since people and journalists often rely on internet information aggregators. The impartial framing of mainstream television and print media, such as the repetition of unverified claims without explanation, unwittingly contributes to bias [11].

Stories and Edited Video Content

Though it is crucial to realize that both images and videos can be modified, people often believe them to be real. Researchers at Stanford unveiled a novel space-time architecture-based artificial intelligence system in 2018. This innovation allows the generation of remarkably lifelike videos using only a single input video. These videos, commonly referred to as "deep fakes," pose a challenge for ordinary individuals to distinguish from genuine content, making it difficult to discern whether the person in the video is authentic Nevertheless, current trends demonstrate that manipulations of speech and video are exploited to smear the reputations of politicians and reach a wide audience.

Political Interference

The utilization of social media for political manipulation has raised significant apprehension in recent times. Diverse strategies are deployed to impact public sentiment, influence election outcomes, and mold political narratives. Some prevalent approaches include:

Dissemination of False Information

Fabricated or deceptive details are circulated across social media platforms with the intent to mislead the public. This encompasses the creation and sharing of deceptive news articles, manipulated visuals, or entirely fictional narratives to bolster a specific political agenda.

Manipulation Through Deepfakes

Advanced technologies for manipulating videos and audio are employed to generate lifelike yet entirely false content. Politicians' speeches or actions can be altered to disseminate inaccurate information or tarnish their reputations.

Monetary Policies

Governments can manipulate economic conditions through monetary policies, affecting inflation, interest rates, and employment. Advertising and marketing strategies can influence societal values and behaviours by promoting certain lifestyles or products.

ESSENTIAL CHARACTERISTICS OF MANIPULATION

Manipulation is the exertion of influence or control over someone or something through clever or unscrupulous means. It can manifest in diverse settings, such as interpersonal relationships, business, politics, and beyond. While manipulation can serve both positive and negative ends, its deceptive or exploitative use frequently carries negative implications [12]. The following outlines key attributes associated with manipulation:

Deception

Manipulation frequently includes employing deceit, as the manipulator hides their actual motives or distorts information to attain their preferred result. This may encompass falsehoods, exaggeration, or the intentional omission of vital details.

Control

Manipulation is motivated by a longing for authority over others or a particular circumstance. Those who engage in manipulation aim to shape the thoughts, emotions, or behaviours of their subject in order to conform to their own objectives.

Exploitation

Manipulation frequently includes taking advantage of the vulnerabilities, fears, or weaknesses of the target. This may be undertaken to secure an edge, extract resources, or accomplish personal objectives, even if it comes at the cost of the manipulated individual.

Planning with a Strategic Approach

Successful manipulation typically demands meticulous planning and strategic thinking. Manipulators may assess their targets, pinpoint vulnerabilities, and devise a plan to attain their goals.

Exerting an Impact on Emotions

Emotional influence involves manipulators using emotions to manipulate their targets. This may include exploiting feelings of guilt, fear, love, or sympathy to impact the behaviour of the target.

It is crucial to recognize that not all forms of influence or persuasion are inherently manipulative. Positive and ethical persuasion relies on clear communication, respect for the autonomy of others, and a sincere intention to foster mutual benefit. A comprehension of the traits associated with manipulation can assist individuals in identifying and protecting themselves against manipulative strategies.

MANIPULATION AND AI

According to the criteria given, some digitally driven sociotechnical phenomena have raised questions about the possibility of manipulation. Pay close attention to the following: social media networks, deepfake technology, tailored search algorithms, and microtargeting advertising.

Online platforms allowing people and organizations to produce, distribute, and trade user-generated content—text, photos, videos, and links—are referred to as social media. Profile building, publishing of content, sharing, commenting, and reacting are just a few of the functions available on these sites. Users' networking, interaction, and communication are intended to be facilitated by their architecture. With its many uses—entertainment, information sharing, political participation, and corporate promotion—social media has become an essential component of modern life. But social media's broad use has also raised important social, cultural, and ethical questions about privacy, cyberbullying, filter bubbles, and the propagation of false information [13]. Specifically, social networking sites have been accused of using algorithms to control the material that appears in users' feeds, therefore advancing particular political or commercial agendas.

ADDRESSING DIGITAL MANIPULATION

Addressing digital manipulation requires proactive measures to safeguard oneself and others from deceitful practices on the internet [14].

Fig. (2) represents some approaches to minimize the impact of digital manipulation:

Critical Thinking and Media Literacy

Cultivate robust critical thinking abilities for evaluating information thoughtfully. Remain mindful of potential biases and scrutinize the origins of information. Dedicate time to engage in media literacy education to comprehend the processes involved in producing, disseminating, and consuming information.

Verify Information

Verify information by consulting several trustworthy sources before accepting or disseminating it.

Employ fact-checking websites to confirm the accuracy of statements and narratives.

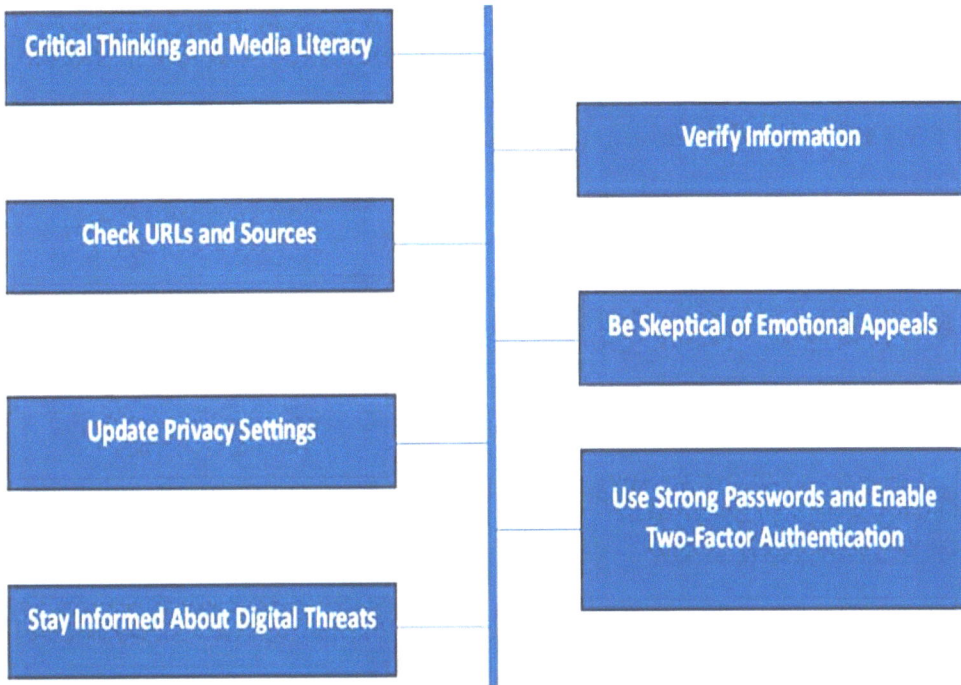

Fig. (2). Steps of address digital manipulation.

Check URLs and Sources

Authenticate websites by examining the URL for misspellings or unusual characters.

Confirm the reliability of sources and exercise caution when encountering information from unfamiliar or dubious websites.

Be Skeptical of Emotional Appeals

Exercise caution regarding content crafted to elicit intense emotions, as it could be a manipulative strategy.

Pause and contemplate the emotional influence of information before responding or disseminating it.

Update Privacy Settings

To manage the information, we disclose and restrict who can access it, and regularly review and adjust your privacy settings on social media sites.

Exercise prudence when sharing personal details on the internet.

Use Strong Passwords and Enable Two-Factor Authentication

Secure your online accounts with robust and distinct passwords.

Enhance your account security by activating two-factor authentication for an additional layer of protection.

Stay Informed About Digital Threats

Stay informed about prevalent techniques employed in digital manipulation, including phishing, misinformation, and social engineering. Acquaint yourself with common cybersecurity risks and fraudulent schemes.

DISINFORMATION DETECTION AND COMBATING DISINFORMATION

In recent years, the issue of disinformation and misinformation has gained significant attention. Social media's accessibility and anonymity have made it simple for users to share information, but they have also rendered the platforms more vulnerable to harmful activity. Although the transmission of misinformation and disinformation has been studied in journalism, social media's openness and automation's potential allow for the quick spread of this false information to wide audiences, creating hitherto unheard-of difficulties. To clarify, disinformation refers to intentionally spreading false or inaccurate information with the aim of misleading or deceiving, whereas misinformation involves false content shared unknowingly by individuals who are unaware of its inaccuracy or misleading nature [15].

The examination of news content and social context is usually the main focus of techniques for spotting fake news [16]. The examination of news content is necessary to distinguish between fake and real news, with news content-based elements acting as the most direct markers for fake news identification. The requirement for content-based fake news identification is that the substance of false information should show quantifiable variations from the truth since the assessed news on social media is primarily textual [17].

The features of content-based techniques can be classified as either visually based or linguistically based. Linguistic elements, including lexical and syntactic data, capture the unique writing styles and attention-grabbing headlines that are typical of false news articles. However, it is not easy for these algorithms to generalize linguistic qualities that are hand-crafted across different domains, languages, and topics. Furthermore, individuals have a hard time making good use of the abundant contextual and semantic data that is accessible to them [4].

To overcome the limitations of linguistic-based approaches, there has been extensive exploration of deep neural network methods, including recurrent neural networks (RNNs), convolutional neural networks, and variational autoencoders (VAEs) in recent years. This is explained by their capacity to recognise complex contextual patterns in news material and to automatically acquire latent textual representations [4].

Visually based features seek to identify photos that have been purposefully altered or that have certain traits linked to photos of fake news. Information will spread more widely if news has visual components since users of social media are more likely to notice it. The combination of visual and linguistic features has demonstrated superior performance compared to using a single modality of features. For instance, the author introduced an automatic multimodal fake news detection model based on recurrent neural networks (RNNs), which integrates visual and textual information through an attention mechanism [3]. Additionally, an innovative fake news detection method is introduced that considers the correlations across different modalities.

ETHICAL OBLIGATIONS AND SOCIETAL RESPONSIBILITIES OF AI DEVELOPERS

AI developers have ethical obligations and societal responsibilities that stem from the potential impact of their creations on individuals and communities [5]. Here are some key aspects to consider:

Transparency and Responsibility

Developers ought to prioritize transparency throughout the AI system's design, development, and deployment, ensuring that decision-making processes and algorithms are comprehensible to individuals without technical expertise. Additionally, it is essential to institute accountability mechanisms in cases where AI systems result in harm. Developers must acknowledge responsibility for rectifying unintended consequences and gaining insights from errors.

Equity and Impartiality

We need to make sure that AI systems are crafted and trained with a focus on fairness and impartiality. This entails recognizing and mitigating biases in training data and algorithms to prevent discrimination against specific groups. We must consistently evaluate and audit AI systems to identify and rectify any biased outcomes. The use of fairness metrics and diverse datasets can contribute to achieving impartial results.

Privacy

Safeguarding the rights to privacy by incorporating robust data protection measures is necessary. This limits the gathering and utilization of personal data to the essential requirements for the intended purpose. This let us communicate with users about the intended use of their data and secure explicit consent for data collection, ensuring adherence to privacy regulations.

Security

Give precedence to the security of AI systems to deter unauthorized access or misuse. Introduce strong security measures to guard against cyber threats and attacks. We consistently update and apply patches to AI systems, addressing vulnerabilities and proactively managing evolving security risks.

Empowering Users

Empowering users by offering transparent details on the functioning of AI systems and the decision-making process is another important aspect. This grants users control over their data, providing customization options and transparency. User-friendly AI interfaces promote responsible usage, steering clear of deceptive practices or manipulative behaviours.

Evaluation of Societal Repercussions

Conduct comprehensive assessments of the social impact before implementing AI systems. Take into account potential effects on employment, education, and various societal facets. Involve a wide range of stakeholders, including impacted communities, to collect feedback and perspectives regarding the potential influences of AI technologies.

Ongoing Observation and Enhancement

Consistently observe and assess the functionality of AI systems in real-world situations. Employ feedback loops to recognize and resolve issues that may emerge over time. Dedicate to continuous learning and enhancement, staying abreast of ethical best practices and integrating them into the development process.

Cooperation and the Exchange of Knowledge

Encourage partnerships with fellow AI developers, researchers, and stakeholders to exchange insights, best practices, and ethical methodologies in AI development. Contribute to the establishment of industry-wide standards and guidelines, ensuring a unified dedication to ethical AI practices.

By embracing these ethical principles and societal obligations, AI developers can actively contribute to the responsible and advantageous implementation of AI technologies across diverse domains.

SOCIETAL RESPONSIBILITIES OF REGULATORY BODIES

Regulatory bodies bear distinct duties and societal roles in guaranteeing the appropriate operation, safety, and ethical utilization of diverse industries [5, 8]. These responsibilities may include the following:

Implementation of Criteria

Set and uphold standards within the industry to ensure the excellence, safety, and dependability of products and services.

Safeguarding the Rights and Interests of Consumers

Protect consumers' rights by overseeing and resolving concerns such as fraud, misinformation, and unjust business practices.

Ensuring the Safety of the Public

Enforce rules to secure public safety, especially in sectors with potential risks, such as healthcare, transportation, and environmental preservation.

Ethical Reflections

Consider ethical ramifications in regulatory choices, especially in realms like human rights, privacy, and the conscientious application of technology.

Promotion of Knowledge and Consciousness

Supply the public and businesses with information and educational materials to elevate understanding of regulations and compliance obligations.

Engagement with Global Organizations

Cooperate with regulatory bodies on the international stage to tackle global issues and align standards where feasible.

Regulatory bodies have a pivotal role in striking a balance between fostering economic growth and safeguarding the welfare of individuals and the environment. Their duties and responsibilities adapt to the shifting dynamics of societal needs and technological landscapes.

CONCLUSION

The rise of digital and AI-powered systems, including social media, targeted marketing, and personalized search tools, has introduced innovative ways to interact with users and collect data. However, concerns about potential manipulation have arisen due to the unique capabilities of these systems in targeting and influencing individuals through automation. Social media algorithms create user profiles based on online activities, enabling tailored recommendations to specific audience segments. This amplifies the risk of propaganda and misinformation impacting individuals' perspectives and choices, particularly in electoral contexts. The chapter emphasizes the function of artificial intelligence and associated technologies while giving a thorough assessment of the body of knowledge on manipulation. It also delves into the ethical responsibilities of AI developers, social media platforms, and regulatory bodies in addressing these concerns and mitigating negative impacts.

REFERENCES

[1]   N. Bontridder, and Y. Poullet, "The role of artificial intelligence in disinformation", *Data Policy,* vol. 3, no. 3, p. e32, 2021.
[http://dx.doi.org/10.1017/dap.2021.20]

[2]   M. Ienca, "On Artificial Intelligence and Manipulation", *Topoi (Dordr.),* vol. 42, no. 3, pp. 833-842, 2023.
[http://dx.doi.org/10.1007/s11245-023-09940-3]

[3]   K. Shu, "Combating disinformation on social media: A computational perspective", *BenchCouncil Transactions on Benchmarks, Standards and Evaluations,* vol. 2, no. 1, p. 100035, 2022.
[http://dx.doi.org/10.1016/j.tbench.2022.100035]

[4]   U. Reisach, "The responsibility of social media in times of societal and political manipulation", *Eur. J. Oper. Res.,* vol. 291, no. 3, pp. 906-917, 2021.
[http://dx.doi.org/10.1016/j.ejor.2020.09.020] [PMID: 32982027]

[5]   E. Gideon, A. Rifqi, M. Jerome, N. Fathia, M. Noor, and M. Masrom, *Sains Humanika Social Media Identity Manipulation: A Review in the Context of Industry 4. 0* vol. 1. , 2023, no. 2024, pp. 1-7.

[6]   M. Carroll, A. Chan, H. Ashton, and D. Krueger, "Characterizing Manipulation from AI Systems", *ACM Int. Conf. Proceeding Ser,* 2023.
[http://dx.doi.org/10.1145/3617694.3623226]

[7]   M. Vangeli, *The Philosophy of Algorithmic Manipulation.*.

[8]   L. Illia, E. Colleoni, and S. Zyglidopoulos, "Ethical implications of text generation in the age of artificial intelligence", *Bus. Ethics Environ. Responsib.,* vol. 32, no. 1, pp. 201-210, 2023.
[http://dx.doi.org/10.1111/beer.12479]

[9]   S. Karnouskos, "Artificial Intelligence in Digital Media: The Era of Deepfakes", *IEEE Trans. Technol. Soc.,* vol. 1, no. 3, pp. 138-147, 2020.
[http://dx.doi.org/10.1109/TTS.2020.3001312]

[10]   N. Helberger, M. Van Drunen, S. Eskens, M. Bastian, and J. Moeller, "A freedom of expression perspective on AI in the media-with a special focus on editorial decision making on social media platforms and in the news media", *Eur. J. Law Technol.,* vol. 11, 2020no. 3, .Available from: https://lawreview.law.ucdavis.edu/issues/51/3/Essays/51-3_Balkin.pdf

[11]   C. Wu, F. Wu, T. Qi, W.Q. Zhang, X. Xie, and Y. Huang, "Removing AI's sentiment manipulation of personalized news delivery", *Humanit. Soc. Sci. Commun.,* vol. 9, no. 1, p. 459, 2022.
[http://dx.doi.org/10.1057/s41599-022-01473-1]

[12]   A. Knott, *Responsible AI for Social Media,* 2021.

[13]   N.A. Farooqui, M. Pandey, R. Mirza, S. Ali, and A.N. Khan, "8 Exploratory study of the parental perception of social learning among school-aged children based on augmented and virtual reality", *Augmented and Virtual Reality in Social Learning: Technological Impacts and Challenges,* vol. 3, pp. 117-140, 2023.
[http://dx.doi.org/10.1515/9783110981445-008]

[14]   N.A. Farooqui, and A.S. Ritika, "Sentiment analysis of twitter accounts using natural language processing", *Int. J. Eng. Adv. Technol.,* vol. 8, no. 3, pp. 473-479, 2019.

[15]   Wasim Khan *et al*, *Anomalous node detection in attributed social networks using dual variational autoencoder with generative adversarial networks,* 2023.
[http://dx.doi.org/10.1016/j.dsm.2023.10.005]

[16]   W. Khan, M. Ishrat, M. Haleem, A.N. Khan, M.K. Hasan, and N.A. Farooqui, An Extensive Study and Review on Dark Web Threats and Detection Techniques.*Advances in Cyberology and the Advent of the Next-Gen Information Revolution.* IGI Global, 2023, pp. 202-219.
[http://dx.doi.org/10.4018/978-1-6684-8133-2.ch011]

[17]   Mohd. Haleem, Md. Faizan Farooqui, Md. Faisal"Cognitive impact validation of requirement uncertainty in software project development", *International Journal of Cognitive Computing in Engineering,* vol. 2, pp. 1-11, 2021.
[http://dx.doi.org/10.1016/j.ijcce.2020.12.002]

CHAPTER 5

Recent Trends in AI-Driven Human Detection Tactics

Mohd. Aquib Ansari[1], **Khalid Anwar**[1,*], **Arvind Mewada**[1] and **Aasim Zafar**[2]

[1] *SCSET, Bennett University, Greater Noida, U.P., India*

[2] *Department of Computer Science, Aligarh Muslim University, Aligarh, India*

Abstract: In the age of technology, the main function of video surveillance is to detect and track individuals in dynamic environments. This chapter extensively explores and reviews comprehensive literature on various human detection methodologies and datasets, focusing on frameworks that detect human presence through object detection methods by processing video sequences.

The object detection techniques discussed include face detection, motion detection, frame differencing, histogram-based, and geometry-based approaches. These techniques classify objects as human or non-human using different deep learning and machine learning models. This survey explores current technological advancements and their frameworks, revealing insights from studies addressing challenges such as occlusion, pose variation, and environmental complexities.

An overview of prominent human detection datasets, such as INRIA, MIT, CAVIAR, CALTECH, and others, offers valuable resources for training and evaluating detection models. This comprehensive exploration aims to provide researchers and practitioners with a cohesive understanding of human detection methodologies, challenges, and diverse datasets for advancing this critical field in computer vision and surveillance technology.

Keywords: Benchmark datasets, Fuzzy and neutrosophic logic, Human detection, Image analysis, Machine learning, Video surveillance.

INTRODUCTION

Recent advancements in computational intelligence approaches have led to the development of automated systems in several real-life applications, including natural language processing (NLP), recommender systems (RS), sentiment analysis (SA), and computer vision (CV) [1]. The automation of surveillance systems has improved the efficiency of many organizations, and it has gained

---

* **Corresponding author Khalid Anwar:** SCSET, Bennett University, Greater Noida, U.P., India; E-mail: khalid35amu@gmail.com

Asif Khan, Mohammad Kamrul Hasan, Naushad Varish & Mohammed Aslam Husain (Eds.)

wide acceptance in many real-life applications, including gender recognition, counting and identifying persons entering highly secure and crowded places, detecting road traffic signals, recognizing number plates, violence detection, and many more. Video surveillance systems are highly effective in crime prevention by detecting violence and illegal activities. Traditional surveillance systems rely on humans, leading to delays in detecting criminal activities [2]. Automating surveillance eliminates the delay in manual surveillance and improves the effectiveness of real-time surveillance systems and detection.

Generally, object detection is figuring out if there is an instance of a particular object class in a scene. The CV systems use human detection and tracking to find and follow individuals in video footage [3]. Finding the instance of a person in an image is known as "human detection". It has most commonly been achieved by looking for human occurrences at every size and position in the picture and comparing a small portion of each with known human patterns or templates. Creating permanent routes, or trajectories, for individuals in a video series by temporally linking the person detections is known as "human tracking." In a video surveillance pipeline, human identification and tracking are typically regarded as the initial two steps. These techniques, such as action recognition and dynamic scene analysis, may be included in higher-level reasoning modules.

Fig. (1) shows the basic human detection framework that can be used in surveillance and many more applications. The camera takes the input in the form of video sequences. The object detection process is done on these input sequences, which detect the intended objects by analyzing each sequence. Then, these objects are classified, whether the object is human or not, through various classification algorithms.

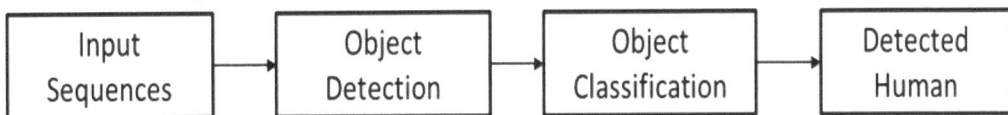

Input Sequences	→	Object Detection	→	Object Classification	→	Detected Human

Fig. (1). Human Detection Framework.

Detecting humans in real-time video sequences is challenging due to constraints such as occlusion, cluttered environment, noise, *etc*. Several researchers have worked in this area, and research has been published. The identification of persons is important for many kinds of applications in visual monitoring systems [4], such as person detection and identification, elderly fall detection, aberrant surveillance, gender classification, crowd analysis, and person gait analysis. This chapter aims to provide a comprehensive guide for human detection in surveillance videos. It is believed that the researchers working in the area of CV in general and human detection in particular will find this work useful. The contributions of this chapter are summarised in the following points.

- It presents and discusses different classification techniques used for human detection.
- It overviews the machine-learning approaches used for human detection.
- It elaborates on different benchmark data sets used to train human detection models.
- It discusses potential future research directions in the area of human detection.

The remaining sections of the chapter are organized as follows: Section 2 discusses different human detection techniques and their classification. Chapter 3 covers various machine-learning algorithms used for human detection. Chapter 4 presents the different available datasets for training human detection classifiers. Future research opportunities are discussed in Section 5. Finally, Section 6 provides the conclusion.

CLASSIFICATION OF HUMAN DETECTION TECHNIQUES

Several researchers have provided various methods in the area of human detection. These methods can be broadly classified based on the nature of the algorithm. The classification tree of human detection algorithm is shown in Fig. (**2**). The human detection algorithms are classified into modules, each containing several algorithms, as outlined below.

a. Face Detection Based Human Detection algorithms classify a segment of the face as a person if a human's face is found in that portion.
b. Motion-Based Human Detection Algorithms: the pixel movement vectors are traced in the successive frames, and these pixels are classified into human body or background pixels.
c. Human Detection using Frame Differencing Algorithms: it detects the human by subtracting the current frame from the reference frame.
d. Histogram-Based Human Detection Algorithms: based on various attributes, the histogram vector is made for the image and then trains a classifier using histogram characteristics for the human body.
e. Geometry-Based Human Detection Algorithm: It uses information about the human body, its components, curves, and straight-line information to make a classifier for the human body.

While examining some techniques, many challenges may have to be faced due to shadow, cluttered areas, the wind causing reflections, illumination, noises, object overlapping, the slow movement of objects, *etc*. They may affect the algorithm badly and produce inappropriate results. Table **1** presents the summary of various human detection techniques.

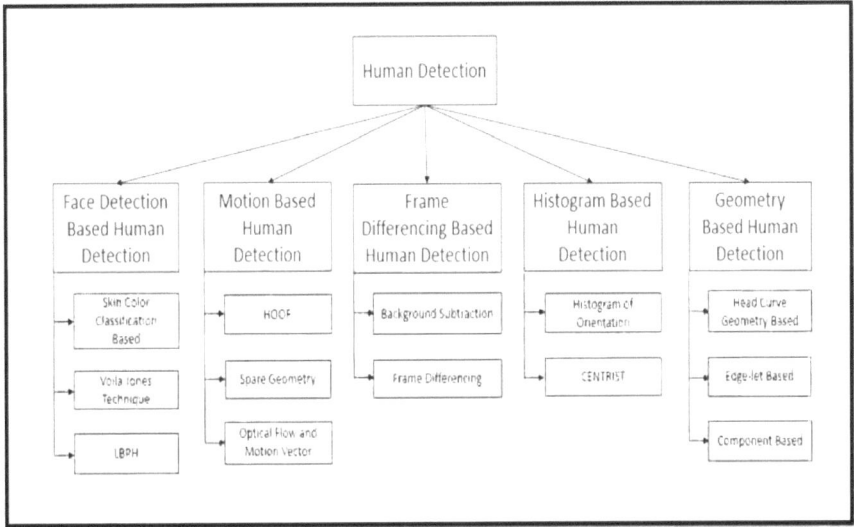

Fig. (2). Human Detection Technique's Classification.

Table 1. Human Detection Techniques.

Category	Description	Techniques	Concept	Remarks
Face Detection Based Human Detection	It classifies a segment of the face as a person if a human's face is found in that portion.	Skin Color Modelling [6]	Extract the face based on skin pixels.	☐ It is simple and fast. ☐ It is sensitive to illumination, cluttered backgrounds, ethnicity, *etc*.
		Voila Zones [7]	It uses the Haar descriptor to evaluate the features of the face. Further, these features are used to build a classifier.	☐ 15 times quicker than Skin based techniques ☐ It is effective only for frontal face images.
		Local Binary Pattern Histogram (LBPH) [8, 9]	First, LBP features are evaluated, and then a histogram is produced on these features to help build a Classifier.	☐ This model provides effective frontal face features in low computational time. ☐ It can't detect the face under varied expressions.
Frame Differencing-Based Human Detection	It detects the human by subtracting the current frame from the reference frame.	Background Subtraction [10, 11]	It detects the human by subtracting the current frame from the fixed background frame.	☐ It is a direct pixel-based subtraction technique. ☐ The background needs to be stationary.
		Frame Differencing [12]	It detects the human by subtracting the current frame from the previous frame.	☐ It can resist light interference up to some extent. ☐ This algorithm turns an object into the background if it simply stops moving.

(Table 1) cont.....

Category	Description	Techniques	Concept	Remarks
Motion-Based Human Detection	The pixel movement vectors are traced in successive frames, and these pixels are classified into human body pixels or background pixels.	Spare Geometry [13]	Detect human by region segmentation and Classification	☐ It can identify humans amidst all the moving objects. ☐ Not as accurate as optical flow.
		Optical Flow and Motion Vector [14, 15]	Optical flow combined with motion vector estimates is used for object detection and tracking in the video frame sequences.	☐ It provides an estimation of object position from consecutive frames that increases the accuracy. ☐ Unable to detect very slow-moving objects.
		Histogram of Oriented Optical Flow (HOOF) [16]	It uses motion extraction, segmentation, and histogram generation to detect human presence before classifying them.	☐ It is scale-invariant and combines the advantages of motion and shape features. ☐ High computational cost.
Histogram-Based Human Detection	The histogram vectors are created for the human body based on various attributes, which are then used to build the classifier.	Histogram of Oriented Gradient (HOG) [17, 18]	This method counts instances of gradient orientation in specific areas of an image.	☐ It can deal with occlusion. ☐ Because of the HOG's extremely long feature length, computing costs are exceedingly expensive.
		Census Transform Histogram [19]	It extracts the local features of the images by comparing each pixel with all its 8-connected neighbours.	☐ It can be used with thermal images/video and is much more time-efficient than HOG. ☐ It can't deal with high-dimensional sparse databases.
Geometry-Based Human Detection	It uses information about the human body, its components, curves and straight-line information to make a classifier for the human body.	Head Curve Geometry [20]	Human detection is performed using point searching and curve drawing algorithms.	☐ It can deal with thermal images. ☐ It cannot detect multiple humans in the same frame.
		Edgelet Based [21]	It detects humans by evaluating Edgelet features, which helps build the classifier.	☐ It is invariant to reflection, shadows and clothing differences. ☐ It is not accurate to deal with the harsh environment.
		Component-Based [22]	Each separated component is detected first and then combined using some geographical configuration.	☐ It can identify partially occluded people within the video sequences. ☐ It can't deal with noisy and harsh environments.

(Table 1) cont.....

Category	Description	Techniques	Concept	Remarks
CNN	It excels in detecting and precisely locating individual or multiple objects within an image. In terms of its operation, the image is first segmented into different regions, and subsequently, each region is classified into specific categories.	R-CNN [23]	The utilization of the Selective Search algorithm facilitates the generation of region proposals. Convolutional Neural Networks (CNN) are applied for feature extraction, while Support Vector Machines (SVM) serve the purpose of object classification.	☐ Due to its significant computational demands, this approach cannot be executed in real-time, as approximately 47 seconds are required to process a test image.
		Faster RCNN [24]	Faster R-CNN swaps out the old Selective Search algorithm for the Region Proposal Network.	☐ Its performance hinges on the preceding systems, causing delays in object proposals.
		Yolo v3 [25]	YOLOv3 utilizes Darknet-53 to extract features while employing multiscale prediction to generate more detailed and refined information. Logistic regression and binary cross-entropy loss functions are applied to forecast the score and classes.	☐ YOLOv3 encounters challenges when identifying small objects within clustered groups.
		SSD [26]	SSD builds upon the VGG16 architecture as its fundamental framework. It utilizes multiscale feature maps and default bounding boxes to detect objects independently.	☐ Like YOLOv3, it suffers from similar problems.
		Marks R-CNN [27]	It enhances Faster R-CNN by integrating an extra branch that predicts the mask of an object alongside the primary branch responsible for detecting bounding boxes.	☐ It doesn't match the speed of Faster R-CNN.
		F-YOLO [28]	Its foundational approach is Tiny-Darknet. F-YOLO improves performance by using a distillation loss function in a single pass detector, transferring knowledge from the teacher network's feature maps to the student network.	☐ It's faster but sacrifices some accuracy compared to other methods.

CLASSIFIERS

This section presents different machine and deep learning classifiers used for human detection [5, 12, 15, 16, 20, 25, 29, 40]. The identified classifiers are Naïve Bayes, Nearest Neighbour, Logistics Regression, decision tree, random forest, neural networks and many more. A brief description of the classifiers is given in the subsequent subsections.

Naive Bayes Classifier (Generative Learning Model)

This classification method assumes predictor independence and is based on the Bayes theorem. Simply put, a Naive Bayes classifier assumes that a feature's presence in a class is independent of the existence of any other feature. Each of these attributes individually increases the chance, even if they depend on the other traits or their existence. The Naive Bayes model is especially helpful for large data sets and is simple to construct. Naive Bayes is recognized to perform better than even quite complex classification techniques, and it is simple.

Nearest Neighbor

As a supervised classification method, the k-nearest-neighbors algorithm takes a set of labelled points and uses them to teach itself how to classify new points [3]. When a new point must be labelled, it first looks at the labelled points closest to it (*i.e.*, its nearest neighbours) and asks them to vote. The new point is then assigned the label that most of its neighbours have (the number of neighbours it checks is "k") [30].

Logistic Regression (Predictive Learning Model)

This statistical technique analyses data collection where one or more independent factors determine a result. A dichotomous variable with only two potential outcomes is used to quantify the result. Logistic regression aims to find the best-fitting model to explain the connection between a collection of independent (predictor or explanatory) factors and the dichotomous feature of interest. Since it also provides a quantitative explanation of the elements that influence categorization, this binary classification is superior to others, such as the closest neighbour [31].

Decision Trees

A decision tree uses a tree structure to construct models for regression or classification. It partitions a data set into ever smaller sections and simultaneously builds an accompanying decision tree piecemeal. A tree containing decision nodes and leaf nodes is the end product. A decision node comprises two or more branches, with a decision or classification represented by a leaf node. The root node of a tree is the highest decision node, corresponding to the best predictor. Decision trees may handle both numerical and categorical data [32].

Random Forest

During training, many decision trees are constructed. In the end, the class representing the mean prediction (regression) or mode of each tree's class (classification) is the output. Random forests are an ensemble learning method for problems such as regression and classification. These are often referred to as random decision forests. Random decision forests correct the tendency of decision trees to over-match their training set [33].

Neural Network

A neural network comprises layers of units called neurons that process input vectors and produce outputs. Every unit receives an input, processes it using a (often nonlinear) function, and then forwards the result to the subsequent layer. In general, networks are designed to be feed-forward, meaning no feedback is sent back to the previous layer; instead, a unit feeds its output to every unit on the next layer. In order to tailor a neural network to the specific task at hand, weightings are added to the signals sent between units. These weightings are adjusted throughout the training phase.

DATASETS FOR HUMAN DETECTION

Table **2** summarises prominent human detection datasets, detailing their characteristics regarding training and testing data. These datasets differ in the number of positive and negative samples, the types of data they contain (such as images or videos), and additional information such as creation year and specific features. They serve as crucial resources for evaluating and advancing human detection algorithms by offering diverse and challenging scenarios for assessment.

In 2005, the National Institute for Research in Digital Science and Technology (INRIA) built a benchmark dataset for human detection research [34]. The INRIA dataset was annotated with bounding boxes, with 3,634 images distributed into positive (human-containing) and negative (background) samples. This dataset facilitates the training and testing of human detection algorithms in various real-world scenarios. Despite its age, it remains widely used due to its quality annotations and relevance. Available for academic use, it aids reproducibility and comparability in CV research.

Table 2. Human Detection Datasets.

Dataset	Training Data		Testing data		Video Sequences/Image	Remark
	Positive Data	Negative Data	Positive Data	Negative Data		
INRIA	2416	1218	1127	453	Images	Different versions of cropped humans generated in 2005.
MIT	Total 924 images without separating positive and negative				Images	The uncompressed version, with a size of 22 Mbytes, was created in 2000.
CAVIAR	Videos in the "People Walking Alone" class are typically between 6 and 12 MB in size.				Video	Video is captured at different positions, such as in a corridor or front view. Created in 2004.
CALTECH	61000	61000	56000	65000	Video	Detailed detection results are also incorporated, with a total size of 11 GB, created in 2009.
NICTA	187000	5200	6900	50000	Video	Created in 2008
TUD-Brussels	1092	192	508		Video	Produced in an urban environment in 2009.
CVC	six datasets, CVC 01 through CVC 06, produced between 2007 and 2013.				Video	Pedestrian annotations and partial occlusions are part of the package.
PETS 2009	Three testing datasets with varying video sizes and one training dataset				Video	Include inter-object occlusion. Created in 2009.

Researchers at the Massachusetts Institute of Technology (MIT) researched human identity in 2000 [35]. They collected 924 images of positive and negative samples as well as human and background images. This dataset from MIT needs compatibility with modern deep learning techniques and addresses biases arising from dated image characteristics. Despite the lack of explicit annotations, it is a large collection of images suitable for training and testing human recognition algorithms. However, there are also potential limitations due to its age and lack of annotated ground truth data.

Robert Fischer *et al.* [36] published a research article titled "The Context-Aware Vision Using Image-Based Active Recognition (CAVIAR) on Human Detection" in 2004. For this research, they created a dataset called CAVIAR that contained video sequences capturing individuals walking alone in different environments, which provides rich temporal information important for human recognition research. These sequences vary in size, typically between 6 and 12 MB, and depict people walking in scenarios such as corridors or open spaces. This dataset provides a realistic representation of human movement and behaviour, which is valuable for evaluating and training human recognition algorithms in dynamic settings.

As the research was performed in the field of human detection day by day, a new dataset, NICTA, was introduced by researchers at the National Information and Communications Technology Authority (NICTA) in 2008 [38]. This dataset has significant resource features due to a large collection of annotated video samples. The images of this dataset offer diverse scenarios and environments for machine learning model evaluation and training. It contains 187,000 training and 5,200 testing samples and provides ample data for developing robust model human detection capable of handling various real-world challenges and scenarios.

Researchers at the California Institute of Technology created a popular dataset called CALTECH for human recognition in 2009 [37]. This dataset has established itself as a standard for human recognition research, consisting of annotated video sequences. This dataset includes a wide range of pedestrian scenarios captured in real-world environments. With a total size of 11 GB, it includes detailed annotations to evaluate the detection algorithms accurately. CALTECH presents various challenges, such as occlusion and varying lighting conditions, making it an invaluable resource for training and testing advanced human recognition models.

In 2009, the TUD-Brussels dataset captured real-world surveillance scenarios and human behaviour in urban environments [39]. It also captures the activities of pedestrians in the city, so this dataset is valuable for training and evaluating human recognition algorithms. This dataset contains 1,092 training samples and 192 testing samples, facilitating the development of algorithms for urban monitoring and security applications.

The Computer Vision Center (CVC) dataset amalgamates CVC-01 to CVC-06, built between 2007 and 2013. Each dataset includes annotated video sequences with pedestrian annotations and occlusion information, providing valuable resources for human detection research. These datasets offer diverse scenarios and challenges, aiding in developing robust algorithms capable of handling occlusions and varying environmental conditions.

In 2009, J. Ferryman *et al.* [5] conducted a performance evaluation of the tracking and monitoring (PETS) dataset presented in the published research. It includes testing datasets with different video sizes and an extensive training dataset for human recognition research. This dataset includes inter-object occlusion, which enhances the practicality of surveillance evaluation. Due to the annotated ground truth and diverse scenarios, the PETS 2009 dataset is a benchmark for evaluating human identification algorithms in complex surveillance environments, and it facilitates advances in video-based human identification technologies.

FUTURE RESEARCH OPPORTUNITIES

This section discusses possible future research opportunities. These research directions aim to push the boundaries of AI-based human detection systems by harnessing the capabilities of fuzzy logic and neutrosophic reasoning. By exploring innovative methodologies and addressing real-world challenges, researchers can contribute to developing more robust, adaptable, and trustworthy human detection technologies with broad applications in diverse domains.

Exploring Fuzzy Logic in Human Detection

Investigating the integration of fuzzy logic into AI-based human detection systems presents an intriguing avenue for future research [31]. Fuzzy logic enables modelling uncertainty and imprecision inherent in human detection tasks, offering a more nuanced approach to decision-making [32]. Future studies could explore incorporating fuzzy logic techniques, such as fuzzy inference systems, fuzzy clustering, and fuzzy rule-based classifiers, to enhance the robustness and adaptability of human detection algorithms.

Neutrosophic Deep Learning Architectures for Multimodal Human Detection

Investigating the development of neutrosophic deep learning architectures capable of integrating information from multiple modalities holds promise for advancing human detection in complex scenarios [33]. Future studies could explore the design of novel neural network architectures that incorporate neutrosophic representations of multimodal data, such as combining visual, thermal, and depth information for improved human detection performance in challenging environments.

Adaptive Fusion of Fuzzy and Neutrosophic Techniques

Future research directions could focus on developing adaptive fusion strategies for combining fuzzy and neutrosophic techniques in dynamic environments. By dynamically adjusting the weights assigned to fuzzy and neutrosophic components based on the level of uncertainty and contradiction in the data, researchers can create more flexible and adaptive human detection systems capable of robust performance across diverse environmental conditions.

Explainable AI for Human Detection

Exploring explainable AI techniques in the context of human detection can enhance transparency and interpretability, which is critical for building trust in AI-based systems. Future research could investigate the integration of fuzzy and neutrosophic explanations within human detection algorithms, enabling users to understand the reasoning behind the system's decisions and facilitating effective human-machine collaboration in applications such as surveillance and security.

Cross-Domain Transfer Learning with Fuzzy and Neutrosophic Models

Transfer learning techniques can explore the transferability of fuzzy and neuro-sophisticated models trained on one domain to improve human recognition in different domains in future research. By transferring knowledge learned from well-labelled domains to domains with limited labelled data, researchers can mitigate the need for extensive annotation efforts and adapt human detection systems to new environments more efficiently.

Combating Cyber Attacks in Human Detection System

The rapid advancement and widespread adoption of AI-based human detection technology have brought unprecedented capabilities in various sectors, ranging from surveillance and security to healthcare and retail. However, this technological progress has also attracted the attention of malicious actors seeking to exploit vulnerabilities for nefarious purposes. Cyber attacks targeting human detection AI systems pose significant threats, compromising data integrity and user privacy. Adversarial attacks, wherein adversaries manipulate input data to deceive AI models, can lead to erroneous detections or the evasion of detection altogether. Furthermore, data poisoning attacks, which involve the injection of malicious data into training datasets, can compromise the accuracy and reliability of AI models, resulting in biased or discriminatory outcomes. Addressing these cybersecurity challenges requires a comprehensive approach encompassing robust threat detection mechanisms, secure model training protocols, and ongoing vulnerability assessments. By understanding the evolving nature of cyber threats and implementing proactive measures, researchers and practitioners can mitigate the risks associated with AI-based human detection technology and ensure its continued effectiveness and trustworthiness in real-world applications.

CONCLUSION

In conclusion, investigating human identification in video surveillance demonstrates various approaches, difficulties, and datasets essential to advancing computer vision. In order to recognize human presence inside video sequences, object detection and classification play a crucial role, as shown by the essential framework. Different categorization approaches, such as motion-based algorithms, geometry-based models, and face identification, provide different problems and benefits, requiring customized solutions for certain use cases.

The accuracy of human identification systems is greatly enhanced by essential classifiers that distinguish between human and non-human objects based on feature extraction, such as Naive Bayes, Nearest Neighbor, Logistic Regression, Decision Trees, Random Forest, and Neural Networks. The literature review outlines current developments, with noteworthy research putting forth elaborate frameworks that tackle issues like variance and occlusion.

Datasets assembled from different sources are useful tools for training and testing human detection algorithms in various settings. Improving these techniques will be essential to raising the efficacy and efficiency of video surveillance systems as technology develops. Researchers, practitioners, and other stakeholders engaged in developing and deploying human detection technologies might use this summary as a reference.

REFERENCES

[1]　G. Bhola, and D.K. Vishwakarma, "A review of vision-based indoor HAR: state-of-the-art, challenges, and future prospects", *Multimedia Tools Appl.*, vol. 83, no. 1, pp. 1965-2005, 2024.
[http://dx.doi.org/10.1007/s11042-023-15443-5]

[2]　Z. Zou, "Object detection in 20 years: A survey", *Proceedings of the IEEE,* 2023.
[http://dx.doi.org/10.1109/JPROC.2023.3238524]

[3]　A. Gupta, A. Anpalagan, L. Guan, and A.S. Khwaja, "Deep learning for object detection and scene perception in self-driving cars: Survey, challenges, and open issues", *Array,* vol. 10, p. 100057, 2021.
[http://dx.doi.org/10.1016/j.array.2021.100057]

[4]　M. Antoun, and D. Asmar, "Human object interaction detection: Design and survey", *Image Vis. Comput.,* vol. 130, p. 104617, 2023.
[http://dx.doi.org/10.1016/j.imavis.2022.104617]

[5]　M.A. Ansari, and D.K. Singh, "Human detection techniques for real time surveillance: a comprehensive survey", *Multimedia Tools Appl.,* vol. 80, no. 6, pp. 8759-8808, 2021.
[http://dx.doi.org/10.1007/s11042-020-10103-4]

[6]　S. Maheswari, "Enhanced skin tone detection using heuristic thresholding", *Biomedical Research, Biomed Res- India,* vol. 28, no. 9, 2017.

[7]　P. Viola, and M. Jones, *Robust Real-time Object Detection using a Boosted Cascade of Simple Features.* IJCV, 2001.

[8]　A. Ahmed, J. Guo, F. Ali, and F. Deeba, "LBPH Based Improved Face Recognition At Low

Resolution", *International Conference on Artificial Intelligence and Big Data (ICAIBD),* 2018 China [http://dx.doi.org/10.1109/ICAIBD.2018.8396183]

[9]   T. Ahonen, A. Hadid, and M. Pietikäinen, "Face recognition with local binary patterns", *Computer Vision-ECCV 2004: 8th European Conference on Computer Vision, Prague, Czech Republic, May 11-14, 2004. Proceedings, Part I 8. Springer.* Berlin Heidelberg 2004.

[10] A. Roshan, and Y. Zhang, "Improved frame differencing based moving object detection using feet-step sound", *Airborne Intelligence, Surveillance, Reconnaissance (ISR) Systems and Applications XI,* vol. 9076, 2014.

[11] A.H. Ahmed, K. Kpalma, and A.O. Guedi, "Human Detection Using HOG-SVM, Mixture of Gaussian and Background Contours Subtraction", *13th International Conference on Signal-Image Technology & Internet-Based Systems (SITIS),* pp. 334-338, 2017. [http://dx.doi.org/10.1109/SITIS.2017.62]

[12] X. Zhao, G. Wang, Z. He, and H. Jiang, "A survey of moving object detection methods: A practical perspective", *Neurocomputing,* vol. 503, pp. 28-48, 2022. [http://dx.doi.org/10.1016/j.neucom.2022.06.104]

[13] A. Ioannidou, E. Chatzilari, S. Nikolopoulos, and I. Kompatsiaris, "Deep Learning Advances in Computer Vision with 3D Data: A Survey", *ACM Comput. Surv.,* vol. 50, no. 2, p. 20, 2017.

[14] H. Wang, and C. Schmid, "Action recognition with improved trajectories", *Proceedings of the IEEE international conference on computer vision,* pp. 3551-3558, 2013.

[15] S. Ershadi-Nasab, E. Noury, S. Kasaei, and E. Sanaei, "Multiple human 3D pose estimation from multiview images", *Multimedia Tools Appl.,* vol. 77, no. 12, pp. 15573-15601, 2018. [http://dx.doi.org/10.1007/s11042-017-5133-8]

[16] X. Chen, and A. Yuille, "Articulated pose estimation by a graphical model with image dependent pairwise relations", In: *Proceedings of the 27th International Conference on Neural Information Processing Systems* vol. Volume 1. MIT Press: Cambridge, MA, USApp. 1736-1744.

[17] A.F. Khalifa, E. Badr, and H.N. Elmahdy, "A survey on human detection surveillance systems for Raspberry Pi", *Image and Vision Computing,* vol. 85, pp. 1-13, 2019.

[18] K Seemanthini, and S.S. Manjunath, "Human Detection and Tracking using HOG for Action Recognition", *Procedia Computer Science,* vol. 132, 2018.

[19] F. de Souza, and H. Pedrini, "Detection of Violent Events in Video Sequences based on Census Transform Histogram", *30th SIBGRAPI Conference on Graphics, Patterns and Images (SIBGRAPI),* 2017. [http://dx.doi.org/10.1109/SIBGRAPI.2017.49]

[20] W.W. Kit, and H.J. How, "Face Detection in Thermal Imaging Using Head Curve Geometry", *Image and Signal Processing IEEE International Congress,* pp. 881-884, 2012.

[21] V. Gaikwad, and S. Lokhande, "Vision-based pedestrian detection for advanced driver assistance", *International Conference on Information and Communication Technologies, Procedia Computer Science,* pp. 321-328, 2015.

[22] D-S. Huang, "Partially Obscured Human Detection Based on Component Detectors Using Multiple Feature Descriptors", ICIC 2014", *LNCS,* vol. 8588, pp. 338-344, 2014.

[23] R. Girshick, J. Donahue, T. Darrell, and J. Malik, "Rich feature hierarchies for accurate object detection and semantic segmentation", *Proceedings of the IEEE Conference on Computer Vision and Pattern Recognition,* pp. 580-587, 2014. [http://dx.doi.org/10.1109/CVPR.2014.81]

[24] I. Riaz, J. Piao, and H. Shin, "Human detection by using centrist features for thermal images", *International Conference Computer Graphics, Visualization, Computer Vision and Image Processing,* 2013.

[25] Q.M. Haq, S-J. Ruan, M.A. Haq, S. Karam, J.L. Shieh, P. Chondro, and D-Q. Gao, "An incremental learning of YOLOv3 without catastrophic forgetting for smart city applications", *IEEE Consum. Electron. Mag.,* vol. 11, no. 5, pp. 56-63, 2022.
[http://dx.doi.org/10.1109/MCE.2021.3096376]

[26] W. Liu, "Ssd: Single shot multi-box detector", *14th European Conference,* 2016 Amsterdam, The Netherlands.

[27] K. He, "Mask r-cnn", *Proceedings of the IEEE international conference on computer vision,* 2017.

[28] R. Mehta, and C. Ozturk, "Object detection at 200 frames per second", *Proceedings of the European Conference on Computer Vision (ECCV) Workshops,* 2018.

[29] G.A.P. Singh, and P.K. Gupta, "Performance analysis of various machine learning-based approaches for detection and classification of lung cancer in humans", *Neural Computing and Applications,* vol. 31, no. 10, pp. 6863-6877, 2019.
[http://dx.doi.org/10.12785/ijcds/120146]

[30] Khalid Anwar, Jamshed Siddiqui, and Shahab Saquib Sohail, "Machine learning-based book recommender system: a survey and new perspectives", *International Journal of Intelligent Information and Database Systems,* pp. 231-248, 2020.
[http://dx.doi.org/10.1504/IJIIDS.2020.109457]

[31] Khalid Anwar, Aasim Zafar, and Arshad Iqbal, "Neutrosophic MCDM approach for performance evaluation and recommendation of best players in a sports league", *International Journal of Neutrosophic Science,* pp. 2690-6805, 2023.
[http://dx.doi.org/10.54216/IJNS.200111]

[32] S. Tian, L. Li, W. Li, H. Ran, X. Ning, and P. Tiwari, "A survey on few-shot class-incremental learning", *Neural Netw.,* vol. 169, pp. 307-324, 2024.
[http://dx.doi.org/10.1016/j.neunet.2023.10.039] [PMID: 37922714]

[33] K. Anwar, A. Zafar, A. Iqbal, S.S. Sohail, A. Hussain, Y. Karaca, M. Hijji, A.K.J. Saudagar, and K. Muhammad, "Artificial intelligence-driven approach to identify and recommend the winner in a tied event in sports surveillance", *Fractals,* vol. 31, no. 10, p. 2340149, 2023.
[http://dx.doi.org/10.1142/S0218348X23401497]

[34] M.A. Ansari, and D.K. Singh, "A Review of Machine Learning Approaches for Human Detection through Feature Based Classification", *International Journal of Computing and Digital Systems,* vol. 12, no. 3, pp. 569-586, 2022.
[http://dx.doi.org/10.12785/ijcds/120146]

[35] S.K. Choudhury, P.K. Sa, R. Prasad Padhy, S. Sharma, and S. Bakshi, "Improved pedestrian detection using motion segmentation and silhouette orientation", *Multimedia Tools Appl.,* vol. 77, no. 11, pp. 13075-13114, 2018.
[http://dx.doi.org/10.1007/s11042-017-4933-1]

[36] M.A. Ansari, and D.K. Singh, "Monitoring social distancing through human detection for preventing/reducing COVID spread", *International Journal of Information Technology,* vol. 13, no. 3, pp. 1255-1264, 2021.
[http://dx.doi.org/10.1007/s41870-021-00658-2] [PMID: 33870073]

[37] Neeti A. Ogale, *A survey of techniques for human detection from video.,* 2006.

[38] R. Matsumura, and A. Hanazawa, "Human detection using colour contrast-based histograms of oriented gradients", *Int. J. Innov. Comput., Inf. Control,* vol. 15, no. 4, 2019.

[39] Miao He, "Pedestrian Detection with Semantic Regions of Interest", *Sensors (Basel, Switzerland),* vol. 17,11, p. 2699, 2017.
[http://dx.doi.org/10.3390/s17112699]

[40] K. Anwar, J. Siddiqui, and S.S. Sohail, "Machine learning techniques for book recommendation: an

overview", *Proceedings of International Conference on Sustainable Computing in Science, Technology and Management (SUSCOM), Amity University Rajasthan, Jaipur-India,* 2019. [http://dx.doi.org/10.2139/ssrn.3356349]

CHAPTER 6

A Review of Sentiment Analysis Opinion Mining and Using Machine Learning

Nadiya Parveen[1,*] and **Mohd Waris Khan**[1]

[1] *Department of Computer Application, Faculty of Engineering, Integral University, Lucknow, India*

Abstract: Recently, sentiment analysis and opinion mining have drawn a lot of interest. Because user-generated content on the internet is becoming more and more influential, this research examines the various machine learning (ML) techniques used in opinion mining and sentiment analysis applications. The opinion mining and sentiment analysis utilizing machine learning approaches are thoroughly reviewed in this research article. The objective of this comprehensive review is to find the most accurate and efficient models that can automatically classify and analyze sentiments expressed in textual data. A range of machine learning techniques are utilized and assessed according to performance measures including precision and accuracy. The dataset used consists of real-world text data collected from social media platforms, product reviews, and online forums. The findings indicate that Support Vector Machine (SVM)and Naïve Bayes (NB) achieved exceptionally high values of accuracy. SVM and NB achieved an accuracy of 95%. On the other hand, Logistic Regression (LR) and K-Nearest Neighbor (KNN) demonstrated comparatively lower accuracy scores of 57% respectively. Among all the evaluated techniques, KNN exhibited the lowest precision score of 57%. Overall, ML techniques have proven to be valuable in sentiment analysis and opinion mining.

Keywords: Opinion mining, Sentiment analysis, Social media, Sentiment classification, Supervised learning techniques.

INTRODUCTION

There are numerous significant subfields within natural language processing, two of which are sentiment analysis and opinion mining. These topics focus on autonomously obtaining and evaluating subjective data through textual sources. Because of the expansion of online platforms and social media, there is an increasing need to analyze and comprehend the thoughts, feelings, and attitudes that individuals have regarding a variety of subjects, goods or best services [1].

* **Corresponding author Nadiya Parveen:** Department of Computer Application, Faculty of Engineering, Integral University, Lucknow, India; E-mail: nadiyaparveen@iul.ac.in

Asif Khan, Mohammad Kamrul Hasan, Naushad Varish & Mohammed Aslam Husain (Eds.)

Machine learning (ML) techniques are emerging as potent tools in this field that enable quick and automatic analysis of large amounts of textual data in search of patterns of interest. Sentiment analysis is a branch of natural language processing that measures sentiment based on opinion and cognition.

Opinion mining goes deeper into understanding the exact opinions, sentiments, or emotions represented within the text, however, sentiment analysis is a well-known scientific field that has seen a lot of recent effort. Billions of individuals have come to social media to engage with one another. These days, a lot of people utilize social media on a daily basis to share thoughts, insights, and experiences in addition to serving as a forum for social interaction. We find phrases that are neutral, negative, or positive to determine the sentiment polarity of a text. This is the aim of sentiment analysis. Individuals can automatically categorize, measure, and analyze attitudes and opinions expressed in a wide variety of textual sources, including customer reviews, social media posts, news articles, and online forums, by applying ML techniques for the classification of sentiments and opinions [2].

Sentiment classification can be done in different ways and opinion mining is made easier with the use of machine learning techniques, which use large-scale annotated datasets to learn patterns. Among the many steps that these methods take, pre-processing the text, extracting features from that text, training the algorithm, and classifying the user's emotions are the most crucial steps [3]. Among the popular supervised learning algorithms used in sentiment analysis are Naive Bayes (NB), Random Forest (RF), and Support Vector Machines (SVM). Opinions in a dataset are discovered and sorted using unsupervised learning strategies like clustering and topic modeling. Deep learning models are remarkably successful at sentiment analysis tasks because of their ability to extract the context and define the semantic information contained in the text [4]. In order to better classify opinions and extract meaningful insights from large amounts of data, these models excel at learning intricate patterns and connections. Fig. (**1**) depicts the process flow of sentiment analysis and opinion mining for applying different machine learning techniques [5].

Machine learning-driven opinion mining and sentiment analysis find extensive practical applications in various real-world scenarios. Brand monitoring, reputation management, social media analysis, and tracking political mood are just a few of the many examples. An organization can improve customer satisfaction, respond quickly to market changes, and cater to individual tastes by automating the study of customer feelings and reviews. Problems with sarcasm, irony, and context-dependent emotions, as well as multilingual and noisy text, remain challenges in the domains of sentiment analysis and opinion mining. Analyzing sentiments is becoming increasingly relevant in fields like healthcare, finance, and social sciences, and future studies will hopefully find ways to make these models more accurate and resilient while also examining how they may be used in these and other growing fields.

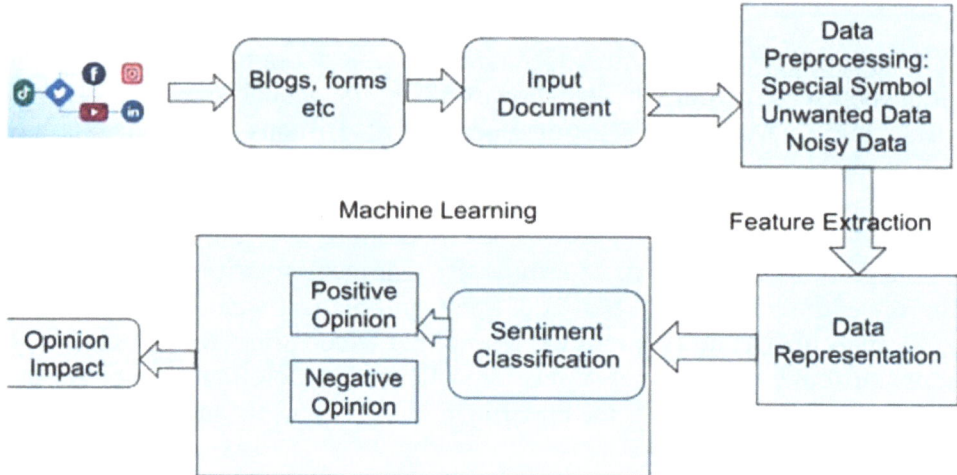

Fig. (1). Opinion mining and Sentiment analysis.

Sentiment Analysis

Automatically identifying a text's underlying emotional state is referred to as sentiment analysis and opinion mining is sometimes called sentiment classification or sentiment polarity detection. Sentiment analysis is the process of categorizing text data as positive, negative, or neutral and assigning scores based on the intensity of the sentiment expressed. Social media posts, online evaluations, client comments, and other types of user-generated material have increased the demand for sentiment analysis in recent years [6]. Fig. (2) given below illustrates the classification of sentiments based on their polarity.

analytics, and reputation management. Businesses can use sentiment analysis to make data-driven decisions, uncover new patterns, comprehend client feelings, and enhance their goods and services in response to customer feedback [8]. Despite the advancements, sentiment analysis still faces challenges. The presence of sentiment detection and opinion extraction using Applications for machine learning can be found in a number of fields, such as market available research, branded monitoring, consumer feedback analysis, social media of sarcasm, irony, or subtle sentiment expressions, which can be difficult to detect accurately. Handling domain-specific language and sentiment lexicons, managing large-scale data, and addressing class imbalance are other challenges that researchers are actively working on [7].

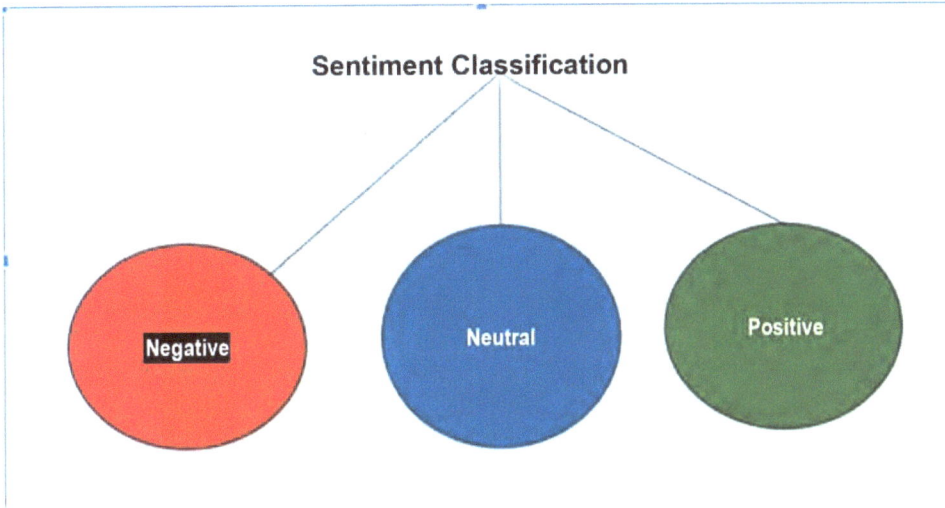

Fig. (2). Sentiment classification.

Sentiment Analysis Applications

- Social media monitoring
- Movie review
- Product review
- Brand monitoring
- Politics

Role of Machine Learning in Sentiment Analysis

Machine learning is pivotal in sentiment analysis and opinion mining as it facilitates the automated and precise examination of extensive amounts of text data. ML algorithms may be trained to discover correlations and trends between phrases, words, and feelings conveyed in the text by using labeled datasets as the basis for training.

These algorithms can then be applied to unlabeled data to classify and extract sentiments, opinions,

and emotions. Through the utilization of methods like natural language processing, extracting features, and employing classification models, machine learning empowers the recognition of sentiment polarity—whether positive, negative, or neutral—and identifies subjective expressions within the text. The ability to automatically analyze sentiments and opinions at scale using machine learning greatly assists businesses, researchers, and organizations in understanding customer feedback, social media sentiment, market trends, and public opinion [9].

In sentiment analysis, supervised learning techniques are frequently utilized. Labeled data, which assigns a sentiment label to each sentence, is used to train these algorithms. Popular supervised learning algorithms for sentiment analysis include SVM, NB, LR, and DT [10]. These algorithms learn to classify new, unseen text by generalizing patterns learned from the training data. Unsupervised learning algorithms are also employed in sentiment analysis, especially for tasks such as sentiment polarity discovery or topic-based sentiment analysis. Unsupervised techniques do not rely on labeled training data but instead discover sentiment patterns and clusters within the text [11]. In tasks including sentiment analysis, deep learning models have also demonstrated encouraging performance. Recurrent Neural Networks (RNN), specifically Long Short-Term Memory (LSTM) and Gated Recurrent Unit (GRU) networks have demonstrated effectiveness in capturing sequential dependencies in text data. Local patterns and characteristics can be extracted from the text by Convolutional Neural Networks (CNNs) *via* convolutional techniques. These deep learning models, when combined with word embeddings, can effectively learn and represent complex sentiment patterns in text data [12, 13].

Overall, sentiment evaluation and mining of opinions, both of which make use of various ML approaches, have developed as strong tools that can interpret and extract emotion from textual data [14]. In this study, various approaches from machine learning are utilized to dive into the complexities of sentiment evaluation and opinion extraction. The study investigates several different machine learning approaches, provides a comparative analysis of these techniques, and then addresses the applications, problems, and potential future possibilities for enhancing opinion mining and sentiment analysis using machine learning.

REVIEW OF LITERATURE

This section provides an overview of relevant publications by various authors in the fields of sentiment analysis and opinion mining using machine learning techniques.

Behera *et al.*, (2021) [13] In this paper, we emphasize the value of analyzing social media reviews from customers for many uses in business. To handle the vast volumes of data generated by these types of assessments, the authors propose a novel deep-learning architecture that combines CNNs and LSTMs. While LSTM networks perform well while analyzing sequential data, CNNs excel at selecting local features. Sentiment analysis of big social datasets presents unique obstacles, which are tested on four different review datasets and show that the ensemble model performs better than traditional machine learning techniques in terms of accuracy and other crucial parameters. These are partly offset by the proposed Co-LSTM model [15, 16].

A. Jeelani *et al.* **(2020) [9]** performed sentimentanalysis in this work to analyze news articles that are scraped from different online news sources. This method's drawback is that it observed the performance of sentiment analysis on English words while ignoring terms in other languages, such as Italian, Arabic, and so forth. The investigation of sentiment analysis and opinions mining is carried out as a test method for sentiment analysis of news stories from different news sources.

H. Alatabi *et al.***, (2020) [14],** studied the massive online data sets created by the proliferation of social media, which has drawn billions of users around the world. Sentiment analysis, a form of data classification, is used to make sense of this information. The study developed a novel sentiment analysis method based on machine learning techniques with the goal of gathering sentiment polarity from texts on social media. The application of ML to sentiment analysis methods has met with widespread success around the world. In this paper, the feature extraction techniques can be used as part of speech feature techniques. This study looked at the problem and suggested a sentiment analysis approach based on the Bayesian Rough Decision Tree (BRDT) method. The testing results illustrate the efficacy of the strategy, with an accuracy rate of over 95% when gathering data from social media networks.

D. Gamal *et al.***, (2018) [21]** performed a review of the literature on sentiment analysis and a natural language processing (NLP) subtask that looks for intent or determines whether a document is intended to be interpreted positively or negatively. The study centered on analyzing sentiments with ML methods. Various ML techniques such as NB, SVM, Partial Approximation (PA), LR, *etc.* were employed for classification alongside two feature extraction techniques applied for Term Frequency-Inverse Document (TF-IDF) and N-gram. PA with a unigram performed best among these four different datasets, with the accuracy of 87%

When the sentiment analysis of student comments is discussed, the precise sentiment of the students is not revealed. **D. Daneena,** *et al.* **(2019) [22]** provide textual feedback to pupils by utilizing machine learning algorithms. To address the drawbacks of grading-based feedback, textual feedback is utilized, as it provides a more accurate representation of students' sentiments.

Alomari *et al.***, (2017) [16]** presented a newly annotated Twitter corpus in Arabic from Jordan to analyze user sentiment. In order to identify the appropriate technique for sentiment analysis in the Arabic corpus, the authors investigated a wide range of pre-processing approaches and ML algorithms. Different pre-processing techniques were used to evaluate SVM and NB classifiers. In terms of accuracy, the SVM classifier scored 88.72% and the F1-score was 88.27%, whereas the NB classifier scored 83.61% and the F1-score was 84.73%. According to the study's findings, the SVM classifier is the superior ML approach over the NB classifier in terms of accuracy and F1 score.

Singh *et al.*, (2017) [17] investigated a technique known as sentiment analysis, which entails gleaning positive or negative thoughts from the text of social media posts. For the purpose of improving sentiment analysis, the study employed four sophisticated machine learning classifiers. These classifiers were named Naive Bayes, J48, BFTree, and OneR. There were three datasets utilized, two of which were obtained from Amazon, while the third was obtained from IMDB movie reviews. Comparing the classifiers revealed that Naive Bayes was the most adept at learning new information, while OneR showed the most potential with an accuracy of 91.3%, 97% in F- measure, and 92.34% in properly categorized instances.

Dey *et al.*, (2016) [18] examined how the rise of Web 2.0 has altered sentiment analysis and the pressing need to quickly unearth emotional web content. For fast content identification and analysis, they focused on movie and hotel reviews as a target area for developing a sentiment-focused web crawling system. Sentence polarity and other subjective aspects were captured through statistical analysis in this work. Accuracy, precision, and recall were examined using several different metrics for two supervised machine learning algorithms: K-NN and NB. For movie review evaluations, NB fared better than K-NN, whereas, for hotel reviews, both systems produced equivalent, lower accuracy.

Islam *et al.*, (2016) [16] presented a visual framework for analyzing and predicting the emotional tone of pictures. With the proliferation of social media platforms, internet users now rely heavily on visual representations of their feelings. Models for analyzing visual sentiment have not received as much attention as sentiment analysis of text-based data. In order to prevent overfitting, the study offers a new framework that combines a deep convolutional neural network (DCNN) with transfer learning. The results acquired on a Twitter image dataset demonstrate that the proposed model outperforms the state-of-the-art model.

Kharde *et al.*, (2016) [20] assessed the sentiment analysis of Twitter data in light of the ever-increasing amount of data being produced and shared online. The study was designed to analyze the good, negative, and neutral tweets that users posted. The study summarized and compared several opinion mining methods, such as machine learning and lexicon-based methods, and gave assessment criteria. The authors studied Twitter data streams using several machine-learning techniques. These included NB, Maximum Entropy (ME), and SVM. The benefits and limitations of using Twitter sentiment analysis were also explored.

Bilal *et al.*, (2016) [17] analyzed the existing research on sentiment mining, which employs text-mining methods to ascertain people's feelings on a variety of topics. The analysis brought to light the difficulties of opinion mining, such as the use of numerous languages and the dearth of studies examining sentiment categorization in languages except for English. Opinions were taken from a blog written in Roman Urdu and English and then categorized using three different categorization techniques used in WEKA, the Waikato Environment for Knowledge Analysis. The models were tested on a dataset that included 150 positive and negative comments and 150 comments in between. Comparing the NB model to the DT model and the KNN model, the findings showed that the NB had superior precision, recall, f-measure, and accuracy.

Duwairi *et al.*, (2014) [18] executed literature research on sentiment analysis, an algorithm for identifying the written work's emotional tone as neutral, negative, or positive. The study discussed how machine learning and lexicons are two ways to attack the issue. Sentiment analysis in Arabic reviews was the focus of the study, and they utilized a machine learning approach. Three classifiers - NB, SVM, and KNN were used for a dataset that was produced in-house and consisted of tweets and comments. According to the data, SVM had the best recall, while KNN with a K=10 parameter value had the best precision.

Table 1. Comparison Table.

Ref, Year	Factor/Feature	Model	Accuracy	Limitation
S.Jaspreet *et al.* (2017)	State-of-the-art	Naïve Bayes J48 , BFTree OneR	91.3%	Restricted to extracting emoticons, and foreign words, and extended the following words along with the associated feelings.
D.Gamal *et al.* (2018)	TF-IDF and N-gram	NB, SGD, SVM, PA, ME, LR	99.96%	To manage and deal with the textual categorization.
J.S Rajkumar, *et al.* (2019)	Dictionary-based approach Lexicon-based approach	Naïve Bayes SVM	98.17% 93.54%	It improves the business strategy.
Johnson *et al.*(2018)	Word Embeddings	LSTM	0.92%	High computational cost

(Table 1) cont.....

		Bayesian Rough Decision Tree (BRDT)	95%	To take the polarity out of texts on social media.
H.Alatabi *et al.*(2020)	Part of speech	Bayesian Rough Decision Tree (BRDT)	95%	To take the polarity out of texts on social media.
F.Jemai *et al.*2021	Stop words embedding	Naïve Bayes, Multinomial NB, Bernoulli NB	99.73% 99.70% 99.67%	Requires large amounts of data
Singh *et al.* (2023)	State-of-the-art	NB, MP, LR	89.4% 98%	The most recent techniques to enhance the usefulness and effectiveness of the generated emotion are included in the state-of-the-art.
Noura *et al* (2024)	BOW, TF-IDF,ngrams, Word2Vec, Hashing vectorizer.	Random forest	70%	It offers helpful information for determining the advantages and disadvantages of certain features and helping users make the best decisions.
Ravinder *et al.* (2019)	TF-IDF, N-Gram	LR, NB, SVM, KNN, DT, Random Forest.	57%	It requires the data in the form of text.

COMPARATIVE ANALYSIS

A variety of studies have explored sentiment analysis employing different factors, models, and techniques across various years. In 2017, Jaspreet *et al.* employed Naïve Bayes, J48, BFTree, and OneR models, achieving a 91.3% accuracy but faced limitations in extracting certain elements like emoticons and foreign words. Gamal *et al.* (2018) utilized TF-IDF and N-gram techniques with multiple models, achieving an impressive 99.96% accuracy, aiming to enhance textual categorization. Rajkumar *et al.* (2019) focused on dictionary-based and lexicon-based approaches, achieving accuracies of 98.17% and 93.54%, respectively, with a focus on improving business strategies. However, Johnson *et al.* (2018) faced high computational costs with an LSTM model achieving only 0.92% accuracy using word embeddings. Alatabi *et al.* (2020) utilized part-of-speech techniques with a Bayesian Rough Decision Tree model, achieving a 95% accuracy in extracting polarity from social media texts. Jemai *et al.* (2021) explored stop-word embedding with multiple Naïve Bayes models, obtaining high accuracies but requiring large datasets. Singh *et al.* (2023) incorporated recent techniques into their state-of-the-art approach, achieving accuracies of 89.4% to 98%. Noura *et al.* (2024) employed various vectorization methods with a Random Forest model but achieved a lower accuracy of 70%, offering insights for feature evaluation. Ravinder *et al.* (2019) utilized TF-IDF and N-Gram techniques with multiple models but achieved a lower accuracy of 57%, highlighting the necessity of text data for analysis (Fig. **3**).

Table 2. Comparative Analysis.

Ref work	*Parameter*	*Model/Technique*	*Accuracy %*
Ravinder *et al.*	02	KNN,DT,RF,SVM,LR	57%
Noura *et al.*	06	Random Forest	70%
Singh *et al.*	01	Naïve Bayes	85.30%
S. Jaspreet *et al.*	01	Naïve Bayes J48 ,BFTree OneR	91.3%
Proposed Analysis	04	NB, SVM	95%

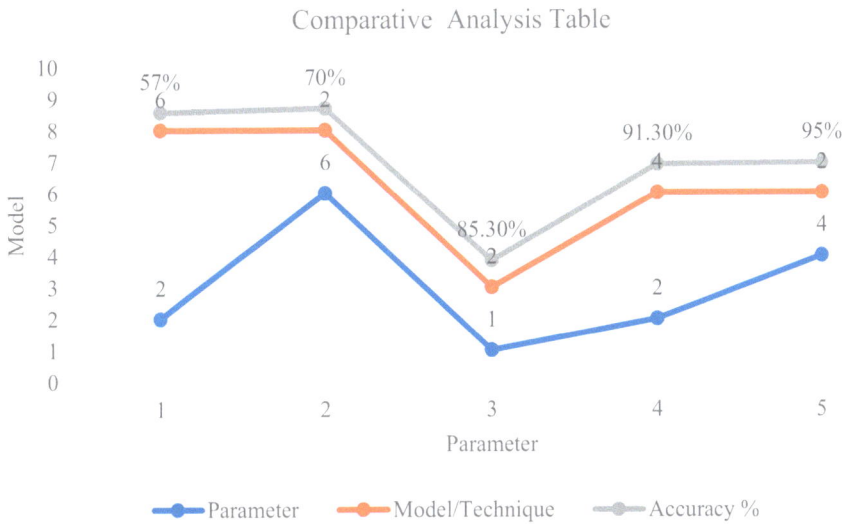

Fig. (3). Comparative Analysis.

It could be observed from the above comparative analysis that the techniques of Logistic Regression, Naïve Bayes SVM, KNN, Random Forest OneR, and Decision Tree demonstrate high accuracy scores, with Naïve Bayes and SVM achieving 95%, J48, BFtree and OneR achieving 91.3%, and Random Forest achieving 70%. These techniques display reliable overall performance in sentiment analysis and opinion-mining tasks. SVM and Naïve Bayes exhibit exceptionally high accuracy values, achieving 95% and DT achieving 98.95%.

These techniques outperform others in terms of accuracy. However, Logistic Regression shows comparatively lower accuracy scores of 57%, respectively.

Overall, the advantages and disadvantages of several machine learning methods for sentiment analysis and opinion mining are highlighted by this comparison analysis. SVM, Naïve Bayes, Random Forest, Decision Tree, and DT are some of the techniques that show great accuracy and are hence good options for sentiment analysis jobs. However, the selection of a technique should consider the specific requirements and characteristics of the dataset and application context [17].

Methods and Approaches Used for Sentiment Analysis

Sentiment analysis has been carried out in many different ways, as was mentioned in the introduction. Three categories were created from these approaches: lexicon-based, machine learning, and hybrid. Upon reviewing several studies, it was found that only one employed a hybrid approach, while the rest made use of machine and lexical learning methods [18]. Almost all studies use machine learning techniques. When it came to machine learning algorithms, the SVM was the most popular. Naive Bayes classifiers, K-NN, and decision trees were also used. These days, deep learning techniques are widely used since they are excellent at extracting characteristics. Sentiment analysis employs a number of approaches and strategies, each with unique advantages and disadvantages.

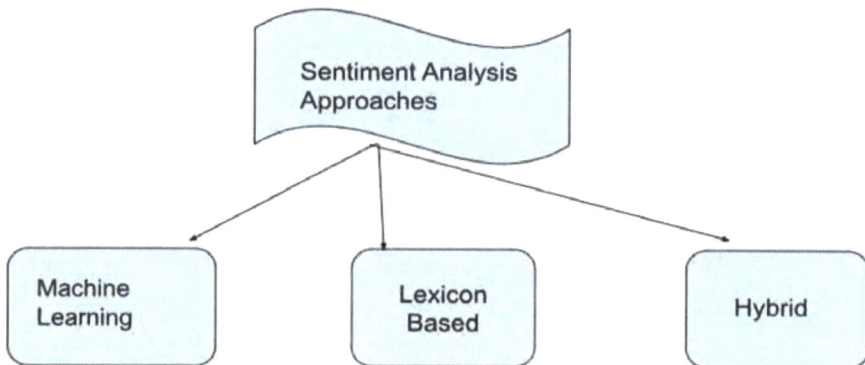

Fig. (4). Sentiment Analysis Approaches.

MACHINE LEARNING TECHNIQUES

Naïve Bayes (NB)

The probability classification technique known as the Naïve Bayes classifier algorithm is primarily grounded in the Bayes theorem. The naïve Bayes classifier operates under the assumption that each feature inside a class is independent of every other feature. Mangos and bananas, for instance, are examples of fruits.

These fruits may have the following characteristics The vast number of data sets can be easily calculated using naïve Bayes. A Naïve Bayes classifier is often the outcome mostly sophisticated classification methods [19]. The Naïve Bayes theorem can be used to calculate the posterior probability p(A/B) from p(A), P(B), and p(B/A), utilizing the given formula.

$$P(B/A) = P(A/B). \, P(A) \, / \, p(B)$$

The posterior probability is denoted by P(A/B), where A represents the class and B represents attribute.

The prior probability of class is P(A).

The likelihood, or probability, of the predictor for a given class is expressed as P(B/A).

The predictor prior probability is P(B).

Support Vector Machine (SVM)

Another method for supervised machine learning is Support Vector Machines (SVMs). In SVM, they can be used both methods that are applicable to regression and classification. SVM is mainly used as a classification problem. Support Vector Machines are used linearly and non-linearly for classification and regression problems. In the support vector machine, there are two label classes separated by the hyperplane or decision boundary. These two classes are nearest close to each other and are called SVM. Margins are the separations between the hyperplane and the support vector machine [20].

H=W. X +b=0 ....(01)

W is a weight vector for $W_1 \, W_2 \, W_3 \ldots \ldots W_n$

X is a training tuple

b is a scalar vector

Decision Tree (DT)

A decision tree is also a supervised machine-learning technique that can be used for both classification and also used for regression [21]. A decision tree is a nonlinear function. Decision trees are the supervised machine learning algorithm. The decision tree consists of two nodes: decision nodes and the rest nodes are leaf nodes. Each leaf node is assigned to one class and that represents the target value.

Decision trees define a document in a top-down manner *i.e.* it starts from the root of the tree and moves down the branches of the leaf node. Each node is labeled with the feature/attribute it tests, and the branches are labelled with different values.

Dataset Domain

Since datasets offer the labeled data required for training as well as assessing sentiment analysis models, they are an essential part of the field. After the articles were examined, it became clear that researchers used a variety of datasets in various fields [22]. These domains include online discussion platforms like Quora, political battles, novels, goods, e-commerce applications, movie reviews, tweets, and books. Research paper summaries provide information about the different dataset domains that are used in sentiment analysis studies [23]. These domains show how sentiment analysis is flexible and can be used in a variety of contexts by encompassing a broad range of themes, languages, and sources. The choice of datasets from domains significantly affects the sentiment analysis algorithms' performance and contextual relevance. Sentiment expressions, linguistic variations, and contextual subtleties are all understood by sentiment analysis algorithms.

Challenges of Sentiment Analysis

Ambiguity and Sensitivity to Context: Natural language is by nature ambiguous and sensitive to context. The context in which a word or phrase is used might give it a distinct meaning. Understanding the context in which words and phrases are used is crucial for correctly identifying sentiment [24].

Subjectivity: Sentiments and opinions are subjective and can vary greatly from person to person. This subjectivity makes it difficult to create a universal model that accurately captures the sentiment of all individuals.

Data Quality and Quantity: In machine learning models, both the volume and quality of training data are critical components of sentiment analysis. Accurately labeling huge volumes of data for sentiment analysis can be difficult, particularly for resource-constrained languages or specialized fields [25].

Lack of labeled data: Large amounts of labeled data are usually needed for the training of sentiment analysis algorithms. Nevertheless, acquiring labeled data can be a costly, time-consuming, and resource-intensive procedure. Creating reliable and accurate sentiment analysis algorithms is continuously hampered by the dearth of labeled data, especially for some subjects or languages [26].

CONCLUSION AND FUTURE SCOPE

In conclusion, an essential component of comprehending and categorizing the attitudes portrayed in textual material is opinion mining and sentiment analysis. Through this comparative analysis. The effectiveness of many machine learning methods is assessed for tasks involving the analysis of sentiment and opinion mining. The results highlighted several techniques that exhibited high accuracy and precision values, indicating their effectiveness in identifying and classifying sentiments. CNN, Naïve Bayes, and Decision Tree demonstrated exceptional performance in accuracy and showcasing their suitability for sentiment analysis tasks. These techniques exhibited reliable overall performance and strong precision in identifying positive sentiments. While other techniques such as PA, SVM, J48, BFTree, OneR, NB, and CNN show moderate to good accuracy and precision scores, they still provide viable options for opinion mining and sentiment analysis applications. It is essential to keep in mind that the selection of an ML method needs to be determined by the specific requirements, characteristics of the dataset, and the application context. Furthermore, it is advisable to consider other factors such as computational complexity, training time, and interpretability of the models when making a decision. Sentiment analysis as well as opinion mining machine learning algorithms have generally demonstrated efficacy in extracting meaningful information from textual input. Further research and development in this field will lead to more precise and effective sentiment analysis systems as technology develops, improving our ability to comprehend public opinion, consumer feedback, and social media sentiments, among other applications.

REFERENCES

[1]   M. Birjali, M. Kasri, and A. Beni-Hssane, "A comprehensive survey on sentiment analysis: Approaches, challenges and trends", *Knowl. Base. Syst.,* vol. 226, p. 107134, 2021.
[http://dx.doi.org/10.1016/j.knosys.2021.107134]

[2]   E. Elgeldawi, A. Sayed, A.R. Galal, and A.M. Zaki, Hyperparameter tuning for machine learning algorithms used for Arabic sentiment analysis.*Informatics* vol. 8. Multidisciplinary Digital Publishing Institute, 2021, no. 4, p. 79.
[http://dx.doi.org/10.3390/informatics8040079]

[3]   X. Zhang, and X. Zheng, "Comparison of text sentiment analysis based on machine learning", In: *In 2016 15th international symposium on parallel and distributed computing (ISPDC)* IEEE, 2016, pp. 230-233.
[http://dx.doi.org/10.1109/ISPDC.2016.39]

[4]   L.M. Rojas-Barahona, "Deep learning for sentiment analysis", *Language and linguistics compass,* vol. 10, no. 12, pp. 701-719, 2016.

[5]   N.C. Dang, M.N. Moreno-García, and F. De la Prieta, "Sentiment analysis based on deep learning: A comparative study", *Electronics (Basel),* vol. 9, no. 3, p. 483, 2020.
[http://dx.doi.org/10.3390/electronics9030483]

[6]   S Chandra Kala, and C. Sindhu, "Opinion Mining and sentiment classification a survey", *ICTACT*

journal on soft computing, vol. 3, no. 1, pp. 420-425, 2012.

[7]   P. Mehta, and S. Pandya, "A review on sentiment analysis methodologies, practice and applications", *International Journal of Scientific and Technology Research,* vol. 9, no. 2, pp. 601-609, 2020.

[8]   S. Saad, and B. Saberi, "Sentiment Analysis Or Opinion Mining: A Review", *International Journal of Advanced Science Engineering Information Technology,* vol. 17, 2017.

[9]   J. Ahmed, and M. Ahmed, "A framework for sentiment analysis of online news articles", *International Journal on Emerging Technologies,* vol. 11, no. 3, pp. 267-274, 2020.

[10]   Z. Li, Y. Fan, B. Jiang, T. Lei, and W. Liu, "A survey on sentiment analysis and opinion mining for social multimedia", *Multimedia Tools Appl.,* vol. 78, no. 6, pp. 6939-6967, 2019.
[http://dx.doi.org/10.1007/s11042-018-6445-z]

[11]   Mohamed Alloghani, "A systematic review on supervised and unsupervised machine learning algorithms for data science", *Supervised and unsupervised learning for data science,* pp. 3-21, 2020.
[http://dx.doi.org/10.1007/978-3-030-22475-2_1]

[12]   Q.T. Ain, M. Ali, A. Riaz, A. Noureen, M. Kamran, B. Hayat, and A. Rehman, "Sentiment analysis using deep learning techniques: a review", *Int. J. Adv. Comput. Sci. Appl.,* vol. 8, no. 6, 2017.

[13]   R.K. Behera, M. Jena, S.K. Rath, and S. Misra, "Co-LSTM: Convolutional LSTM model for sentiment analysis in social big data", *Inf. Process. Manage.,* vol. 58, no. 1, p. 102435, 2021.
[http://dx.doi.org/10.1016/j.ipm.2020.102435]

[14]   Hayder A. Alatabi, and Ayad R. Abbas, "Sentiment analysis in social media using machine learning techniques", *Iraqi Journal of Science,* pp. 193-201, 2020.
[http://dx.doi.org/10.24996/ijs.2020.61.1.22]

[15]   F. Jemai, M. Hayouni, and S. Baccar, "Sentiment analysis using machine learning algorithms", In: *2021 International Wireless Communications and Mobile Computing (IWCMC).* IEEE, 2021.

[16]   J. Singh, G. Singh, and R. Singh, "Optimization of sentiment analysis using machine learning classifiers. Human-centric Computing and information", *Sciences (New York),* vol. 7, pp. 1-12, 2017.

[17]   L. Dey, S. Chakraborty, A. Biswas, B. Bose, and S. Tiwari, "Sentiment analysis of review datasets using naive bayes and k-nn classifier", *arXiv preprint arXiv:1610.09982,* .

[18]   J. Islam, and Y. Zhang, "Visual sentiment analysis for social images using transfer learning approach", In: *In 2016 IEEE International Conferences on Big Data and Cloud Computing (BDCloud), Social Computing and Networking (SocialCom), Sustainable Computing and Communications(SustainCom)(BDCloud- SocialCom-SustainCom)* IEEE, 2016, pp. 124-130.
[http://dx.doi.org/10.1109/BDCloud-SocialCom-SustainCom.2016.29]

[19]   M. Bilal, H. Israr, M. Shahid, and A. Khan, "Sentiment classification of Roman-Urdu opinions using Naïve Bayesian, Decision Tree and KNN classification techniques", *Journal of King Saud University - Computer and Information Sciences,* vol. 28, no. 3, pp. 330-344, 2016. [1].
[http://dx.doi.org/10.1016/j.jksuci.2015.11.003]

[20]   R.M. Duwairi, and I. Qarqaz, "Arabic sentiment analysis using supervised classification", In: *2014 International Conference on Future Internet of Things and Cloud* IEEE, 2014, pp. 579-583.

[21]   D. Gamal, "Analysis of machine learning algorithms for opinion mining in different domains", *Machine Learning and Knowledge Extraction,* vol. 1, no. 1, pp. 224-234, 2018.
[http://dx.doi.org/10.3390/make1010014]

[22]   D. Dsouza, "D P Nayak, E J Machado, A N.D. "Sentimental analysis of student feedback using machine learning techniques."", *International Journal of Recent Technology and Engineering,* vol. 8, no. 14, pp. 986-991, 2019.

[23]   R.S. Jagdale, V.S. Shirsat, and S.N. Deshmukh, "Sentiment analysis on product reviews using machine learning techniques", *Cognitive Informatics and Soft Computing: Proceeding of CISC,* 2019 Springer Singapore.

[http://dx.doi.org/10.1007/978-981-13-0617-4_61]

[24]   N. Singh, and U.C. Jaiswal, "Sentiment Analysis Using Machine Learning", *ADCAIJ: Advances in Distributed Computing and Artificial Intelligence Journal,* vol. 12, pp. e26785-e26785, 2023.
[http://dx.doi.org/10.14201/adcaij.26785]

[25]   A. Semary, ""Enhancing machine learning-based sentiment analysis through feature extraction techniques", *Plos one,* vol. 19.2, p. e0294968, 2024.

[26]   R. Ahuja, A. Chug, S. Kohli, S. Gupta, and P. Ahuja, "The impact of features extraction on the sentiment analysis", *Procedia Comput. Sci.,* vol. 152, pp. 341-348, 2019.
[http://dx.doi.org/10.1016/j.procs.2019.05.008]

CHAPTER 7

State-of-the-Art Techniques in Visual Analysis for Image Processing and Pattern Recognition: A Systematic Review

Santoshachandra Rao Karanam[1,*], Naresh Tangudu[2], Kalangi Praveen Kumar[3], T.N.S. Padma[4], Illa Mahesh Kumar Swamy[3] and **P. Nagamani[3]**

[1] *Department of CSE, GITAM (deemed to be) University, Hyderabad, India*

[2] *Department of IT, Aditya Institute of Technology and Management, Tekkali, Andhra Pradesh, India*

[3] *Department of IT, Anurag University, Hyderabad, India*

[4] *Department of CSE-DS, Sreenidhi Institute of Science and Technology, Hyderabad, India*

Abstract: Visual analysis of human motion has emerged as a frontier vicinity in computer vision in up-to-date years. In visual sequences, it can identify, track, and recognize individuals. It can also comprehend and characterize their movements. With the quick growth and widespread use of information technology, the application of computer vision technology to the study of image processing, pattern recognition, and the efficient extraction and identification of human motion elements from video images has gained significant attention. In order to enhance the capacity to evaluate the attributes of moving human bodies, this work introduces the extraction function method, examines the properties of the extraction function, and proposes a technique for doing so based on picture recognition. The periodic motion in each motion is segmented using the hierarchical clustering approach to obtain precise segmentation. The tests employed self-built data and several benchmark datasets. Tests demonstrate that the method can extract less feature data and retain low computational complexity while producing high classification and recognition results. Additionally, it is capable of naturally integrating both the static and dynamic aspects of human gait.

Keywords: Feature extraction, Image processing, Image segmentation, Image compression, Image classification, Neural networks.

INTRODUCTION

Computer vision, or image recognition, is the process of classifying objects, people, places, or behaviours in digital photographs or video frames. In order to

---

[*] **Corresponding author Santoshachandra Rao Karanam:** Department of CSE, GITAM (deemed to be) University, Hyderabad, India; E-mail: kschandra.rao@gmail.com

enable computers to study and comprehend visual input similarly to humans, it entails the creation and application of algorithms and methodologies. To identify patterns and features in images, image recognition systems usually use convolutional neural networks (CNNs), deep learning models, and erstwhile machine learning approaches. Numerous industries use image recognition technology, including driverless cars, surveillance, medical imaging, facial identification, augmented reality, and satellite imagery analysis. The field of pattern recognition is more expansive and includes more than just visual data; it also includes the identification, categorization, and interpretation of patterns in data. Pattern recognition applies to several forms of data, including signals, noises, texts, and more, whereas image recognition is primarily concerned with visual patterns. Machine learning algorithms, statistical techniques, neural networks, and other computer methodologies are examples of pattern recognition techniques [1-4]. These techniques seek to identify patterns or commonalities in data so that judgments or predictions can be based on them. Many fields use pattern recognition: bioinformatics, speech recognition, handwriting recognition, anomaly detection, fraud detection, and natural language processing. Everywhere you look, you see patterns. It is a part of all that we do in our everyday lives. From the style and colour of our clothing to the use of voice assistants with intelligence, everything involves some kind of pattern.

Overview of Image Processing and Pattern Recognition

The two image processing and pattern recognition, each with a distinct application and focus, are essential elements of Information Technology. Image processing is the use of mathematical techniques and algorithms for the manipulation and analysis of images. Improving the visual appeal of photos or deriving valuable information from them is its main goal. This covers a broad spectrum of jobs, ranging from simple adjustments like cropping and resizing to more complex procedures like feature extraction, segmentation, restoration, and image enhancement. Image processing has several uses in a wide range of industries, including digital photography, biometrics, remote sensing, medicine, and industrial automation. It helps with duties like environmental monitoring, security, and quality control as well as medical diagnostics [3, 4].

Contrarily, pattern recognition is the process of locating, categorizing, and deciphering patterns in data—which could be text, photos, signals, or other types of information. Pattern recognition systems employ algorithms to scan input data for patterns or regularities; they frequently do this by comparing the data to templates or models that have already been created. Pattern recognition has several uses, such as object identification, biometric identification, verbal communication detection, natural language processing, and handwriting recognition. Virtual assistants, security systems, document processing, and many more industries where pattern recognition is automatic find applications for these technologies.

Importance

- Information Extraction: Image processing makes it possible to extract important information from pictures, which mold it to introspect and analyze, comprehend, and make sense of data.
- Automation: The ability of systems to identify patterns or objects in images without the need for human intervention makes pattern recognition a useful tool for task automation.
- Enhancement and Restoration: Through the removal of noise, the correction of distortions, or an improvement in quality, image processing techniques can enhance and restore images.
- Decision Making: By offering insights and spotting patterns in huge datasets, pattern recognition algorithms support decision-making processes and enable the making of well-informed choices.
- Efficiency: Through task automation, a decrease in manual intervention, and workflow streamlining, image processing techniques can enhance efficiency across a range of operations.

Applications

- Medical Imaging: Pattern recognition for illness detection, image enhancement, diagnosis, and segmentation (finding structures within images) are just a few of the many uses of image processing in medical imaging [5].
- Biometrics: Biometric systems use pattern recognition techniques to identify and authenticate people based on their distinct physiological or behavioural qualities, such as facial features, iris patterns, and biometrics [6].
- Image processing is essential to the investigation of GIS Data for uses in agriculture, urban planning, disaster relief, and environmental monitoring [7].
- Security and Surveillance: Surveillance systems employ image processing and pattern recognition to follow objects or people, identify suspicious activity, and improve public safety [8].
- Automotive Industry: Image processing is being used more and more for tasks like object detection, lane tracking, and collision avoidance in automotive applications including driver assistance systems, autonomous cars, and traffic monitoring [9].

Below word-cloud shows applications where image process and pattern recognition play a vital role (Fig. **1**).

Fig. (1). Word-cloud of Image processing and Pattern recognition Applications.

FUNDAMENTALS OF IMAGE PROCESSING

In computer vision, image processing is a basic subject that deals with modifying digital images to enhance their quality or extract relevant data. It includes several different methods, like compression, restoration, and visual enhancement, among others [10]. Developing techniques and applications in domains like computer vision, medical imaging, and remote sensing requires a solid understanding of the principles of image processing.

Basics of Digital Images

Digital images are representations of visual data that have been digitally saved. Each pixel in the grid that makes up the image represents a little component. Knowledge of terms like resolution, colour depth, and picture formats is necessary to grasp the fundamentals of digital images. These ideas are essential to applying software tools and algorithms for digital image processing and analysis [11].

Image Representation (Pixel, Colour Models)

The term "image representation" describes the digital encoding and storing of visual data. The fundamental units of digital images are called pixels, and each pixel has a numerical value that represents colour or intensity. Colour models that specify how colours are represented and shown in digital images include Cyan, Magenta, Yellow, and Black (CMYK) and Red, Green, and Blue (RGB) [12].

Comprehending various colour models is crucial for the precise representation and manipulation of colours in the image processing software (Table **1**)

Table 1. Color Models RGB and CMYK.

RGB	Red	
	Green	
	Blue	
	White	
CMYK	Cyan	
	Magenta	
	Yellow	
	Black	

Image Enhancement Techniques

Techniques for image enhancement seek to raise the contrast, brightness, and sharpness of digital images in order to increase their overall quality. Redistributing pixel intensities in an image is known as histogram equalization, and it is a technique used to increase contrast. The technique of contrast stretching aims to improve visual contrast by extending the range of pixel intensities. Images can be sharpened and noise-reduced for greater clarity and detail by applying filtering techniques in the frequency and spatial domains.

Histogram Equalization

The process of shifting pixel intensities in an image to enhance contrast is called histogram equalization (Fig. **2**). In order for it to function, the pixel intensities' cumulative distribution function must be mapped to a new, more uniformly distributed histogram. Extending the image's intensity range effectively increases overall contrast by making dark areas darker and bright areas brighter.

Fig. (2). Sample Image before & after Histogram Equalization.

Contrast Stretching

Contrast stretching is a straightforward image enhancement technique that increases the range of intensity of pixels in an image to improve its contrast [13]. It is sometimes referred to as contrast normalization or intensity rescaling. In order to achieve this, the pixel values are linearly scaled from their initial range to a new range that encompasses the entire dynamic range of the display device. This can aid in bringing to light details that would otherwise be hidden by poor contrast in both bright and dark regions of the picture (Fig. **3**).

Original Image   Contrast Stretched Image

Fig. (3). Before and After Contrast Stretched Image.

Filtering (Spatial and Frequency Domain)

An image's pixel values are altered during filtering, a basic image processing procedure, in accordance with a predetermined filter kernel or mask. There are primarily two kinds of filtering:

- **Spatial Domain Filtering:** Smoothing filters (like Gaussian blur), edge enhancement filters (like the Sobel operator), and noise reduction filters (like the median filter) are examples of common spatial filters.
- **Frequency Domain Filtering:** The picture is first converted to the frequency domain using techniques such as the Fourier transform, after which filtering operations are carried out, and the filtered image is then returned to the spatial domain. This procedure is known as frequency domain filtering. Noise reduction and picture sharpening are two common applications for frequency domain filtering.

Image Restoration

The recovery of damaged or corrupted images due to noise, blur, or compression artifacts is accomplished through the employment of image restoration techniques (Fig. **4**). With these methods, undesired distortions are reduced or removed in an effort to return the image to its original quality. Two popular approaches include spatial domain filtering, which uses filters to eliminate blur or noise, and frequency domain approaches like Wiener filtering, which eliminates noise while keeping image information.

Fig. (4). Noisy and Restoration Image.

Image Compression

The technique of lowering the size of digital photos in order to free up storage space or enable faster transmission over networks is known as image compression. Depending on whether an exact reconstruction of the original image can be made from the compressed form, compression can be either lossless or lossy. While lossy compression techniques compromise some image quality in order to attain larger compression ratios, lossless compression techniques maintain every bit of the image without any loss. In picture compression algorithms, methods like discrete cosine transform (DCT), run-length encoding, and Huffman coding are frequently employed (Fig. **5**).

Lossless Compression

Lossless compression techniques seek to minimize the dimensions of digital images while preserving all of their information, enabling precise reconstruction of the source image. In order to compress the visual data, these techniques take advantage of statistical features and redundancy. Lempel-Ziv-Welch (LZW) compression is a common lossless compression technique that is used in formats such as TIFF and GIF, whereas DEFLATE compression is used in the PNG picture format.

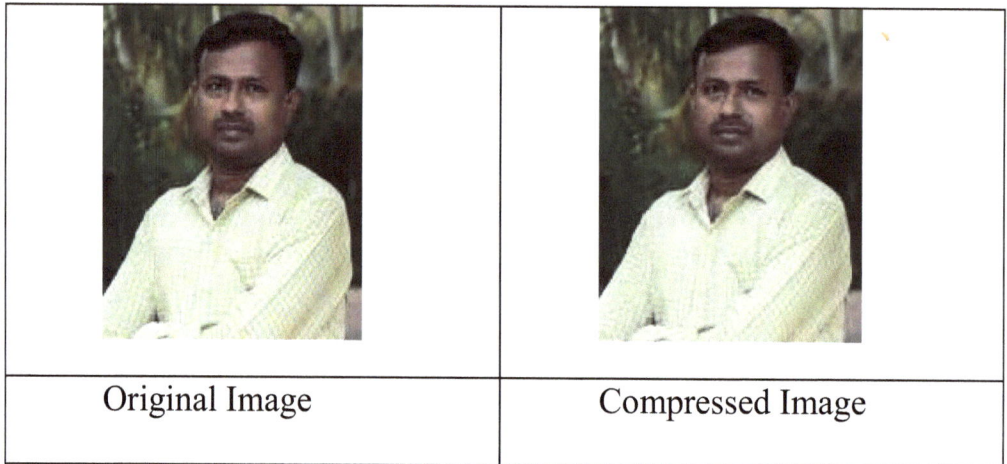

| Original Image | Compressed Image |

Fig. (5). Image before and after Compression.

Lossy Compression

Techniques for lossy compression compress digital images by removing details that are judged unimportant or unperceptually small. With lossy compression, you can get larger compression ratios than with lossless compression, but at the expense of some image quality loss. Well-known lossy compression algorithms include JPEG (Joint Photographic Experts Group), which achieves compression without sacrificing visual quality appropriate for online and photography photos through the use of methods like quantization and chroma subsampling.

Image Transform

A 3-stage hierarchical image [14] where 3 feature descriptors are calculated at three different stages using adaptive tetrolet transform with less overhead and better accuracy.

IMAGE SEGMENTATION

Thresholding Techniques

A simple yet powerful technique for segmenting images is thresholding. In order to categorize each pixel in the image according to whether its intensity value is above or below the threshold, a threshold value must be set. Pixels are then categorized as background or foreground (object of interest), creating a binary image [15]. Typical methods [16, 17] for thresholding include (Fig. **6**).

- **Global Thresholding:** The entire image is subject to a single threshold value.
- **Adaptive Thresholding:** To accommodate for differences in illumination or contrast, various threshold values are applied to different sections of the image.
- **Otsu's Method:** Maximizes the between-class variation of pixel intensities to automatically determine the ideal threshold value.

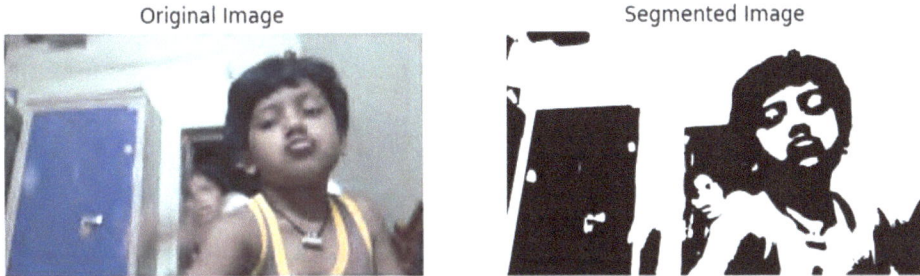

Fig. (6). Image before and after segmentation.

Edge Detection

Algorithms for edge identification pinpoint borders or edges in a picture where notable variations in intensity take place. These margins frequently line up with the borders of objects or areas of interest. Typical methods for detecting edges include (Fig. **7**):

- **Sobel Operator:** The Sobel Operator is a gradient-based technique for highlighting edges by determining the gradient magnitude at each pixel.
- **Canny Edge Detector:** A multi-stage technique that uses hysteresis thresholding, non-maximum suppression, gradient computation, and Gaussian smoothing to identify edges.
- **Prewitt Operator:** This operator is comparable to the Sobel operator but computes gradients using a slightly different kernel.

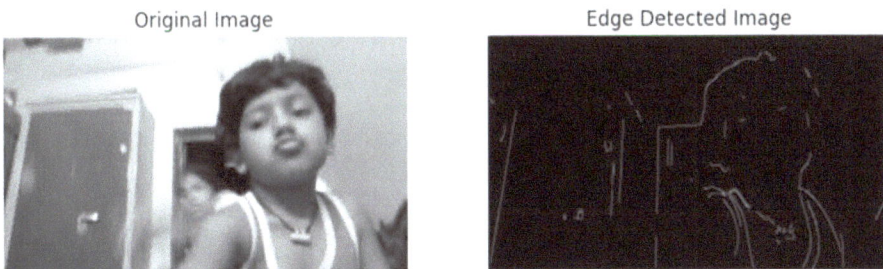

Fig. (7). Original Image Vs Edge Detected Image.

Region-based Segmentation

Methods of segmenting an image based on specific characteristics, including homogeneity of colour, texture, or intensity, divide it into meaningful parts or objects. Typical methods of region-based segmentation include the following:

- **Region Growing:** Region growth is an iterative process that begins with seed points and adds surrounding pixels that meet specific similarity requirements to expand regions.
- **Split and Merge:** This technique separates the image into smaller sections before combining neighbouring areas that satisfy particular homogeneity requirements.
- **Mean-Shift Clustering:** This non-parametric clustering algorithm divides similar pixels into regions by repeatedly shifting data points in the direction of their local density distribution's mode (Fig. **8**).

Fig. (8). Original Image vs Segmented Regions.

Clustering Techniques

Clustering algorithms use specific similarity metrics to group together data elements that are comparable. Clustering algorithms are frequently employed in the context of image segmentation to divide pixels into discrete clusters that represent various objects or regions. Typical clustering methods include the following:

- **K-means Clustering [18]:** By reducing the sum of squared distances between each data point and the cluster centroids, the clustering procedure divides the data into K clusters.
- **Gaussian Mixture Models (GMM):** depicts the probability distribution of the data using a number of Gaussian distributions, each of which relates to a cluster.
- **Hierarchical clustering:** Iteratively combines or divides clusters according to specific parameters, like similarity or distance, to create a hierarchy of clusters.

Watershed Transform

The watershed transform image segmentation technique treats the grayscale picture as a topographic surface. Pixels with high-intensity values indicate peaks, whereas pixels with low-intensity values indicate troughs. The algorithm floods these valleys with water, filling basins little by bit until they combine at watershed lines—the borders of objects in the image. The watershed transform is very helpful for separating items in an image that overlap or contact.

FEATURE EXTRACTION

Basics of Feature Extraction

The process of identifying and extracting pertinent data from visual sequences is known as feature extraction in the domain of human motion analysis. Components of the human body that serve as landmarks or important locations include joints and other body components. Features are then extracted from the body based on their temporal and spatial properties. Edge detection, motion estimation [19], and optical flow analysis are common methods utilised in feature extraction. In order to facilitate further analysis and identification tasks, these approaches [38] seek to capture significant motion signals and patterns (Table **2**).

Feature Selection Methods

Feature selection is critical to improving human motion analysis systems' efficacy. This section examines a number of feature selection strategies, including filter, wrapper, and embedding approaches [20, 21]. Filter approaches include ranking features based on how relevant they are to the classification objective, whereas wrapper techniques use a particular classifier to evaluate feature subsets. Embedded techniques integrate feature selection directly into the learning process, optimizing both classification and feature selection simultaneously. Furthermore, techniques like Principal Component Analysis (PCA) and Linear Discriminant Analysis (LDA) may be utilized to reduce the dimensionality of feature space while preserving discriminative information.

Texture Analysis

A crucial component of feature extraction is texture analysis, especially when it comes to identifying minute differences and patterns in human movements. A variety of texture analysis methods, such as statistical, structural, and model-based approaches, are covered in this section. While structural approaches concentrate on examining the physical relationships between adjacent pixels, statistical methods analyse the statistical characteristics of pixel intensity distributions.

Model-based methods describe texture patterns in photos using pre-built models or filters. These approaches capture textural information that may be missed by more conventional feature extraction techniques, leading to a more thorough knowledge of human motion.

Table 2. Different features extracted from the image.

Input Image	
Features Extracted	Image Area: 921600 Image Mean Intensity: 134.88041449652778 Image Standard Deviation of Intensity: 48.66757002855642 Image Aspect Ratio: 1.7777777777777777 Color Histogram: [[[0. 0. 0. ... 0. 0. 0.] [0. 0. 0. ... 0. 0. 0.] [0. 0. 0. ... 0. 0. 0.] ... [0. 0. 0. ... 0. 0. 0.] [0. 0. 0. ... 0. 0. 0.] [0. 0. 0. ... 0. 0. 0.]] [[0. 0. 0. ... 0. 0. 0.] [0. 0. 0. ... 0. 0. 0.] [0. 0. 0. ... 0. 0. 0.] ... [0. 0. 0. ... 0. 0. 0.] [0. 0. 0. ... 0. 0. 0.] [0. 0. 0. ... 0. 0. 0.]] ... ... [0. 0. 0. ... 0. 0. 0.] [0. 0. 0. ... 0. 0. 0.] [0. 0. 0. ... 0. 0. 0.]]] LBP Histogram: [6886 30531 8933 109760 139354 241361 58777 78947 247051] Number of Contours: 1

Shape Analysis

Capturing the geometrical characteristics and arrangements of human body components in motion is made possible through the use of shape analysis. Many shape analysis methods, such as model-based, skeleton-based, and contour-based methods, are covered in this section [22]. While skeleton-based approaches concentrate on examining an item's underlying skeletal structure, contour-based approaches use object boundaries to extract form data. Model-based methods compare and describe forms in photos using pre-made shape models or templates. Enhancing the overall accuracy of human motion analysis systems, these approaches allow the extraction of shape-based characteristics that are resistant to changes in appearance and attitude.

Feature Descriptors (SIFT, SURF, *etc.*)

To characterise local visual structures in a compact and discriminative way, feature descriptors are crucial building blocks of feature extraction. This section covers a wide range of feature descriptors, such as Scale-Invariant Feature Transform (SIFT), Speeded Up Robust Features (SURF), and Histogram of Oriented Gradients (HOG) [23]. Both SIFT and SURF can capture unique aspects of human motion since they are resistant to changes in rotation and size. By contrast, HOG descriptors are useful for identifying characteristics linked to motion and form since they concentrate on collecting gradient orientations within small picture patches. For tasks involving recognition and analysis, later on, these feature descriptors are essential in encoding and containing important motion information (Fig. **9**).

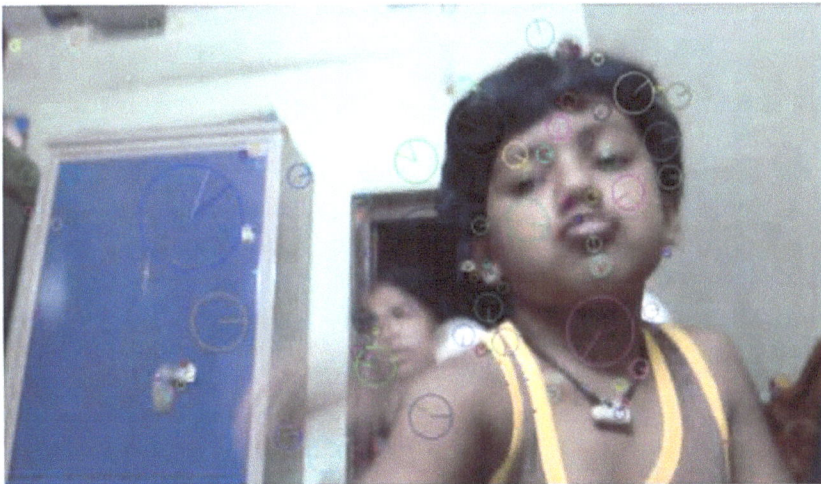

Fig. (9). Sift Keypoints in given Input Image.

PATTERN RECOGNITION

An essential component of image processing, pattern recognition is vital to the analysis of human movements from visual data. In order to make sense of complicated information and get valuable insights, it entails the detection and interpretation of patterns within data. Pattern recognition techniques are used in the context of human motion studies to categorise and identify certain motion patterns or behaviours from visual sequences.

Introduction to Pattern Recognition

The study of different approaches and strategies for finding patterns in data is known as pattern recognition. These patterns might appear as signals, pictures, or sequences, among other formats. Pattern recognition is used to analyse visual sequences taken from cameras or sensors in the context of human motion analysis in order to comprehend and describe human motions. ☐Generally speaking, there are two types of learning algorithms for pattern recognition: supervised(learning by example) and unsupervised(learning by observation). In learning by example, a model is trained using labelled data, where each point of data is connected to a particular class or category. Unsupervised learning, on the other hand, concentrates on finding patterns or structures in the data without the need for explicit direction and does not require labelled data.

Supervised and Unsupervised Learning

In supervised learning, a model is trained using labeled data, where each point of data is connected to a particular class or category. By extrapolating patterns from the annotated training data to previously unseen cases, the model gains the ability to predict outcomes. Support Vector Machines (SVM), Decision Trees, Neural Networks, and k-nearest Neighbors (k-NN) are examples of common supervised learning algorithms. These algorithms use several techniques to learn from annotated data and forecast future occurrences.

Unsupervised learning, on the other hand, does not require labelled data and focuses on identifying patterns or structures within the data without explicit guidance. Unsupervised learning algorithms look for underlying patterns, clusters, or correlations in the data rather than making predictions about particular results. Clustering algorithms like K-means, hierarchical clustering, and density-based clustering are examples of common unsupervised learning approaches. Principal Component Analysis (PCA) and t-distributed Stochastic Neighbour Embedding (t-SNE) are examples of dimensionality reduction techniques. These algorithms enable the exploration and discovery of hidden patterns and structures within unlabelled data, facilitating tasks such as data visualization, anomaly detection, and data pre-processing for supervised learning tasks.

Classification Techniques

Classification techniques are a subset of supervised learning methods that involve categorizing input data into predefined classes or categories. This subsection explores various classification techniques commonly used in pattern recognition for human motion analysis.

Support Vector Machines (SVM)

A potent classification technique called Support Vector Machines (SVM) divides input data into distinct groups by identifying the ideal hyperplane that maximises the margin between classes. SVMs are frequently used in human motion analysis because of their ability to handle high-dimensional data and nonlinear decision restrictions. They excel in distinguishing between different motion patterns or behaviors because they convert input data into a high-dimensional feature space (Fig. **10**).

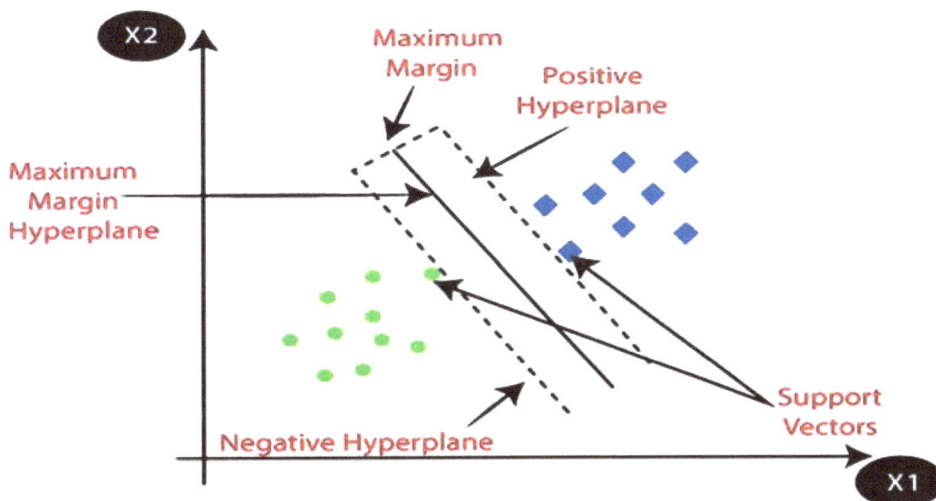

Fig. (10). Support Vector Machine.

SVM can be a powerful tool for image classification by extracting features using HOG, SIFT, and CNN [24] and training SVM [25], where it iteratively adjusts this decision boundary to maximize the margin between the closest data points from each class.

Decision Trees

Decision trees have become more and more popular due to their capacity to effectively capture non-linear relationships within data, in addition to their ease of use and interpretability. Because of this, they work especially effectively on jobs with complicated or ill-defined decision limits. Decision trees are useful for a number of tasks in the analysis of human motion patterns from visual sequences, including action detection, gesture recognition, and human posture estimation (Fig. **11**).

One of the key advantages of using decision trees for analyzing human motion patterns is their ability to handle features of varying importance. Decision trees are able to automatically identify the most discriminative features for differentiating distinct motion patterns by recursively dividing the feature space depending on the importance of various attributes. This not only simplifies the feature selection process but also helps in identifying the key.

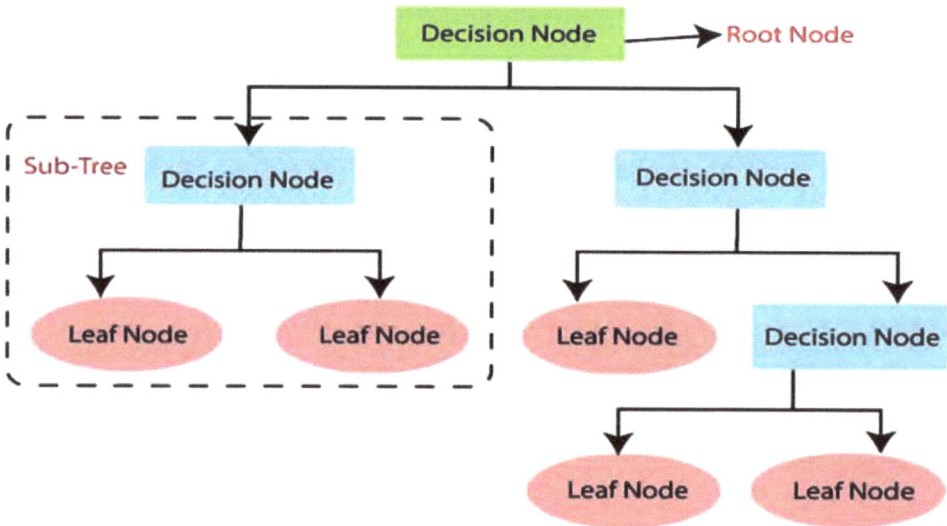

Fig. (11). Decision Tree [26].

Similarly, SVM in decision tree-based image classification starts with feature extraction with HOG/SIFT/CNN followed by training where the decision tree algorithm [27] starts with the root node iteratively splitting the data into subsets based on a decision rule that best separates the data points belonging to different classes.

Neural Networks

By replicating the intricate structure and functions of the human brain through the connected structure of biological neurons, Neural Networks are transforming machine learning. These networks comprise layers of interconnected nodes, or neurons, each processing input signals and transmitting them to subsequent layers. With the capability to learn intricate patterns and relationships from input data, Neural Networks have proven highly effective in human motion analysis tasks, boasting remarkable accuracy in recognizing and classifying complex motion patterns. Among Neural Network architectures, Convolutional Neural Networks (CNNs) stand out for their aptitude in processing visual sequences. Specifically designed for analysing images and video data, CNNs excel in detecting and categorizing human motion patterns captured from video streams. Leveraging convolutional layers to extract hierarchical features, CNNs effectively capture spatial and temporal nuances inherent in human motion, rendering them essential instruments in the fields of human motion analysis and computer vision (Fig. **12**).

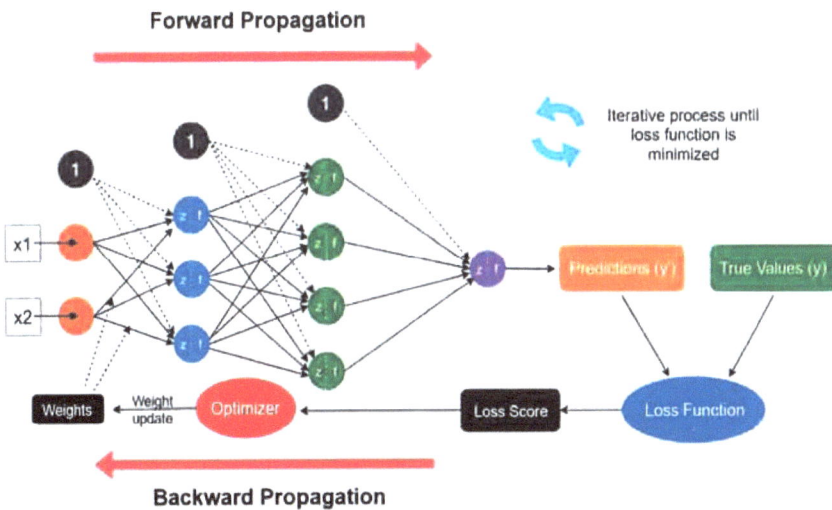

Fig. (12). Neural Networks.

k-Nearest Neighbors (k-NN)

k-Nearest Neighbors (k-NN) is an uncomplicated yet powerful classification algorithm commonly employed in human motion analysis due to its simplicity and robustness. When dealing with non-parametric data distributions, such as those seen in human motion data, k-NN efficiently detects patterns by labeling data points according to the majority class among their k-nearest neighbors in feature space [28]. Its non-parametric nature eliminates the need for explicit model training, making it particularly appealing for scenarios where labeled data is limited or where the underlying data distribution is not well understood. Moreover, k-NN's adaptability to changes in the input data distribution renders it suitable for dynamic environments, where human motion patterns may evolve over time (Fig. **13**). However, its reliance on a distance metric and the choice of k can significantly impact its performance, requiring careful selection and optimization to achieve optimal results. Despite these considerations, k-NN remains a versatile and widely used algorithm in human motion analysis.

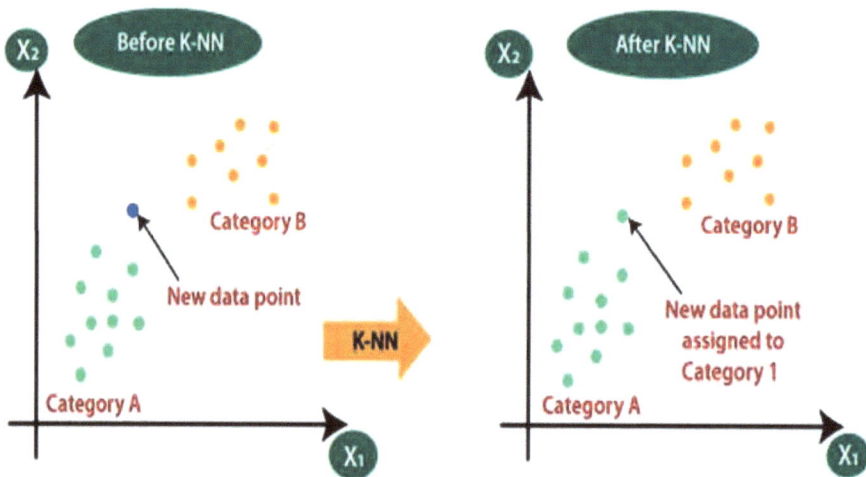

Fig. (13). k-Nearest Neighbors (k-NN) [29].

Performance Evaluation Metrics

Performance evaluation metrics are used to assess the effectiveness and accuracy of pattern recognition algorithms in classifying and recognizing human motion patterns. Common metrics include precision, accuracy, F1-score, recall, and receiver operating characteristic (ROC) graph curve. These metrics offer numerical assessments of algorithm performance and facilitate the comparison of various methods for human motion analysis. Additionally, performance evaluation techniques such as cross-validation and confusion matrix analysis are used to validate the robustness and generalization capability of pattern recognition models.

OBJECT DETECTION AND RECOGNITION

In computer vision, object detection and recognition are crucial tasks, especially when analysing visual sequences that involve human motion. With an emphasis on their uses in human motion analysis, this section examines several approaches [30] and methods for identifying and locating objects in visual data.

Object Detection Techniques

Object detection is the process of locating and recognising certain items or areas of interest in images. Two widely used object detection methods in computer vision are covered in this topic.

Haar Cascades

A cascade of classifiers trained on Haar-like characteristics is used in the machine learning-based object recognition method known as Haar Cascades. To differentiate between areas that include objects and those that don't, these characteristics, which show local intensity differences in the picture, are employed. Because of their computational efficiency and resilience to changes in scale and direction, Haar Cascades are especially useful for real-time object identification applications.

Histogram of Oriented Gradients (HOG)

An object identification and recognition feature descriptor approach called Histogram of Oriented Gradients (HOG) is employed. It entails calculating gradient orientation histograms inside certain picture areas and expressing them as feature vectors. HOG descriptors capture information about the shape and texture of objects, making them suitable for detecting objects with distinctive visual characteristics, such as human bodies and body parts.

Object Recognition

Object recognition is the process of identifying specific objects or classes within visual data. This subsection explores two approaches to object recognition commonly used in computer vision applications.

Template Matching

Template Matching is a straightforward technique for object recognition that involves comparing a template image with regions of interest within the input image. The template image represents the object of interest, and matching scores are computed to determine the similarity between the template and the image regions [31]. Template Matching is commonly used in scenarios where objects have consistent appearance and are relatively simple to detect.

Deep Learning-based Approaches

Deep Learning -based techniques, which leverage neural networks' capacity to construct hierarchical representations of visual data, have fundamentally altered the way objects are identified. Convolutional Neural Networks (CNNs) are highly helpful for applications involving object identification because they can automatically learn discriminative features from raw pixel data.CNNs have been extensively used in human motion analysis for detecting and recognizing human bodies, body parts, and motion patterns from visual sequences.

Applications in Computer Vision

Object detection and recognition techniques have numerous applications in computer vision, including surveillance, human-computer interaction, and augmented reality. In the context of human motion analysis, these techniques are used for various applications such as tracking and recognizing individuals, analyzing gait patterns, and monitoring human activities in surveillance systems. By accurately detecting and recognizing objects within visual data, computer vision systems can extract meaningful information about human motion and behavior, leading to advancements in various fields such as healthcare, and sports analytics.

CASE STUDIES AND APPLICATIONS

Medical Image Processing

Medical image processing utilizes computer vision techniques to analyze and interpret medical images, aiding in diagnosis, treatment planning, and medical research. It involves various tasks such as image segmentation, registration, and feature extraction to extract valuable information from medical images. Applications include tumor detection, organ segmentation, and image-guided surgery, contributing to advancements in healthcare and medical technology.

Biometric Recognition

Identification of people by their distinct biological characteristics, such as fingerprints, iris patterns, or facial features, is known as biometric recognition. Biometric data is captured and analyzed using computer vision methods, opening up applications like identity verification, access control, and forensic investigation. It is essential for improving privacy and security in a variety of areas, including financial transactions, border control, and law enforcement (Fig. **14**).

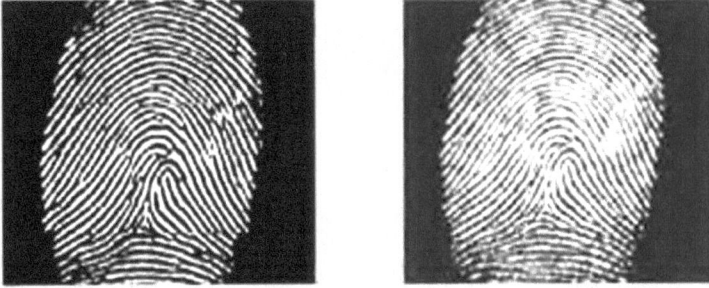

Fig. (14). Biometric Recognition.

Remote Sensing

Remote sensing involves the utilization of a variety of sensors and imaging devices to gather data about the Earth's surface from a distance, enabling comprehensive observation and analysis of large geographic areas. These sensors capture electromagnetic radiation across different wavelengths, ranging from visible light to microwaves and beyond, allowing for the collection of diverse types of data. Computer vision techniques play a crucial role in processing and examining data from remote sensing, making it easier to extract important details about different features of the Earth's surface, such as vegetation density, urban development, land cover, and environmental changes over time. By leveraging advanced algorithms and machine learning models, computer vision systems can automatically identify and classify different features within remote sensing imagery, enabling applications such as environmental monitoring, disaster management, urban planning, and agricultural assessments. For instance, remote sensing data can be used to monitor deforestation, track changes in land use patterns, assess the impact of natural disasters such as wildfires or floods, and optimize agricultural practices through precision farming techniques. These applications not only contribute to better understanding and management of the Earth's resources but also support sustainable development efforts by providing valuable insights into the state of the environment and guiding informed decision-making processes at local, regional, and global scales (Fig. **15**).

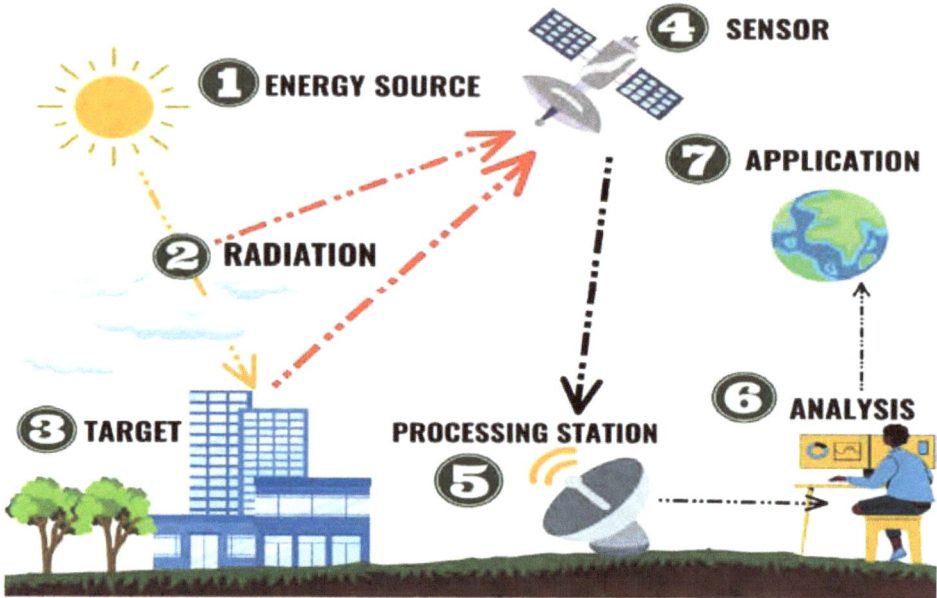

Fig. (15). Remote Sensing.

Autonomous Vehicles

Autonomous vehicles rely on computer vision systems to perceive and interpret the surrounding environment, enabling navigation and decision-making without human intervention [32]. Computer vision techniques such as object detection, tracking, and scene understanding are used to detect obstacles, recognize traffic signs, and navigate complex traffic scenarios. Transportation might undergo a revolution thanks to autonomous cars, which increase accessibility, efficiency, and safety (Fig. **16**).

Security and Surveillance

Security and surveillance systems utilize computer vision technologies to monitor and analyze video data for detecting suspicious activities, identifying individuals, and ensuring public safety. Applications like video surveillance, crowd monitoring, and facial identification use computer vision methods including object detection, tracking, and behavior analysis. Security and surveillance systems play a crucial role in law enforcement, homeland security, and public safety, helping to prevent crime and protect communities (Fig. **17**).

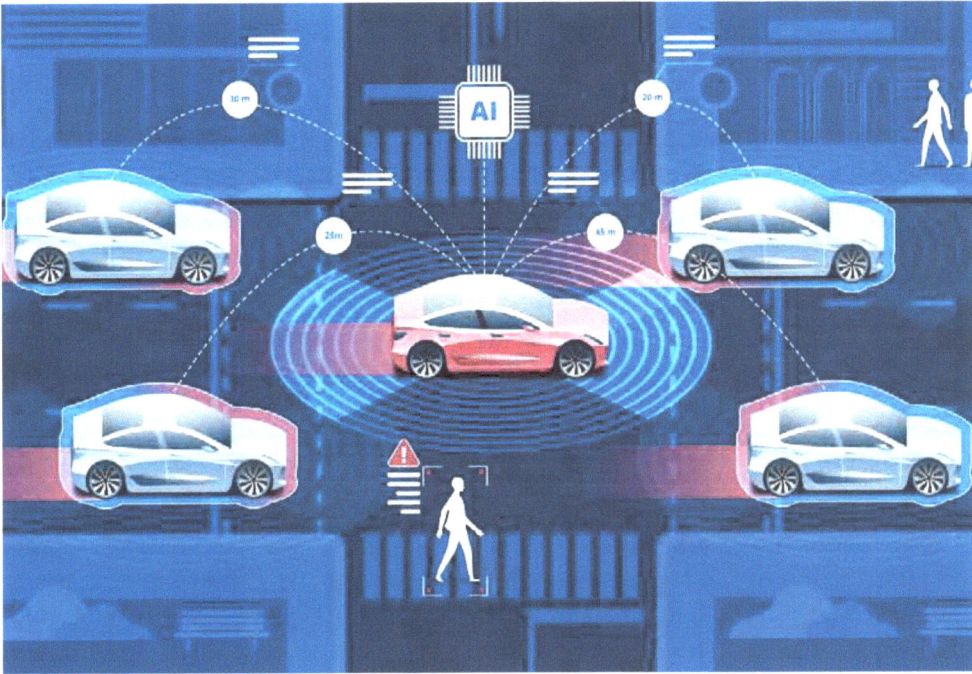

Fig. (16). Autonomous Vehicles.

Fig. (17). Security and Surveillance.

CHALLENGES AND FUTURE DIRECTIONS

Current Challenges in Image Processing and Pattern Recognition

In the realm of image processing and pattern recognition, several challenges persist despite significant advancements. One primary challenge is the complexity and variability of human motion, which can vary significantly based on factors such as lighting conditions, occlusions, and background clutter. Additionally, the extraction of meaningful features from visual sequences poses a challenge, particularly in scenarios where motion patterns are subtle or non-uniform. Another challenge lies in the computational complexity of algorithms, especially for real-time applications where efficiency is crucial. Furthermore, the integration of static and dynamic aspects of human gait remains challenging, as capturing both spatial and temporal information accurately requires sophisticated techniques [33].

Emerging Technologies

Emerging technologies hold the potential to address existing challenges and push the boundaries of image processing and pattern recognition in human motion analysis. Convolutional neural networks (CNNs), which have demonstrated outstanding performance in a variety of computer vision applications, including object identification and recognition, are one example of this technology. CNNs can automatically learn hierarchical representations of visual data, enabling more accurate and robust feature extraction for human motion analysis. Another emerging technology is 3D vision, which allows for the capture and analysis of depth information, enhancing the understanding of three-dimensional human motion [34]. Additionally, advancements in sensor technologies, such as depth sensors and wearable devices, provide new opportunities for capturing and analysing human motion data in diverse environments [35-36].

Potential Future Trends

Looking ahead, several potential future trends are expected to shape the landscape of image processing and pattern recognition in human motion analysis. One trend is the integration of multi-modal data sources, such as combining visual data with inertial sensors or physiological signals, to capture a more comprehensive view of human motion. This integration can improve the accuracy and robustness of motion analysis systems, particularly in challenging conditions. Another trend is the development of adaptive and personalized systems that can tailor the analysis and recognition process to individual characteristics and preferences. This personalized approach can enhance the usability and effectiveness of human motion analysis systems in diverse applications, including healthcare, sports performance analysis, and assistive technologies. Furthermore, the growing emphasis on ethical considerations, such as privacy protection and bias mitigation, is expected to influence the design and deployment of image processing and pattern recognition systems in human motion analysis, ensuring fairness and accountability in their use [37-40].

CONCLUSION

The study underscores the significance of image processing and pattern recognition within the realm of computer vision, particularly in the analysis of human motion. Through visual sequences, computer vision technology can effectively identify, track, and recognize individuals while comprehensively characterizing their movements. The rapid growth and widespread adoption of information technology have spurred considerable attention towards leveraging computer vision for tasks such as image processing, pattern recognition, and efficient extraction of human motion elements from video data. The introduction of the extraction function method and its subsequent examination has led to the proposal of a picture recognition-based technique aimed at enhancing the evaluation of moving human bodies. By employing a hierarchical clustering approach, the study successfully segmented periodic motion within each movement, facilitating precise segmentation and enabling accurate analysis of human motion patterns. Tests conducted on both self-built data and benchmark datasets have demonstrated the method's ability to extract minimal feature data while maintaining low computational complexity, thereby yielding high classification and recognition results. Furthermore, the proposed method exhibits the natural integration of both static and dynamic aspects of human gait, contributing to a comprehensive understanding of human motion characteristics. Overall, the study emphasizes the critical role of image processing and pattern recognition in advancing computer vision technology and its applications in various domains such as healthcare, sports analytics, security, and surveillance. Continued research and innovation in this area are crucial for addressing complex challenges and unlocking new opportunities in the future.

SUMMARY OF KEY POINTS

In conclusion, this paper has explored the frontier area of visual analysis of human motion within the realm of computer vision. Through the utilization of visual sequences, the ability to identify, track, and recognize individuals has been highlighted, showcasing the potential of computer vision technology in understanding human behaviour. The introduction of the extraction function method and its examination of properties, along with the proposed technique based on picture recognition, has demonstrated a novel approach to enhancing the evaluation of moving human bodies.

The segmentation of periodic motion using a hierarchical clustering approach has been discussed, showcasing its effectiveness in achieving precise segmentation of human motion elements from video sequences. Furthermore, the tests conducted on self-built data and benchmark datasets have shown promising results, indicating the method's capability to extract less feature data while maintaining low computational complexity and achieving high classification and recognition accuracy. All things considered, the main ideas covered in this work highlight how important it is to use image processing and pattern recognition methods when analyzing human motion.

IMPORTANCE OF IMAGE PROCESSING AND PATTERN RECOGNITION

It is impossible to exaggerate the significance of pattern recognition and image processing in the context of human motion analysis. These technologies, which have implications in everything from sports analytics and healthcare to security and surveillance, are vital to improving our understanding of human behavior and movement patterns. By leveraging advanced computer vision techniques, such as the ones discussed in this paper, researchers and practitioners can extract valuable insights from visual data, leading to advancements in various fields and improving the quality of life for individuals.

Significant implications for the development of cutting-edge technologies like virtual reality, augmented reality, and driverless cars may be found in image processing and pattern recognition. Through precise analysis and interpretation of visual data, these technologies may improve user experience, safety, and efficiency across a range of applications. Furthermore, there are new avenues for problem-solving and social advancement when image processing and pattern recognition are combined with other cutting-edge technologies like artificial intelligence and the Internet of Things (IoT).

FINAL REMARKS

The future of image processing is crammed with many possibilities. As technology continues to evolve, the integration of image processing and pattern recognition holds immense promise for addressing complex challenges and improving the quality of life for individuals around the world. Researchers can design deeper and more efficient architectures for image processing tasks and future work will be more focused on medical image analysis to ensure better medical diagnosis and treatment planning, on autonomous vehicles to ensure more secure self-driving cars, and on generative image models to have realistic simulations and creative content generation. However,ethical considerations, biases and privacy needs are to be addressed as image processing continues to reshape the entire world.

CONSENT FOR PUBLICATION

I would like to confirm that the individuals in these images are Naresh Tangudu, the second co-author of the paper, and his daughter. Mr. Tangudu. They have provided permission for these images to be used in the publication.

REFERENCES

[1]   K. Simonyan, and A. Zisserman, Two-stream convolutional networks for action recognition in videos.*In Advances in neural information processing systems*, 2014, pp. 568-576.

[2]   C. Feichtenhofer, A. Pinz, and A. Zisserman, "Convolutional two-stream network fusion for video action recognition", *Proceedings of the IEEE Conference on Computer Vision and Pattern Recognition,* pp. 1933-1941, 2016.
[http://dx.doi.org/10.1109/CVPR.2016.213]

[3]   G. Gkioxari, J. Malik, and J. Johnson, "Contextual action recognition with R* CNN", *Proceedings of the IEEE International Conference on Computer Vision,* pp. 1080-1088, 2015.

[4]   D. Weinland, R. Ronfard, and E. Boyer, "A survey of vision-based methods for action representation, segmentation and recognition", *Comput. Vis. Image Underst.,* vol. 115, no. 2, pp. 224-241, 2011.
[http://dx.doi.org/10.1016/j.cviu.2010.10.002]

[5]   D.Y. Pimenov, L.R.R. da Silva, A. Ercetin, O. Der, T. Mikolajczyk, and K. Giasin, "State-of-the-art review of applications of image processing techniques for tool condition monitoring on conventional machining processes", *Int. J. Adv. Manuf. Technol.,* vol. 130, no. 1-2, pp. 57-85, 2024.
[http://dx.doi.org/10.1007/s00170-023-12679-1]

[6]   A.Z. Khoirunnisaa, L. Hakim, and A.D. Wibawa, "The Biometrics System Based on Iris Image Processing: A Review", *2019 2nd International Conference of Computer and Informatics Engineering (IC2IE), Banyuwangi, Indonesia,* pp. 164-169, 2019.
[http://dx.doi.org/10.1109/IC2IE47452.2019.8940832]

[7]   K Prakash, P Saravanamoorthi, Mr Sathishkumar, and M. Parimala, "A Study of Image Processing in Agriculture", *International Journal of Advanced Networking and Applications.,* vol. 9, pp. 3311-3315, 2017.

[8]   Deepayan Bhowmik, and Mehryar Emambakhsh, *Image Processing for Surveillance and Security.,* 2017.
[http://dx.doi.org/10.4018/978-1-5225-2498-4.ch003]

[9]   M. Bertozzi, Image Processing for Vehicular Applications.*Handbook of Intelligent Vehicles.,* A. Eskandarian, Ed., Springer: London, 2012.
[http://dx.doi.org/10.1007/978-0-85729-085-4_38]

[10]   K. Soomro, A.R. Zamir, and M. Shah, "UCF101: A dataset of 101 human actions classes from videos in the wild", arXiv:1212.0402v1.

[11]   L. Wang, Y. Qiao, and X. Tang, "Action recognition with trajectory-pooled deep-convolutional descriptors", *Proceedings of the IEEE Conference on Computer Vision and Pattern Recognition,* pp. 4305-4314, 2015.

[12]   J. Carreira, and A. Zisserman, "Quo vadis, action recognition? A new model and the kinetics dataset", *proceedings of the IEEE Conference on Computer Vision and Pattern Recognition,* pp. 6299-6308, 2017.
[http://dx.doi.org/10.1109/CVPR.2017.502]

[13]   H. Wang, A. Kläser, C. Schmid, and C.L. Liu, "Dense trajectories and motion boundary descriptors for action recognition", *Int. J. Comput. Vis.,* vol. 103, no. 1, pp. 60-79, 2013.
[http://dx.doi.org/10.1007/s11263-012-0594-8]

[14]   N. Varish, A.K. Pal, R. Hassan, M.K. Hasan, A. Khan, N. Parveen, D. Banerjee, V. Pellakuri, A.U. Haqis, and I. Memon, "Image Retrieval Scheme Using Quantized Bins of Color Image Components and Adaptive Tetrolet Transform", *IEEE Access,* vol. 8, pp. 117639-117665, 2020.
[http://dx.doi.org/10.1109/ACCESS.2020.3003911]

[15]   Q.B. Rind, G.A. Mallah, I. Memon, and N.A. Shaikh, "Identification of Human & various objects through Image Processing based system", *2020 International Conference on Information Science and Communication Technology (ICISCT),* pp. 1-4, 2020.
[http://dx.doi.org/10.1109/ICISCT49550.2020.9080056]

[16]   N. Goel, A. Yadav, and B. M. Singh, "Medical image processing: A review", *2016 Second International Innovative Applications of Computational Intelligence on Power, Energy and Controls with their Impact on Humanity (CIPECH), Ghaziabad, India,* pp. 57-62, 2016.
[http://dx.doi.org/10.1109/CIPECH.2016.7918737]

[17]   R. Nikhil, "A review on image segmentation techniques", *Pattern Recognition,* vol. 26, no. 9,1993, pp. 1277-1294, 1993.
[http://dx.doi.org/10.1016/0031-3203(93)90135-J]

[18]   A. Shifa, M.S. Afgan, M.N. Asghar, M. Fleury, I. Memon, S. Abdullah, and N. Rasheed, "Joint Crypto-Stego Scheme for Enhanced Image Protection With Nearest-Centroid Clustering", *IEEE Access,* vol. 6, pp. 16189-16206, 2018.
[http://dx.doi.org/10.1109/ACCESS.2018.2815037]

[19]   S.L. Ullo, and A. Siddiqi, Remote Sensing Through Satellites and Sensor Networks.*Women in Telecommunications. Women in Engineering and Science.,* M.S. Greco, D. Cassioli, S.L. Ullo, M.J. Lyons, Eds., Springer: Cham, 2023.
[http://dx.doi.org/10.1007/978-3-031-21975-7_9]

[20]   B. Remeseiro, and V. Bolon-Canedo, "Veronica Bolon-Canedo,A review of feature selection methods in medical applications", *Computers in Biology and Medicine,* vol. 112, 2019.
[http://dx.doi.org/10.1016/j.compbiomed.2019.103375]

[21]   R. Sindhuja, and S. Srinivasan, Efficient Fusion Based Multi-modal Biometric Authentication System Using Machine Learning.*Electronic Systems and Intelligent Computing. Lecture Notes in Electrical Engineering.,* P.K. Mallick, P. Meher, A. Majumder, S.K. Das, Eds., vol. Vol. 686. Springer: Singapore, 2020.
[http://dx.doi.org/10.1007/978-981-15-7031-5_12]

[22]   X. Yang, and Y. Tian, "Super normal vector for activity recognition using depth sequences", *IEEE Trans. Pattern Anal. Mach. Intell.,* vol. 38, no. 3, pp. 501-511, 2016.
[PMID: 27116731]

[23]   K. Kikuchi, K. Ueki, T. Ogawa, and T. Kobayashi, "Video semantic indexing using object detection-derived features", *2016 24th European Signal Processing Conference (EUSIPCO), Budapest, Hungary,* pp. 1288-1292, 2016.
[http://dx.doi.org/10.1109/EUSIPCO.2016.7760456]

[24]   K. Ishfaq, M. Sana, and W.M. Ashraf, "Artificial intelligence–built analysis framework for the manufacturing sector: performance optimization of wire electric discharge machining system", *Int. J. Adv. Manuf. Technol.,* vol. 128, no. 11-12, pp. 5025-5039, 2023.
[http://dx.doi.org/10.1007/s00170-023-12191-6]

[25]   Sai Chaganti, Ipseeta Nanda, Koteswara Pandi, Tavva Prudhvith, and Niraj Kumar, *Image Classification using SVM and CNN,* pp. 1-5, 2020.
[http://dx.doi.org/10.1109/ICCSEA49143.2020.9132851]

[26]   A. Shankhdhar, N. Adnekar, P. Bansal, and R. Agrawal, Healthcare Bot Using Machine Learning Algorithms for Medical Services.*Inventive Systems and Control. Lecture Notes in Networks and Systems.,* V. Suma, J.I.Z. Chen, Z. Baig, H. Wang, Eds., vol. Vol. 204. Springer: Singapore, 2021.
[http://dx.doi.org/10.1007/978-981-16-1395-1_35]

[27]   C. Agarwal, and A. Sharma, "Image understanding using decision tree based machine learning", *ICIMU 2011: Proceedings of the 5th international Conference on Information Technology,* 2011pp. 1-8 Multimedia, Kuala Lumpur, Malaysia.
[http://dx.doi.org/10.1109/ICIMU.2011.6122757]

[28]   Y. Gu, S. Ghosal, and H. Kautz, "AViD: Action video dataset with spatio-temporal keypoints", *Proceedings of the IEEE Conference on Computer Vision and Pattern Recognition,* pp. 947-956, 2018.

[29]   S. Modak, and A.C. Mondal, "Sentiment Analysis of Twitter Data Using Clustering and Classification", *Proceedings of Third International Conference on Computing, Communications, and Cyber-Security. Lecture Notes in Networks and Systems,* vol. 421, Singh, P.K., Wierzchoń, S.T., Tanwar, S., Rodrigues, J.J.P.C., Ganzha, M. (eds) Springer, Singapore., 2023.
[http://dx.doi.org/10.1007/978-981-19-1142-2_51]

[30]   Xinrui Zou, *A Review of Object Detection Techniques,* pp. 251-254, 2019.
[http://dx.doi.org/10.1109/ICSGEA.2019.00065]

[31]   S. Zhang, R. Benenson, M. Omran, J. Hosang, and B. Schiele, "How far are we from solving pedestrian detection?", *Proceedings of the IEEE Conference on Computer Vision and Pattern Recognition,* pp. 1259-1267, 2016.
[http://dx.doi.org/10.1109/CVPR.2016.141]

[32]   J. Liu, J. Luo, and M. Shah, "Recognizing realistic actions from videos "in the wild"", *Proceedings of the IEEE Conference on Computer Vision and Pattern Recognition,* pp. 1996-2003, 2009.
[http://dx.doi.org/10.1109/CVPR.2009.5206744]

[33]   J. Liu, and M. Shah, "Learning human actions via information maximization", *Proceedings of the IEEE Conference on Computer Vision and Pattern Recognition,* pp. 1-8, 2008.

[34]   X. Yang, Y. Tian, and L. Duan, "Eigenjoints-based action recognition using Naive-Bayes-Nearet-Neighbor", *Pattern Recognit. Lett.,* vol. 74, pp. 15-21, 2016.

[35]   C. Chen, R. Jafari, and N. Kehtarnavaz, "UTD-MHAD: A multimodal dataset for human action recognition utilizing a depth camera and a wearable inertial sensor", *Proceedings of the IEEE International Conference on Image Processing,* pp. 1681-1684, 2011.

[36]   J.C. Niebles, C.W. Chen, and L. Fei-Fei, "Modeling temporal structure of decomposable motion segments for activity classification", *Proceedings of the European Conference on Computer Vision,* pp. 392-405, 2010.
[http://dx.doi.org/10.1007/978-3-642-15552-9_29]

[37]   H. Jhuang, J. Gall, S. Zuffi, C. Schmid, and M.J. Black, "Towards understanding action recognition", *Proceedings of the IEEE International Conference on Computer Vision,* pp. 3192-3199, 2013.

[38]   P. Dollar, V. Rabaud, G. Cottrell, and S. Belongie, "Behavior recognition via sparse spatio-temporal features", *Proceedings of the IEEE International Workshop on Visual Surveillance and Performance Evaluation of Tracking and Surveillance,* pp. 65-72, 2005.
[http://dx.doi.org/10.1109/VSPETS.2005.1570899]

[39]   I. Laptev, M. Marszałek, C. Schmid, and B. Rozenfeld, "Learning realistic human actions from movies", *Proceedings of the IEEE Conference on Computer Vision and Pattern Recognition,* pp. 1-8, 2008.

[40]   Y. Yu, C. Wang, Q. Fu, R. Kou, F. Huang, B. Yang, T. Yang, and M. Gao, "Techniques and Challenges of Image Segmentation: A Review", *Electronics (Basel),* vol. 12, no. 5, p. 1199, 2023.
[http://dx.doi.org/10.3390/electronics12051199]

CHAPTER 8

Cyber-Physical Architecture of Smart Grid Network

A.K.M. Ahasan Habib[1], Mohammad Kamrul Hasan[1,*] and Shayla Islam[2]

[1] *Faculty of Information Science and Technology, Universiti Kebangsaan Malaysia (UKM), 43600 Bangi, Selangor, Malaysia*

[2] *Institute of Computer Science and Digital Innovation, UCSI University, Federal Territory of Kuala Lumpur, Malaysia*

Abstract: The smart grid (SG) system is a novel concept that introduced bidirectional power and communication infrastructure to traditional power grid systems at the beginning of the 2000s. To make information and communication technologies (ICTs) available in utility grids at every point throughout the generation, transmission, distribution, and consumption (GTDC) of power are necessary. This chapter explains the fundamental elements and cutting-edge technologies that make up SGs, including sensor networks, intelligent management systems, monitoring, and metering systems, communication technologies, regulations, standards, and security needs for this idea. Two-way intelligent communication and real-time measurements are all used in the "SG", an electrical distribution system. A safe, secure, dependable, robust, effective, and sustainable SG is anticipated. Measuring tools like phasor measurement units (PMUs) could drastically alter how grids are monitored. There are a few obstacles, though, like managing the massive volume of data and deploying an adequate number of PMUs. A fundamental need of the SG is communication in both directions. It is necessary to have a communications network that can handle the data traffic and is secure, devoted, and capable. Renewable energy inclusion will change the grid's characteristics. Enhanced distribution-level management and monitoring are necessary, given the current circumstances.

Keywords: Cyber-physical system, Conventional grid, Smart grid, Smart grid architecture.

INTRODUCTION

The traditional electricity system has degenerated since its inception and widespread usage. The four main components of the power grid are GTDC. Bulk-generating systems include hydropower plants, coal, diesel, gas power plants, thermos generators, solar and wind power plants, and nuclear power. The deteri-

---
[*] **Corresponding author Mohammad Kamrul Hasan:** Faculty of Information Science and Technology, Universiti Kebangsaan Malaysia (UKM), 43600 Bangi, Selangor, Malaysia; E-mail: mkhasan@ukm.edu.my

Asif Khan, Mohammad Kamrul Hasan, Naushad Varish & Mohammed Aslam Husain (Eds.)

orating utility has several flaws affecting electricity quality and dependability. Among well-known power system flaws are voltage variability, blackouts, intermittency, and imbalanced or heavy-load circumstances. Remote control and monitoring technologies have been enhanced and incorporated into the traditional grid [1, 2].

Since the conventional grid was constructed, worldwide energy consumption has risen. Governments and energy providers have upgraded demand-side management (DSM) and numerous energy projects to fulfill the need. Regulations allowing more distributed generation (DG) have existed for decades. Along with DG initiatives, renewable energy sources (RES) usage has grown steadily. Conventional grid research and development have imposed a new necessity on communication arrangements. These communication arrangements improved the SG by managing sources and loads, monitoring GTDC rates, and control systems. The phrase SG, coined in the early 2000s, refers to monitoring and controlling power system management [3 - 5]. The SG combines physical and cyber communication networks and increases power network communication and control. The SG promotes the power network by allowing two-way communication.

The SG infrastructure provides a data communication means for signal monitoring, control, measurement, and management. In addition to microgrids, the SG interface may be incorporated into the grid at any point. The transmission interface and medium must be secure, dependable, and efficient. Many legislation, standards, applications, and reference works have been produced to advance the SG idea. The Energy Independence and Security Act of 2007 defined SG and its characteristics [6]. Instead of only improving technology, SG has acknowledged the goal.

Table 1 compares conventional and SG's most important properties. Enhanced ICT allowed the traditional grid to supply electricity efficiently. Data transmission over a cyber-secure communication gateway is possible for the SG. Thus, computing intelligence is incorporated into the traditional grid, making grid diagnosis and troubleshooting considerably more efficient. Computing intelligence is included in traditional grid GTDA. Thus, the upgraded grid is far safer, dependable, controlled, and efficient. It is decentralized and DG, whereas the traditional grid relies on centralized plants. Because of decentralized generating, SG monitoring and measuring technologies have been developed. Thus, SG improvements now have two-way communication.

Table 1. Compares among traditional grid and SG.

Feature	Conventional Grid	Smart Grid
Grid architecture	Radial	Network
Power Generation	Central	Decentralized
Power flow	Unidirectional	Bi-directional
Communications	Unidirectional	Bi-directional
Restoration	Local and manual	Self-restoration
Control	Passive and limited	Active
Monitoring	Manual	Self-monitoring
Transducers	Limited sensors	Widespread and unlimited
Metering	Electromechanical and digital	Smart meter

This is done by using smart sensors, and networks infinitely and ubiquitously. The intelligence-based innovative electrical grid construction can self-restore and heal, although traditional grid requires manual or local restoration [5, 7, 8].

IEEE Std 2030–2011 supports the National Institute of Standards and Technology (NIST) outline direction and includes many explanations representing a system-level interoperability method. This capability allows any system to connect with another *via* devices, services, applications, networks, and interfaces, all of which are supported by cyber-physical systems (CPSs). Thus, every SG system must combine data transmission, software, and hardware systems, and exchange networks [1]. The ICT enables combination based on the need for compatibility. The NIST-suggested compatibility architecture is shown in Fig. (**1**).

It facilitates interactions between SG applications and imaginary reference representations (see Fig. **1**). A smart grid conceptual reference model defines characteristics, behaviors, needs, and standards for the SG system *via* views and descriptions. Actors, domains, and layered structures are all described in the conceptual reference models. Of the several reference models presented, NIST and IEC are commonly acknowledged [1, 5].

Markets, operations, and service providers are smart grid domains characterized by electrical flow. As demonstrated in Fig. (**2**), the smart grid interacts with existing systems on both electrical and communication levels. Generating power plants make up the majority of the generation. It is linked to other domains through WANs and substations *via* LANs. All transmission level equipment are field devices and substations. In distribution, data collectors offer connectivity between WANs, field area networks, and substation LANs. A FAN connects field equipment to the operational and transmission domains. Energy management systems (EMS) are part of the customer-domain energy storage systems (ESSs).

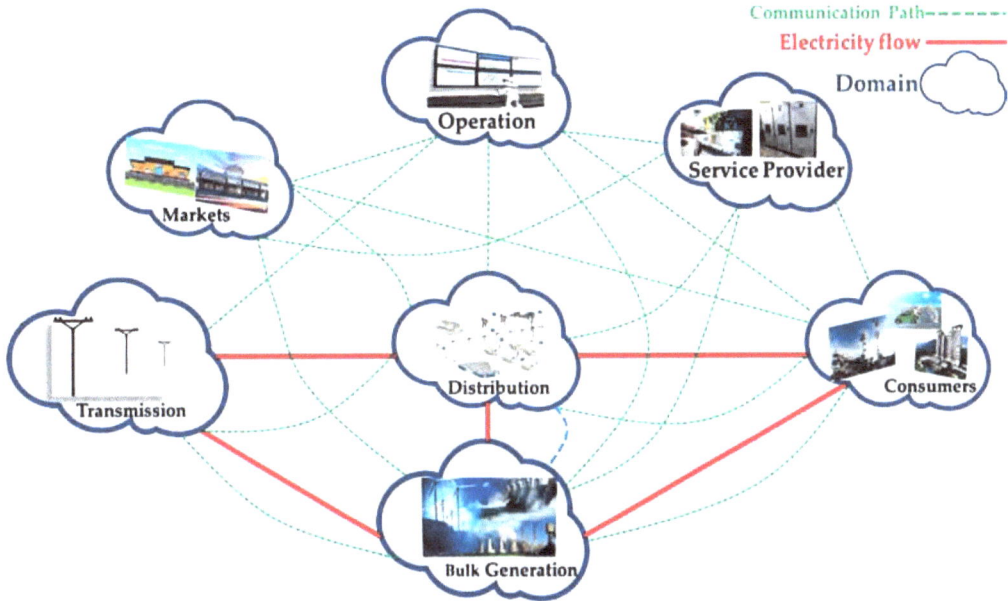

Fig. (1). NIST conceptual model of SG [1].

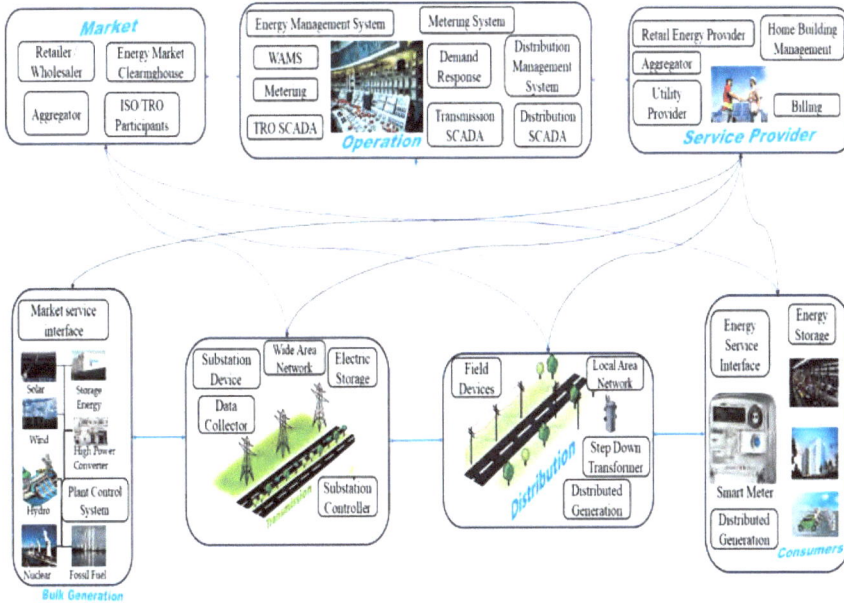

Fig. (2). Smart grid domains characterized.

The utility grid operators and energy market have encouraged the deployment of RES to regulate consumer demand. Administrations and authorities also pushed the deployment of RES to offset greenhouse gas and carbon emissions. Many governments encouraged people to become prosumers by establishing microgrids (MGs). Several DR and DSM schemes have been improved by generating and distributing businesses [3, 9 - 11]. Aside from DG and MG, ESSs are commonly used to balance production and consumption. Smart generating requires technology advancements in GTDC and monitoring. The SG enhancements involve a broad range of grid infrastructure and technology. Fig. (**3**) shows an entire SG architecture. The picture depicts the SG design with all components and system incorporations. The bottom levels represent the electricity system. It defines each element at the bulk GTDC and consumer levels of energy storage. The majority of generation is made up of nuclear, and hydroelectric power facilities, as well as RES like PV and wind.

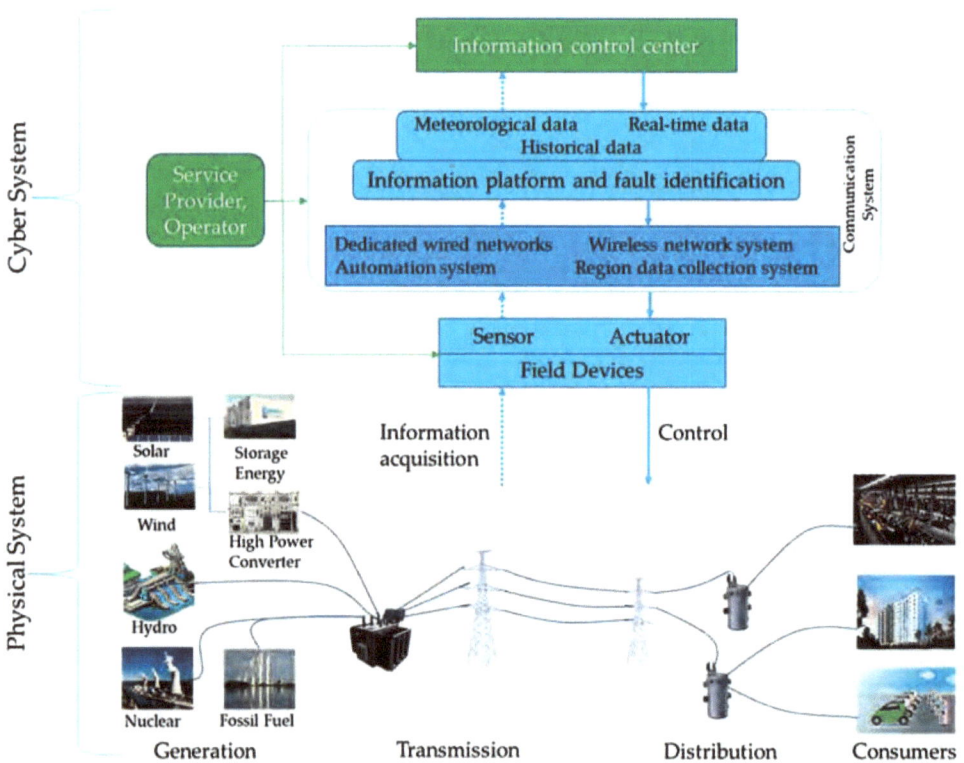

Fig. (3). Entire smart grid cyber-physical architecture [5].

A smart transformer with sensors and IEDs is an example of a transmission or distribution level. Intelligent substations connect energy-generating and DG plants. These may be incorporated into the distribution system and the consumers. Industrial and residential loads represent the utility grid consumption level where whole communication may be accomplished wired or wirelessly. Home management systems (HMS) may control household loads in SG applications enabled by service providers. The ICT sublayer connects supervision and management systems to the power network. Supervisory management, consumer/DSM side management, and control service.

The supervisory management department is in charge of monitoring and controlling bulk generation and transmission. WANs help transmit data and control signals across various tiers. NAN and FAN are used for distribution and MG control. Smart meters help enhance the SG by integrating with the current infrastructure. Smart meters may send and receive data in both directions [5, 12 - 14].

The first research on SG concentrated on decentralized and intelligent generation architecture, interactive system implementations, and plant installations. However, a new study focuses on security, sustainability, dependability, and efficiency. The three primary parts of SG design are structure, administration, and protection [1]. The structure context also handles source penetration shares, decentralized generation, and transmission. Smart communication facilitates connection and data transfer among the SG system. Smart management services include demand profile and response, power quality, energy efficiency, control, and optimization. Smart management also covers communication activities like smart metering. Smart protection is connected to dependability, self-healing characteristics, diagnostics, failure detection, and cyber-physical security.

As a result, ongoing SG development procures new technology and components incorporated into the current grid infrastructure. The most widely used measurement and monitoring equipment includes smart measuring apparatus for both reactive and active power detection, SCADA, and upgraded management systems employing communication interfaces [1, 5, 15]. Many grid services and functions have been updated to work with smart grids and older applications have been modified to work with intelligence-based grids. Several communication systems are established to assure data transmission reliability in monitoring, metering, and control applications.

POWER GRID DEVELOPMENTS

From 1880 through 1930, the electric power grid was evolving. New York's Pearl Street Station became the first central power plant [16, 17]. It was a set of steam generators with a 100V DC generation and distribution. Due to the low voltage, the earliest power systems worked in isolation, only servicing a limited area. In Chicago alone, 45 separate utilities served people with power. Geographically scattered American electric power firms began merging operations in 1910, realizing the economic benefits of developing huge power facilities and distributing energy over more considerable distances. Small areas were soon integrated into more extensive networks, regions, and states. A single, unified power system encompassing a large extent, a country, or possibly one day even a continent, was founded on these ideas. Globally, extensive linked power networks have grown exponentially for over half a century. The 1965 American blackout jolted electrical engineers out of their "golden age" comfort zone. After a minor delay, hundreds of kilometers away failed, and a big metropolitan area lost power within 12 minutes, raising severe concerns about large interconnected power networks' dependability. The linked structure of the grid causes such cascade failures.

The electric power system comprises several linked parts that generate, transfer, and distribute electricity across a vast region. The power system is constantly full of dynamic interactions due to its nature. Interactions may cause diverse disruptions when operating circumstances vary. A disturbance in the electricity system is any unexpected incident, including an outage that causes an irregular operational situation. The interaction of various natural components is an essential factor in power grid dynamics. These phenomena' physical natures and rules are distinct. Also, these occurrences occur in varying time intervals. Wave effect and voltage switching occur in milliseconds. State estimate is done in seconds, but load projection is made in days to months. Some of these dynamics influence certain aspects of the system, while others disturb the whole system. The maximum critical worry for power system workers is how the power system will respond to changes in power demand and other system disruptions.

DIFFICULTIES OF CONVENTIONAL GRID

The electrical grid is a complex network. The grid was developed this way for better economic dependability. In case of a problem, the system has numerous generating and transmission options. Nevertheless, a small fault in a small portion of the grid could cause a blackout due to its mesh network architecture [18, 19]. In a highly meshing network such as the electrical grid, a blackout is caused by the lines' loading limit. If too much power is sent through a network connection due to overload, the line can trip. This may cause a cascade of low-likelihood occurrences leading to a blackout.

Deregulation of the electricity industry has increased the likelihood of grid blackouts. For example, the 2003 Italian blackout was caused by a tree falling on a wire somewhere in the network. The system imported 6000 MW of low-cost electricity from neighbors at the time of the fault, contributing to the disastrous blackout. This blackout, impacting 57 million people, is among the worst in European history. Table **2** summarizes significant global blackouts and their effect in the last three decades.

Table 2. Summary of global blackouts and their effect in the last three decades [20, 21].

Date	Location	Affected People	MW Lost	Restoration Time
2/7/1996	US Western	2 M	11,850	Minutes to hours
10/8/1996	US Western	7.5 M	30,500	Minutes to 9h
11/3/1999	Brazil	75 M	25,000	30min to 4h
14/8/2003	US Northeastern	50 M	61,800	Around 4 days
28/9/2003	Sweden/Denmark	4.85 M	6550	2 to 4.3 h
28/9/2003	Italy	57 M	27,700	2.5 to 19.5 h
31/7/2012	India	670 M	48,000	2 to 8 h
23/12/2015	Ukraine	230k	74	1 to 6 h

No system can entirely avoid large-scale outages. These blackouts are the consequence of occurrences beyond contingency. The power network is designed to handle contingency situations. Due to current economics, developing a power infrastructure that accounts for all low-probability conditions is not viable. Blackouts will continue to occur, according to many modeling and simulation studies. Making measures for early grid failure detection is the way ahead. If a defect arises, it should be isolated rapidly to avoid damage to other system elements. Deregulation of the electricity market has made it increasingly critical to strengthen grid monitoring and control. The deregulated electricity market is also 325 percent more likely to have a blackout than the traditional system. While most blackouts cause low probability, improved sensing, and control strategies may have averted or at least lessened their effects. The utilities also fail to provide the essential power quality for the emerging digital society. Voltage and frequency fluctuations may cause digital equipment to fail [22, 23].

The linked nature of the electrical system is unlikely to alter. To counteract any potential negative impacts caused by the grid's meshed construction, enhanced control and monitoring mechanisms are required. The goal is not to eliminate the risk of blackouts but to control them. Also, the system should recover fast if a significant malfunction or blackout happens. The SG has three core features:

enhanced control, monitoring, management, and issues during grid disturbance. Here are a few key drivers discussed below:

- Energy trading has never been this common across several regional power systems due to deregulation. As a result, new power flow states and reservations have emerged, which the traditional method cannot handle.
- The rising use of renewable energy will need a meshed distribution system, requiring improved monitoring and management.
- Reliable, high-quality power is a requirement of the modern digital economy.
- The possibility of cyber-attacks grows as the power grid is networked and uses more wide-area communications.
- Environmental preservation and sustainable development are currently hot topics. It means building power systems more efficiently, minimizing peak demand, and boosting renewable energy integration.

SMART GRID

The SG has not been officially defined, although several aspects have been suggested. The SG is an electrical system that utilizes sophisticated sensing, control, and communication technologies. The SG is projected to be added resourceful, reliable, and versatile than the traditional grid [1, 5, 24, 25]. Generally, the SG vision comprises:

- Optimal energy grid distribution operations
- Use information technology at all grid levels, including two-way communications. The expression "using megabytes of data to transport megawatts of energy" sums up this demand.
- Encouraging large-scale renewable energy integration.

The Electric Power Research Institute (EPRI) of the USA defines an SG as follows [26 - 28]:

Self-Healing in Nature: The smart grid's self-healing capability involves comprehensive real-time monitoring of the grid's status. The self-healing grid may also isolate problematic pieces from the rest of the system. The smart grid's self-healing capability will improve customer service dependability and enable utility administrators to better manage energy infrastructure.

Resilient to Threats: Physical and cyber threats and natural calamities will not affect the smart grid's resilience.

Involve the Consumers in the Design Process: In contrast to the traditional grid, the smart grid will allow customers to participate in the system actively. By altering how power is bought and utilized, this active engagement will aid in balancing supply and demand and ensure dependability. A new pattern of use is being encouraged by providing incentives to customers.

Quality Power for the Digital Age: The SG will deliver high-quality electricity fit for today's digital age. We can quickly diagnose and solve problems using real-time monitoring and control approaches, including switching surges, line failures, and harmonic sources.

Promotes the use of renewable energy sources: The SG will have a high penetration of environmentally friendly renewable energy sources at the distribution level. The smart grid will accommodate and stimulate these sources' integration.

Market interaction: The SG will help the power trading sector grow. Consumers will be able to pick from a variety of services. The smart grid allows utilities, regulators, and customers to customize operating regulations to meet local needs.

Optimize Assets: Using current monitoring and communication technology to maximize asset utilization is crucial to the SG goal. In the SG, asset maintenance will be condition-based rather than time-based. The US Congress defines the SG as:

- More information controls;
- Grid resource and operation optimization
- Strong renewable energy penetration
- The installation and promotion of distribution automation, load curve flattening technology; and integrated communications;
- Two-way consumer-utility communication for individualized control choices;
- The compatibility of devices and applications linked to the power grid.

The European Commission describes the SG as follows:

- It is adaptable to changes and obstacles.
- Accessible to multiple dispersed generating sources, including renewables.
- In the face of disruptions and uncertainty, security, and power quality are reliable.
- Economical *via* innovation, energy efficiency, and regulation.

Traditional and contemporary power engineering combines sophisticated sensing, processing, information technologies, and secure two-way communications to improve grid performance and customer service. The SG is a self-healing, adaptable, robust, and sustainable digital two-way power flow system with predictive capabilities in Table **3**. It is designed to work with current and future cyber-secure standards of components, devices, and procedures.

Table 3. compares the advantages of the smart grid with the traditional grid.

Characteristic	Smart grid	Traditional grid
Consumer participation	Actively involved and informed	Non-participative
Communication	Two-way communication	One way
Digital currency	Not fit	Suitable
Eco-friendly power generation	Distributed Renewable power source integration is the main vision	Only renewable energy sources are not a paint power source
Asset maintenance	Condition-based minimizing and prevention	Time-based
Self-healing	Damages are not protecting and minimize	Minimizing fault case disruption and prevention
Attack resilience	Natural disasters, cyber and physical attack	Man-made threats and natural vulnerable

SMART GRID KEY TECHNOLOGY

As stated before, the SG will appear after the traditional grid provided certain fundamental fundamentals are realized. Various technologies are required to implement these characteristics. The National Energy Technology Laboratory (NETL) has categorized SG needs into five classes [26, 29, 30]. Decision support and improved interfaces are among the highlighted categories. Integrated communications are required for advanced meter features.

To increase the grid's awareness of its condition, more sophisticated monitoring and measurement are needed. Sensor and measurement data should contain power factors, quality, consumption, outages, temperature, phasor relationships, *etc.* provide the electrical grid expansion, low-cost, simple to maintain, and secure. Several technologies projected to show a dynamic role in developing an SG system are described below.

Distributed Generation and Storage [5, 31 - 33]: Distributed generation (DG) is a critical component of a smart grid. It relies on distributed energy resources, mainly renewable sources, to increase power quality and dependability. The traditional grid uses dispersed generation as backup power and does not integrate it. However, these RES would be easily integrated with a smart grid. This approach reduces the need for expensive peaking equipment and reduces the likelihood of blackouts. Distributed generation is based on smaller generating systems closer to customers. Micro-hydropower, wind, solar, and geothermal energy plants are environmentally friendly RES. The SG concept incorporates eco-friendly distributed energy sources. The DG is cheaper than traditional power systems because it eliminates the need for long-distance transmission and distribution. Technologies have advanced where small kW to large MW distributed generating units can be combined into the power grid.

The DG combination saves operating costs and helps grid developers. Generally combined DGs may minimize peak demand, reducing peak load shortages. Moreover, DG is cost-effective for providing electricity to distant places, particularly in developing nations. The DG systems are generally modest capacity, requiring minimum gestation time, consenting for easier and quicker capacity development.

Distributed energy resources, mainly RES are important to accomplishing SG goals. Because of their ability to produce power at the consumer site, they can better control, operate, and regulate the grid as well as conduct financial analysis by lowering peak demands. Using net metering for grid-connected generating sources will enable users to return extra power to the system. So, system builders don't have to construct additional high-voltage transmission lines to get green energy from traditional facilities to reserved cities. The SG function may be applied using a distributed energy source network. A region might be separated from the grid through a disturbance in supply mode. This function is supposed to help the grid self-heal. When the islanded region regains standard functionality, it may seamlessly synchronize with the grid.

Currently, there are minimal obstacles to large-scale renewable energy system integration. Because these energy sources are intermittent, their impact on grid dynamics is a significant problem. Power quality challenges like as voltage and power fluctuation due to unexpected weather or seasonal fluctuations are some topics being researched.

Real-time controlling and monitoring [34 - 36]: The typical grid generates energy and distributes it radially. Without real-time monitoring, the electric grid is underutilized to prevent overloading. Real-time monitoring is a must for the SG. With the conventional grid, customer engagement is modest. However, consumer participation is projected to be active in SG. Massive sensor deployment throughout the grid may increase performance by better collecting important data about a breakdown. It will also aid in the analysis to create a chronology of events and offer corrective steps to avoid a recurrence failure.

Sensors may be used in SG applications at the end-user, transmission, and distribution levels. These sensors' speedy data sampling will aid in the prompt diagnosis and correction of grid problems. Over a wide area, the configuration will enable real-time element and system effectiveness assessment. It will enable system administrators to act before a more substantial impact. These sensors' data will also aid in smoothly integrating intermittent RES.

Distributed Process: The SG will witness two-way power and information exchange, unlike a normal grid. Implementing and managing such a system involves decentralization, intelligence, and control on all grid sides. This arrangement will consent to real-time monitoring of grid components and dynamic load and resource balancing to enhance energy efficiency and security. Distributed intelligence will be implemented using smart meters, GPS, and mobile computing devices.

Real-time Communication: Real-time management and monitoring of an SG need two-way communication. Smart grids rely on two-way communication that is fast, secure, and dependable. The communication infrastructure is restricted in the traditional grid. Communication is usually used for non-critical needs. The technology also functions in isolation at various grid levels. The smart grid concept necessitates an integrated strategy for communication system deployment [5].

Demand Management: Demand-side management (DSM) is the effectiveness of designing and leading operations to modify the load curve. DSM activities mainly impact consumer behavior relating to power use in the home. DSM operations are predicted to be profitable for customers. DSM actions comprise together operational and planning strategies. They installed modern metering infrastructure with the load-balancing capacity to replace obsolete incandescent light bulbs within the DSM paradigm.

One of the key factors of DSM's development has been the increase in power consumption, primarily from fossil fuels. Promoting energy efficiency is critical for long-term development. Based on the way they affect consumers; DSM approaches can be categorized into the following groups.

- Energy efficiency.
- Time of use.
- Demand response.

One application of DSM technology is peak clipping. It seeks to reduce peak demand to minimize the requirement for costly infrastructure. By lowering peak demand, DG and customer interaction may shorten peak load duration.

Demand Side Response [37 - 40]: Demand response (DR) is another significant smart grid technique. The electrical grid has traditionally been operated by continually balancing supply and demand. Grid administrators and controllers need to close the gap across baseline and peak loads to make the most use of the electrical system. Stated differently, one of the main objectives of SG adoption is to flatten the load curve. The DR programmers attempt to reduce the peak in the demand curve and postpone building new power plants to supply the short-lived peak loads. The benefit of DR is its flexibility at a minimal cost. Fig. (**4**) summarizes SG systems and their impact on power grid operation.

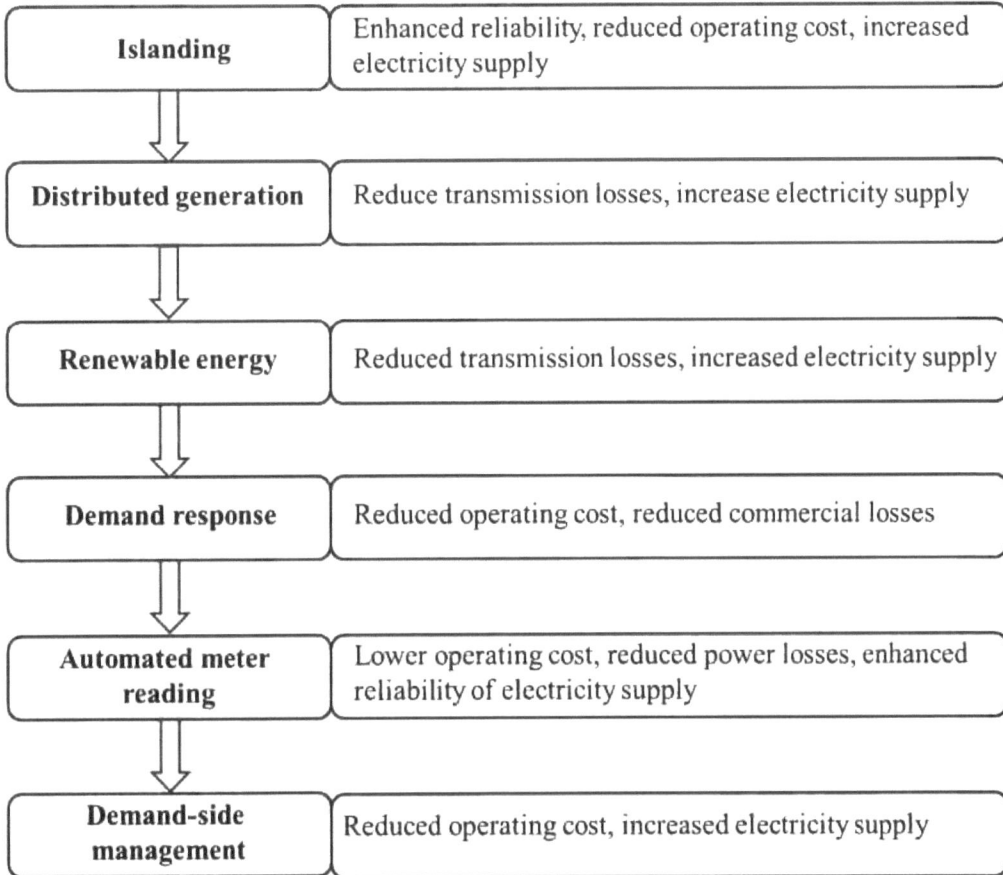

Islanding	Enhanced reliability, reduced operating cost, increased electricity supply
Distributed generation	Reduce transmission losses, increase electricity supply
Renewable energy	Reduced transmission losses, increased electricity supply
Demand response	Reduced operating cost, reduced commercial losses
Automated meter reading	Lower operating cost, reduced power losses, enhanced reliability of electricity supply
Demand-side management	Reduced operating cost, increased electricity supply

Fig. (**4**). Technological impact on smart grid.

ENVIRONMENT AND ECONOMIC IMPACT

Based on these desired qualities, comparing the current electricity system and the proposed SG is required to highlight the grid's strengths and weaknesses. This system will enable consumer participation and improve generation and transmission while reducing system vulnerability, resilience, dependability, and power quality. The SG evolution's targeted aims include training tools and capacity building to manage and run grids, creating new employment possibilities. Research institutes across disciplines must collaborate to develop the first generation of SG [41, 42].

Utilities and SG technology manufacturers can address core causes of vulnerabilities rather than particular threats. Adding security measures to an existing system is complex and often impossible. Therefore, they should be included from the start. The deployed security control base will be regularly reviewed to defend the smart grid from developing threats.

CONCLUSION

To successfully execute controlling, monitoring, and metering activities, utility companies must actively utilize communication networks, according to research and technology advancements relating to the physical components and structure of the traditional grid. This demand was essential for generation and load management, effective monitoring, and metering for all phases of electrical grids, which led to the development of the SG idea. The SG, proposed at the start of the 2000s, represents one of the latest technologies intended to add new capabilities to conventional grids because of these specifications and improvements. This novel idea is appreciated for existing a data communication system for the transportation of diverse signals containing significant information on the fundamentals of control activities monitoring, measurement, and management, and this novel idea is also linked to utility grids at any part that includes GTDC components. One of its most critical components is its communication infrastructure, which must ensure secure data transmission in a dependable, and effective manner. This chapter presents the conventional gird components, SG technology, smart monitoring and control, key components, and environmental impact. Firstly, the transformation of the power grid system was discussed, then the difficulties of the conventional power grid system. Later, distributed generation and storage, real-time controlling and monitoring, demand-side responses, and management were discussed. Each element is thoroughly examined and introduced regarding its difficulties, advancements, and contributions.

ACKNOWLEDGEMENTS

This work has been supported by the Ministry of Higher Education Malaysia, under Grant FRGS/1/2020/ICT03/UKM/02/6. A K M Ahasan Habib thanks the ICT division, Ministry of Posts, Telecommunications and Information Technology, Bangladesh, under the code: 1280101-120008431-3821117 for supporting the research work.

REFERENCES

[1]   M.K. Hasan, A.K.M.A. Habib, Z. Shukur, F. Ibrahim, S. Islam, and M.A. Razzaque, "Review on cyber-physical and cyber-security system in smart grid: Standards, protocols, constraints, and recommendations", *J. Netw. Comput. Appl.,* vol. 209, p. 103540, 2023.
[http://dx.doi.org/10.1016/j.jnca.2022.103540]

[2]   M.S. Alvarez-Alvarado, C. Apolo-Tinoco, M.J. Ramirez-Prado, F.E. Alban-Chacón, N. Pico, J. Aviles-Cedeno, A.A. Recalde, F. Moncayo-Rea, W. Velasquez, and J. Rengifo, "Cyber-physical power systems: A comprehensive review about technologies drivers, standards, and future perspectives", *Comput. Electr. Eng.,* vol. 116, p. 109149, 2024.
[http://dx.doi.org/10.1016/j.compeleceng.2024.109149]

[3]   M. İnci, Ö. Çelik, A. Lashab, K.Ç. Bayındır, J.C. Vasquez, and J.M. Guerrero, "Power system integration of electric vehicles: A review on impacts and contributions to the smart grid", *Appl. Sci. (Basel),* vol. 14, no. 6, p. 2246, 2024.
[http://dx.doi.org/10.3390/app14062246]

[4]   E.D. Ayele, J.F. Gonzalez, and W.B. Teeuw, "Enhancing Cybersecurity in Distributed Microgrids: A Review of Communication Protocols and Standards", *Sensors (Basel),* vol. 24, no. 3, p. 854, 2024.
[http://dx.doi.org/10.3390/s24030854] [PMID: 38339572]

[5]   M.K. Hasan, A.K.M.A. Habib, S. Islam, M. Balfaqih, K.M. Alfawaz, and D. Singh, "Smart grid communication networks for electric vehicles empowering distributed energy generation: Constraints, challenges, and recommendations", *Energies,* vol. 16, no. 3, p. 1140, 2023.
[http://dx.doi.org/10.3390/en16031140]

[6]   G.N. Sorebo, and M.C. Echols, *Smart grid security: an end-to-end view of security in the new electrical grid.* CRC Press, 2012.

[7]   S. S. Sarma, and M. R. P. Reddy, "Assimilation of Sustainable Energy Resources into the Smart Grid: Current Advancements in the Realm of Information and Communication Technologies," 2024.

[8]   M.O. Qays, I. Ahmad, A. Abu-Siada, M.L. Hossain, and F. Yasmin, "Key communication technologies, applications, protocols and future guides for IoT-assisted smart grid systems: A review", *Energy Rep.,* vol. 9, pp. 2440-2452, 2023.
[http://dx.doi.org/10.1016/j.egyr.2023.01.085]

[9]   S. Hossain, M. Rokonuzzaman, K.S. Rahman, A.K.M.A. Habib, W-S. Tan, M. Mahmud, S. Chowdhury, and S. Channumsin, "Grid-vehicle-grid (G2V2G) efficient power transmission: an overview of concept, operations, benefits, concerns, and future challenges", *Sustainability (Basel),* vol. 15, no. 7, p. 5782, 2023.
[http://dx.doi.org/10.3390/su15075782]

[10]   B. Jimada-Ojuolape, J. Teh, and C.M. Lai, "Securing the grid: A comprehensive analysis of cybersecurity challenges in PMU-based cyber-physical power networks", *Electr. Power Syst. Res.,* vol. 233, p. 110509, 2024.
[http://dx.doi.org/10.1016/j.epsr.2024.110509]

[11]   Q. Hassan, A.A. Khadom, S. Algburi, A.K. Al-Jiboory, A.Z. Sameen, M.A. Alkhafaji, H.A. Mahmoud, E.M. Awwad, H.B. Mahood, H.A. Kazem, H.M. Salman, and M. Jaszczur, "RETRACTED: Implications of a smart grid-integrated renewable distributed generation capacity expansion strategy: The case of Iraq", *Renew. Energy,* vol. 221, p. 119753, 2024.
[http://dx.doi.org/10.1016/j.renene.2023.119753]

[12]   M.K. Hasan, A.K.M.A. Habib, S. Islam, N. Safie, S.N.H.S. Abdullah, and B. Pandey, "DDoS: Distributed denial of service attack in communication standard vulnerabilities in smart grid applications and cyber security with recent developments", *Energy Rep.,* vol. 9, pp. 1318-1326, 2023.
[http://dx.doi.org/10.1016/j.egyr.2023.05.184]

[13]   I. Zografopoulos, N.D. Hatziargyriou, and C. Konstantinou, "Distributed energy resources cybersecurity outlook: Vulnerabilities, attacks, impacts, and mitigations", *IEEE Syst. J.,* vol. 17, no. 4,

pp. 6695-6709, 2023.
[http://dx.doi.org/10.1109/JSYST.2023.3305757]

[14] C. Kumar, and P. Chittora, "Deep-Learning and Blockchain-Empowered Secure Data Sharing for Smart Grid Infrastructure", *Arab. J. Sci. Eng.,* vol. 49, no. 12, pp. 16155-16168, 2024.
[http://dx.doi.org/10.1007/s13369-024-08882-1]

[15] M.K. Hasan, R.A. Abdulkadir, S. Islam, T.R. Gadekallu, and N. Safie, "A review on machine learning techniques for secured cyber-physical systems in smart grid networks", *Energy Rep.,* vol. 11, pp. 1268-1290, 2024.
[http://dx.doi.org/10.1016/j.egyr.2023.12.040]

[16] D. Russ, "Deciphering economic futures: Electricity, calculation, and the power economy, 1880–1930", *Centaurus,* vol. 63, no. 4, pp. 631-650, 2021.
[http://dx.doi.org/10.1111/1600-0498.12416]

[17] A. Korkovelos, H. Zerriffi, M. Howells, M. Bazilian, H.H. Rogner, and F. Fuso Nerini, "A retrospective analysis of energy access with a focus on the role of mini-grids", *Sustainability (Basel),* vol. 12, no. 5, p. 1793, 2020.
[http://dx.doi.org/10.3390/su12051793]

[18] E. Longman, O. Cetinkaya, M. El-Hajjar, and G.V. Merrett, "Mesh networking for intermittently powered devices: Architecture and challenges", *IEEE Netw.,* vol. 36, no. 3, pp. 122-128, 2022.
[http://dx.doi.org/10.1109/MNET.105.2000782]

[19] V. Vita, G. Fotis, C. Pavlatos, and V. Mladenov, "A New Restoration Strategy in Microgrids after a Blackout with Priority in Critical Loads", *Sustainability,* vol. 15, p. 1974, 2023.

[20] G. Fotis, V. Vita, and T.I. Maris, "Risks in the European transmission system and a novel restoration strategy for a power system after a major blackout", *Appl. Sci. (Basel),* vol. 13, no. 1, p. 83, 2022.
[http://dx.doi.org/10.3390/app13010083]

[21] H. Haes Alhelou, M.E. Hamedani-Golshan, T.C. Njenda, and P. Siano, "A survey on power system blackout and cascading events: Research motivations and challenges", *Energies,* vol. 12, no. 4, p. 682, 2019.
[http://dx.doi.org/10.3390/en12040682]

[22] W. Shi, H. Liang, and M. Bittner, "Decision Support for Smart Distribution System Against Natural Disasters During Health Pandemics Considering Resilience", *IEEE Access,* vol. 12, pp. 66335-66351, 2024.
[http://dx.doi.org/10.1109/ACCESS.2024.3397892]

[23] A. Pandey, S. Kumar, S. Mohire, P. Pentayya, and F. Kazi, "Dynamic modeling and cascade failure analysis of the mumbai grid incident of october 12, 2020", *IEEE Access,* vol. 10, pp. 43598-43610, 2022.
[http://dx.doi.org/10.1109/ACCESS.2022.3160740]

[24] M. Fotopoulou, D. Rakopoulos, S. Petridis, and P. Drosatos, "Assessment of smart grid operation under emergency situations", *Energy,* vol. 287, p. 129661, 2024.
[http://dx.doi.org/10.1016/j.energy.2023.129661]

[25] M. Jafari, A. Kavousi-Fard, T. Chen, and M. Karimi, "A review on digital twin technology in smart grid, transportation system and smart city: Challenges and future", *IEEE Access,* vol. 11, pp. 17471-17484, 2023.
[http://dx.doi.org/10.1109/ACCESS.2023.3241588]

[26] E. Kabalci, and Y. Kabalci, *Smart grids and their communication systems (no. 1).* Springer, 2019.
[http://dx.doi.org/10.1007/978-981-13-1768-2]

[27] M.A. Khan, T. Khan, M. Waseem, A.M. Saleh, N. Qamar, and H.A. Muqeet, "Investigation and analysis of demand response approaches, bottlenecks, and future potential capabilities for IoT□enabled smart grid", *IET Renew. Power Gener.,* vol. 18, no. 15, pp. 3509-3535, 2024.

[http://dx.doi.org/10.1049/rpg2.13011]

[28]   D.P. Mishra, A.P. Gaur, Y.K. Rai, and S.R. Salkuti, *"Smart Grid and Energy Management Systems: A Global Perspective,"* in *Energy and Environmental Aspects of Emerging Technologies for Smart Grid.* Springer, 2024, pp. 629-649.

[29]   S.S. Uddin, R. Joysoyal, S.K. Sarker, S.M. Muyeen, M.F. Ali, M.M. Hasan, S.H. Abhi, M.R. Islam, M.H. Ahamed, M.M. Islam, S.K. Das, M.F.R. Badal, P. Das, and Z. Tasneem, "Next-generation blockchain enabled smart grid: Conceptual framework, key technologies and industry practices review", *Energy and AI,* vol. 12, p. 100228, 2023. [http://dx.doi.org/10.1016/j.egyai.2022.100228]

[30]   P. Siitonen, S. Honkapuro, S. Annala, and A. Wolff, "Effects of trust and perceived benefits on consumer adoption of smart grid technologies: a mediation analysis", *Int. J. Sustain. Energy,* vol. 43, no. 1, p. 2350756, 2024. [http://dx.doi.org/10.1080/14786451.2024.2350756]

[31]   S. Sarfarazi, S. Mohammadi, D. Khastieva, M.R. Hesamzadeh, V. Bertsch, and D. Bunn, "An optimal real-time pricing strategy for aggregating distributed generation and battery storage systems in energy communities: A stochastic bilevel optimization approach", *Int. J. Electr. Power Energy Syst.,* vol. 147, p. 108770, 2023. [http://dx.doi.org/10.1016/j.ijepes.2022.108770]

[32]   M. Mythreyee, and A. Nalini, "Genetic Algorithm Based Smart Grid System for Distributed Renewable Energy Sources", *Comput. Syst. Sci. Eng.,* vol. 45, no. 1, 2023. [http://dx.doi.org/10.32604/csse.2023.028525]

[33]   R.P. Kumar, and G. Karthikeyan, "A multi-objective optimization solution for distributed generation energy management in microgrids with hybrid energy sources and battery storage system", *J. Energy Storage,* vol. 75, p. 109702, 2024. [http://dx.doi.org/10.1016/j.est.2023.109702]

[34]   F. Wang, and Z. Nishtar, "Real-Time Load Forecasting and Adaptive Control in Smart Grids Using a Hybrid Neuro-Fuzzy Approach", *Energies,* vol. 17, no. 11, p. 2539, 2024. [http://dx.doi.org/10.3390/en17112539]

[35]   M.K. Hasan, M.M. Ahmed, N.F. Wani, A.H. Abbas, L.M. Alkwai, S. Islam, A.K.M.A. Habib, and R. Hassan, "Dynamic load modeling for bulk load-using synchrophasors with wide area measurement system for smart grid real-time load monitoring and optimization", *Sustain. Energy Technol. Assess.,* vol. 57, p. 103190, 2023. [http://dx.doi.org/10.1016/j.seta.2023.103190]

[36]   C. Biswal, B.K. Sahu, M. Mishra, and P.K. Rout, "Real-time grid monitoring and protection: A comprehensive survey on the advantages of phasor measurement units", *Energies,* vol. 16, no. 10, p. 4054, 2023. [http://dx.doi.org/10.3390/en16104054]

[37]   M. Saleem, M. Shakir, M. Usman, M. Bajwa, N. Shabbir, P. Shams Ghahfarokhi, and K. Daniel, "Integrating smart energy management system with internet of things and cloud computing for efficient demand side management in smart grids", *Energies,* vol. 16, no. 12, p. 4835, 2023. [http://dx.doi.org/10.3390/en16124835]

[38]   V. Arumugham, H.M.A. Ghanimi, D.A. Pustokhin, I.V. Pustokhina, V.S. Ponnam, M. Alharbi, P. Krishnamoorthy, and S. Sengan, "An artificial-intelligence-based renewable energy prediction program for demand-side management in smart grids", *Sustainability (Basel),* vol. 15, no. 6, p. 5453, 2023. [http://dx.doi.org/10.3390/su15065453]

[39]   M.S. Bakare, A. Abdulkarim, M. Zeeshan, and A.N. Shuaibu, "A comprehensive overview on demand side energy management towards smart grids: challenges, solutions, and future direction", *Energy Inform.,* vol. 6, no. 1, p. 4, 2023.

[http://dx.doi.org/10.1186/s42162-023-00262-7]

[40]   R. Çakmak, "Design and implementation of a low-cost power logger device for specific demand profile analysis in demand-side management studies for smart grids", *Expert Syst. Appl.,* vol. 238, p. 121888, 2024.
[http://dx.doi.org/10.1016/j.eswa.2023.121888]

[41]   A.K.M.A. Habib, M.K. Hasan, A. Alkhayyat, S. Islam, R. Sharma, and L.M. Alkwai, "False data injection attack in smart grid cyber physical system: Issues, challenges, and future direction", *Comput. Electr. Eng.,* vol. 107, p. 108638, 2023.
[http://dx.doi.org/10.1016/j.compeleceng.2023.108638]

[42]   F. Bandeiras, Á. Gomes, M. Gomes, and P. Coelho, "Exploring energy trading markets in smart grid and microgrid systems and their implications for sustainability in smart cities", *Energies,* vol. 16, no. 2, p. 801, 2023.
[http://dx.doi.org/10.3390/en16020801]

CHAPTER 9

Improving the Hardware Security of Wireless Sensor Network Systems by Using Soft Computing

Masood Ahmad[1,*], Mohd Waris Khan[1], Satish Kumar[1], Mohd Faizan[1], Mohd Faisal[1], Malik Shahzad Ahmad Iqbal[2] and Raees Ahmad Khan[3]

[1] *Department of Computer Application, Integral University, Lucknow, India*

[2] *Department of Computer Science & Engineering, Acharya University, Karakul, Uzbekistan*

[3] *Department of Information Technology Babasaheb Bhimrao Ambedkar University, Lucknow, India*

Abstract: Hardware security is a critical concern for organizations that use information systems to protect their assets from unauthorized access and malicious attacks. Hardware security assessment involves evaluating the security of hardware components and systems to identify vulnerabilities and areas for improvement. This research paper proposes a framework for hardware security assessment using the Analytic Hierarchy Process (AHP) approach. The proposed framework is applied in a case study to evaluate the security of a wireless sensor network (WSN) system. Based on this calculation with respect to each alternative, the author finds that Hardware encryption obtained the highest final weighted score (0.555), which would be the preferred choice according to the AHP method for improving the security of the hardware of WSN. Based on the obtained weight, authors assign the ranks S1<S3<S2 <S4. The results show that the proposed methodology can effectively identify better security algorithms and prioritize actions to improve the security of the WSN system.

Keywords: AHP, Hardware, Malicious attacks, Soft computing, Security, WSN.

INTRODUCTION

Hardware security is becoming an increasingly important concern for organizations that use information systems to protect their assets. The security of hardware components and systems is essential to prevent unauthorized access, data theft, and other malicious attacks [1, 2]. Hardware security assessment involves evaluating the security of hardware components and systems to identify vulnerabilities and areas for improvement. However, hardware security assess-

---

[*] **Corresponding author Masood Ahmad:** Department of Computer Application, Integral University, Lucknow, India; E-mail: ermasood@gmail.com

Asif Khan, Mohammad Kamrul Hasan, Naushad Varish & Mohammed Aslam Husain (Eds.)

ment is a complex task that requires the consideration of multiple criteria and the use of objective evidence to evaluate the security of the hardware [3].

Hardware security refers to the measures and techniques used to protect computer hardware from unauthorized access, tampering, and theft. It involves the use of various physical and logical mechanisms, such as access controls, encryption, and authentication, to ensure the confidentiality, integrity, and availability of hardware resources [4, 5]. One of the key reasons for hardware security is to prevent the theft of valuable hardware, such as servers, laptops, and mobile devices. In addition, hardware security is important for protecting critical infrastructure, such as power grids, transportation systems, and healthcare facilities, from cyber-attacks [6].

There are several approaches to hardware security, including hardware-based security, software-based security, and hybrid approaches. Hardware-based security involves the use of specialized hardware components, such as security chips, to implement security functions. Software-based security, on the other hand, uses software programs to perform security functions, such as encryption and access controls. Hybrid approaches combine hardware and software security mechanisms to provide stronger protection against attacks [7, 8].

The Analytic Hierarchy Process (AHP) is a decision-making framework that can be used to evaluate and prioritize multiple criteria in a hierarchical structure [9, 10]. AHP has been applied in various fields to support decision-making, including hardware security assessment. This research paper proposes a framework for hardware security assessment using the AHP approach and applies it to a case study to evaluate the security of a wireless sensor network (WSN) system [11]. These are the main mathematical equations involved in the AHP approach. Note that there are variations in the AHP method that uses different equations, such as the eigenvector method and the logarithmic least squares method.

Overall, using AHP for hardware security assessment provides a structured approach that can help organizations make informed decisions about hardware security. By identifying and prioritizing criteria, assigning weights, and evaluating components or systems against those criteria, organizations can make data-driven decisions to improve hardware security.

Contribution: Our contributions are follows as:

• Identification of hardware security techniques and definition of criteria for assessment.
• An AHP model for the evaluation of hardware techniques against each criterion.
• Interpretation and effects of factors on the security of the results.

- Identification of better security techniques and required factors that need to be improved.

MATERIAL AND METHOD

There are several approaches to hardware security, including hardware-based security, software-based security, and hybrid approaches. Hardware-based security involves the use of specialized hardware components, such as security chips, to implement security functions. Software-based security, on the other hand, uses software programs to perform security functions, such as encryption and access controls [12]. Hybrid approaches combine hardware and software security mechanisms to provide stronger protection against attacks.

Some of the common hardware security techniques include:

- Secure boot: This technique ensures that the system boots only from trusted sources, preventing malware from executing at startup [13].
- Trusted Platform Module (TPM): TPM is a hardware component that provides a secure environment for cryptographic operations and storage of sensitive information [14].
- Physical locks and barriers: These are physical mechanisms, such as locks and fences, used to prevent unauthorized access to hardware resources [15].
- Hardware-based encryption: This technique uses hardware components, such as encryption chips, to encrypt data stored on hardware devices [16].

Hardware security is a complex and constantly evolving field, as new threats and vulnerabilities emerge. Therefore, it is essential for organizations to stay up-t--date with the latest hardware security technologies and best practices to protect their valuable hardware resources [17].

Assessing hardware security through the Analytic Hierarchy Process (AHP) can help identify and prioritize security measures for the hardware components used in a system [17]. AHP is a structured decision-making technique that allows stakeholders to compare various criteria and alternatives in a systematic and consistent manner.

The proposed model for improving hardware security by using the AHP approach consists of the following steps shown in Fig. (**2**):

- Identification of hardware techniques
- Definition of criteria for assessment
- Establishment of the hierarchy of criteria
- Assignment of weights to the criteria

- Evaluation of hardware techniques or systems against each criterion and assignment of scores
- Calculation of the overall score
- Interpretation of the results

Step 1: Hierarchical Structure

- Define the main goal (G).
- Identify criteria (C1, C2... Cn) that contribute to the goal.
- Identify alternatives (A1, A2... Am) to be evaluated under each criterion.

Step 2: Pairwise Comparison

For criteria comparison:

- Calculate the pairwise comparison matrix for criteria, denoted as Wc: $Wc(i,j)$ = Relative Importance of Criterion Ci compared to $CjWc$ (i,j) = Relative Importance of Criterion Ci compared to Cj (1)

For alternatives under each criterion comparison:

- Calculate the pairwise comparison matrices for alternatives under each criterion, denoted as Wai: $Wai(i,j)$ = Relative Preference of Alternative Ai over Aj under Criterion $Wai(i,j)$ = Relative Preference of Alternative Ai over Aj under Criterion Ck. (2)

Step 3: Calculate Priority Weights

For criteria:

- Normalize the criteria comparison matrix Wc to get the normalized criteria comparison matrix norm Wc norm:

$$Wc \text{ norm } (i,j) = \sum I = 1 \ nWc \ (i,j) \ Wc \ (i,j) \ (3)$$

- Calculate the priority weight of each criterion:

Priority Weight of Criterion

$$Ci = n1 \sum j = 1nWc \text{ norm } (i,j) \ (4)$$

For alternatives under each criterion:

- Normalize the alternative comparison matrices Wai to get the normalized alternative comparison matrices Wai norm:

Wai norm $(i,j) = \sum I = 1mWai\ (i,j)\ Wai\ (i,j)$ (5)

• Calculate the priority weight of each alternative under each criterion:

Priority Weight of Alternative under Criterion 1norm, Priority Weight of Alternative Ai under Criterion $Ck= m1\sum j=1mWai$norm(i,j) (6)

Step 4: Consistency Check

For the criteria comparison matrix Wc:

• Calculate the largest eigenvalue (λmax) of the criteria comparison matrix Wc.
• Calculate the consistency index (CI) for the criteria comparison matrix:

$CI=n-1/\lambda$max$-n$ (7)

• Determine the Random Index (RI) from pre-defined tables based on the number of criteria.
• Calculate the Consistency Ratio (CR): $CR=RI/CI$ (8)

Step 5: Synthesize Results

• Calculate the weighted score for each alternative under each criterion:

Weighted Score of Alternative Ai in Criterion Ck = Priority Weight of Alternative Ai under Criterion $Ck\times$ Normalized Score of Alternative Ai in Criterion Ck Weighted Score of Alternative Ai in Criterion $Ck=$ Priority Weight of Alternative Aiunder Criterion $Ck\times$ Normalized Score of Alternative Ai in Criterion Ck(9)

Step 6: Decision Making

• Calculate the final weighted score for each alternative by summing up the weighted scores across all criteria:

Final Weighted Score of Alternative Ai (Weighted Score of Alternative Ai in criterion Ck). Final Weighted Score of Alternative $\sum k=1$(Weighted Score of Alternative Ai in Criterion Ck). (9)

The alternative with the highest final weighted score is typically considered the preferred choice.

The proposed framework is applied to a case study to evaluate the security of a wireless sensor network (WSN) system. The WSN system consists of multiple nodes that collect and transmit data to a central node [18]. The nodes are equipped with sensors to monitor various environmental parameters, such as temperature, humidity, and light. The WSN system is used in an industrial setting to monitor the condition of a production line.

In this section, we will use the proposed model, based on the Analytic Hierarchy Process (AHP) and the weighted sum method, to assess the security situation of the hardware of WSN [19].

Based on the provided information, we have a remark set R: = {Very Secure, Secure, Ordinary, Dangerous, and Very Dangerous}, denoting the prospective scores of a criterion. This way, we are collecting the scores given by the experts for each remark on each criterion.

Certainly, let us proceed with the assessment of the security situation for the hardware of WSN using the scores provided by the 4 experts. We define security objectives and criteria based on Table 2, we have 4 security criteria: secure boot, Trusted Platform Module (TPM), physical locks and barriers, and hardware-based encryption. The scores are represented in the Table 1 below:

Table 1. Experts given the scores

-	Very Secure	Secure	Ordinary	Dangerous	Very Dangerous
Secure boot	1	3	2	2	1
Trusted Platform Module (TPM)	2	3	3	1	1
Physical locks and barriers	1	3	3	2	1
Hardware-based encryption	1	3	3	2	1

Table 2. Relationship matrix

-	Secure Boot	TPM	Physical Lock	Hardware
Secure Boot	1	4	3	2
Trusted Platform Module (TPM)	¼	1	3	2
Physical Locks	1/3	1/3	1	1/3
Hardware Based Encryption	½	1	3	1

RESULTS AND DISCUSSION

Step 1: Relationship

We proceeded with the Analytic Hierarchy Process (AHP) to derive the normalized score vector based on the experts' judgments and the relative importance of each criterion.

The evaluation of the WSN system using the proposed methodology reveals several security methods, including secure boot, Trusted Platform Module, physical locks, and hardware-based encryption [20 - 23]. Based on the results, several actions are prioritized to improve the security of the WSN system [24 - 26], including the implementation of stronger authentication and encryption mechanisms, the introduction of access control measures, and the improvement of physical security measures shown in Fig. (**1**). By using equation 1 and 2, authors prepared Table **2**.

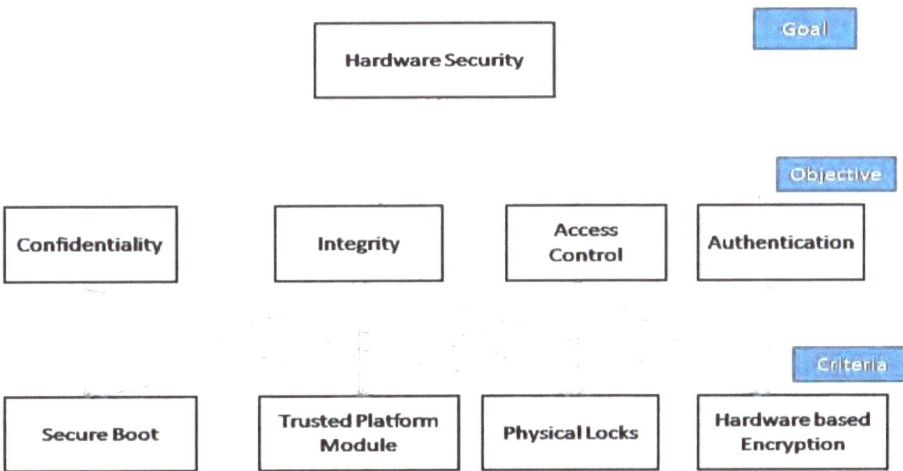

Fig. (1). Hierarchy Security model for improving the security.

Step 2: Normalization

Each column of the matrix is normalized by dividing each element by the sum of its column.

Step 3: Calculate Priority Weights for Criteria

Authors normalized and prioritized the weight Table **3** &4 with the help of equations 3 to 6.

Table 3. Normalized Relation Matrix (pair-wise comparison matrix normalization).

-	Secure Boot	TPM	Physical Locks	Hardware Encryption	Sum
Secure Boot	0.444	0.500	0.375	0.444	1.763
TPM	0.111	0.125	0.375	0.444	1.055
Physical Locks	0.167	0.167	0.128	0.111	0.563
Hardware Encryption	0.278	0.208	0.125	0.500	1.061

Table 4. Normalize the row sums to obtain the priority weights for each criterion.

Criteria	Weight	Priority vector
Confidentiality	1.763 / (1.763 + 1.055 + 0.563 + 1.061)	0.457
Integrity	1.055 / (1.763 + 1.055 + 0.563 + 1.061)	0.273
Access Control	0.563 / (1.763 + 1.055 + 0.563 + 1.061)	0.145
Authentication	1.061 / (1.763 + 1.055 + 0.563 + 1.061)	0.238

Step 4: Calculate Consistency

Calculate the consistency index (CI) and the consistency ratio (CR) to ensure the judgments are consistent [27].

The largest eigenvalue (λmax) for the matrix is approximately 4.02.

CI = (λmax) - n) / (n - 1) $\approx$ (4.02 - 4) / (4 - 1) $\approx$ 0.007

The Random Index (RI) for a matrix of size 4 is 0.9. Therefore,

CR = CI / RI $\approx$ 0.007 / 0.9 $\approx$ 0.008

Since CR is much smaller than 0.1, the consistency is acceptable. Both the values are calculated by using equation 7 & 8.

Step 5: Synthesize Results

The author is determining the weighted scores for the "Secure Boot" alternative under different security criteria such as "Confidentiality," "Integrity," "Access Control," and "Authentication." The weighted scores are calculated by multiplying the priority weight of each criterion with the normalized score of the alternative under that specific criterion.

The weighted score for "Secure Boot" under "Confidentiality" would be

The weighted score for confidentiality is calculated as 0.457 (confidentiality weight) multiplied by 0.444 (normalized score of "Secure Boot" in confidentiality). The resulting weighted score is 0.203.

Weighted Score of Secure Boot in Confidentiality = Confidentiality Weight * Normalized Score of Secure Boot in Confidentiality

$\approx$ 0.457 * 0.444 $\approx$ 0.203

The weighted score for "Secure Boot" under "Integrity" would be

Weighted Score of Secure Boot in Integrity = Integrity Weight * Normalized Score of Secure Boot in Integrity

= 0.444*0.273=0.121

The weighted score for integrity is calculated as 0.444 (integrity weight) multiplied by 0.273 (normalized score of "Secure Boot" in integrity). The resulting weighted score is 0.121.

The weighted score for "Secure Boot" under "Access Control" would be

Weighted Score of Secure Boot in Access Control = Access Control Weight * Normalized Score of Secure Boot in Access Control

=0.444*0.145=0.063

The weighted score for access control is calculated as 0.444 (access control weight) multiplied by 0.145 (normalized score of "Secure Boot" in access control). The resulting weighted score is 0.063.

The weighted score for "Secure Boot" under "Authentication" would be

Weighted Score of Secure Boot in Authentication = Authentication Weight * Normalized Score of Secure Boot in Authentication

=0.444*0.273=0.121

The weighted score for authentication is calculated as 0.444 (authentication weight) multiplied by 0.273 (normalized score of "Secure Boot" in authentication). The resulting weighted score is 0.121.

From the weighted scores, it is evident that the highest impact comes from the "Confidentiality" criterion, with a weighted score of 0.203. This indicates that, according to the given weights, confidentiality has the most significant influence on the overall effectiveness of the "Secure Boot" technique compared to other security factors such as integrity, access control, and authentication.

The statement "confidentiality has a more significant impact compared to other security factors in the secure boot technique" is derived from the higher weighted score in the confidentiality criterion relative to the scores in the other criteria.

The weighted score for "TMP" under "Confidentiality" would be

In the Trusted Platform Module (TPM) under different security criteria, the author is determining the weighted scores for confidentiality, integrity, access control, and authentication. The weighted scores are obtained by multiplying the priority weight of each criterion with the normalized score of TPM under that specific criterion.

Weighted Score of TPM in Confidentiality = Confidentiality Weight * Normalized Score of TPM in Confidentiality

=0.125*0.457=0.057

The weighted score for confidentiality is calculated as 0.125 (confidentiality weight) multiplied by 0.457 (normalized score of TPM in confidentiality). The resulting weighted score is 0.057.

Weighted Score of TPM in Integrity

Integrity= Integrity Weight * Normalized Score of TPM in Integrity
=0.125*0.273=0.034

The weighted score for integrity is calculated as 0.125 (integrity weight) multiplied by 0.273 (normalized score of TPM in integrity). The resulting weighted score is 0.034.

Weighted Score of TPM in Access Control

Access control Access Control Weight * Normalized Score of TPM in Access Control

=0.125*0.145=0.018

The weighted score for access control is calculated as 0.125 (access control weight) multiplied by 0.145 (normalized score of TPM in access control). The resulting weighted score is 0.018.

Weighted Score of TPM in Authentication = Authentication Weight * Normalized Score of TPM in Authentication

=0.125*0.273=0.034

The weighted score for authentication is calculated as 0.125 (authentication weight) multiplied by 0.273 (normalized score of TPM in authentication). The resulting weighted score is 0.034.

The statement "confidentiality has a more significant impact and access control least impact compared to other security factors in TPM" is derived from the higher weighted score in the confidentiality criterion and the lower weighted score in the access control criterion relative to the scores in the other criteria.

Weighted Score of Physical Lock in Confidentiality = Confidentiality Control Weight * Normalized Score of Physical Lock in Confidentiality

= 0.128*0.457=0.058

The weighted score for confidentiality is calculated as 0.128 (confidentiality control weight) multiplied by 0.457 (normalized score of Physical Lock in confidentiality). The resulting weighted score is 0.058.

Weighted Score of Physical Lock in Integrity = Integrity Weight * Normalized Score of TPM in Integrity

=0.128*0.273=0.035

The weighted score for integrity is calculated as 0.128 (integrity weight) multiplied by 0.273 (normalized score of Physical Lock in integrity). The resulting weighted score is 0.035.

Weighted Score of Physical Lock in Access Control = Access Control Weight * Normalized Score of TPM in Access Control

=0.128*0.145=0.018

The weighted score for access control is calculated as 0.128 (access control weight) multiplied by 0.145 (normalized score of Physical Lock in access control). The resulting weighted score is 0.018.

Weighted Score of Physical Lock in Authentication = Authentication Weight * Normalized Score of Physical Lock in Authentication

=0.128*0.273=0.350

Assuming the corrected value, the weighted score for authentication is calculated as 0.128 (authentication weight) multiplied by 0.273 (normalized score of Physical Lock in authentication). The resulting weighted score is 0.035.

In summary, the analysis indicates that the physical lock has a substantial impact on confidentiality, a moderate impact on integrity and authentication, and a relatively lower impact on access control.

Hardware Encryption

Confidentiality (0.228): Weighted Score of Hardware Encryption in Confidentiality = Confidentiality Weight * Normalized Score of Hardware Encryption in Confidentiality

=0.500*0.457=0.228

- The weighted score for confidentiality is calculated by multiplying the confidentiality weight (0.500) with the normalized score of hardware encryption in confidentiality (0.457).
- The result is 0.500 * 0.457 = 0.228.

The weighted score of 0.228 suggests that hardware encryption has a substantial impact on maintaining the confidentiality of information. This is a significant contribution to the overall security of the system in terms of keeping sensitive data secure.

Integrity (0.136): Weighted Score of Hardware Encryption in Integrity = Integrity Weight * Normalized Score of Hardware Encryption in integrity

=0.500*0.273=0.136

- The weighted score for integrity is calculated by multiplying the integrity weight (0.500) with the normalized score of Hardware Encryption in integrity (0.273).
- The result is 0.500 * 0.273 = 0.136.

The weighted score of 0.136 indicates that hardware encryption also contributes significantly to the integrity of the system. It helps ensure the accuracy and consistency of data, adding another layer of security.

Access Control (0.072): Weighted Score of Hardware Encryption in Access Control = Confidentiality Weight * Normalized Score of Hardware Encryption in Confidentiality

=0.500*0.145=0.072

The weighted score for access control is calculated by mistakenly using the confidentiality weight (0.500) instead of the correct access control weight. Assuming the correct access control weight is different; please provide the correct value for accurate analysis.

Authentication   (0.119):   Weighted   Score   of   Hardware   Encryption   in   Authentication = Confidentiality Weight * Normalized Score of Hardware Encryption in Confidentiality

= 0.500*0.238 = 0.119

- The weighted score for authentication is calculated by multiplying the authentication weight (0.500) with the normalized score of Hardware Encryption in authentication (0.238).
- The result is 0.500 * 0.238 = 0.119.

The weighted score of 0.119 suggests that hardware encryption contributes to the authentication aspect of security. It plays a role in verifying the identity of users or devices, enhancing the overall security posture.

Hardware encryption is shown to have a significant impact on confidentiality and integrity, and it contributes to both access control and authentication. The analysis highlights the multifaceted role of hardware encryption in bolstering different aspects of overall system security.

By using equation 9, the authors prepared Table **5** and drew (Figs. **2** to **6**). Confidentiality is a key security factor that influences all security techniques employed to enhance the hardware security of Wireless Sensor Networks. These analyses help stakeholders understand the strengths and weaknesses of each hardware security algorithm in different security aspects, aiding in informed decision-making based on specific security requirements.

Table 5. Security score for each hardware security algorithm.

-	Confidentiality	Integrity	Access Control	Authentication
Secure Boot	0.203	0.121	0.063	0.121
TPM	0.057	0.034	0.018	0.034
Physical Lock	0.058	0.035	0.018	0.350
Hardware Encryption	0.228	0.136	0.072	0.119

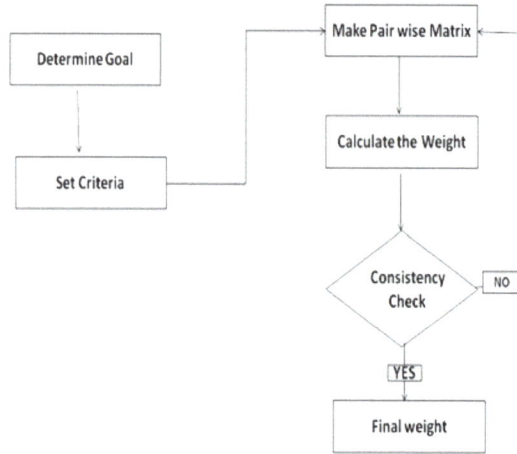

Fig. (2). AHP Flow of work.

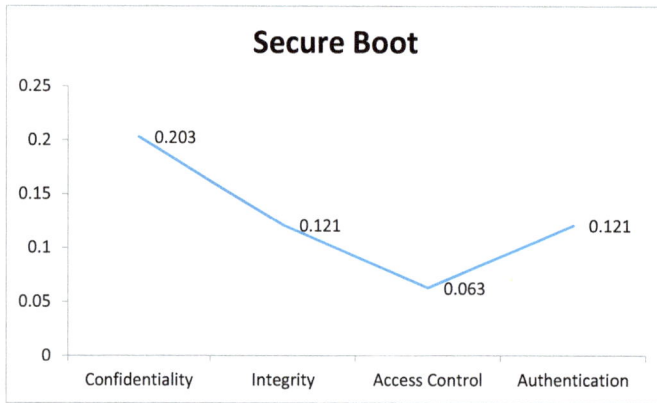

Fig. (3). Security factor effect on secure boot technique.

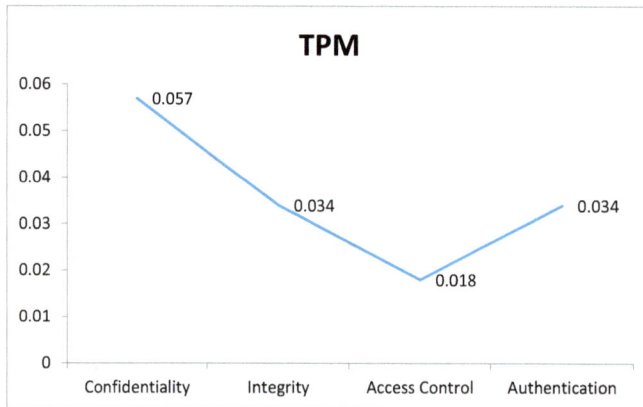

Fig. (4). Security factor's effect on the TMP technique.

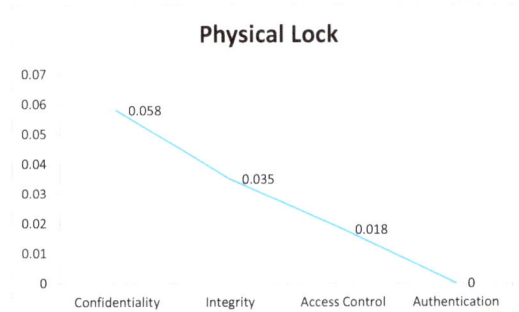

Fig. (5). Security factor's effect on physical lock.

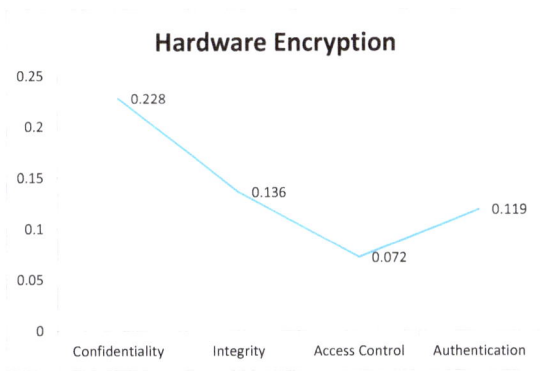

Fig. (6). Security factor effect on hardware encryption.

Step 6: Decision Making

The final weighted scores for each security method are presented (Secure Boot, TPM, Physical Lock, and Hardware Encryption) by summing up the weighted scores across all criteria (Confidentiality, Integrity, Access Control, and Authentication). The final results are then presented in Table **6**, along with the assigned ranks based on the calculated final weights. Herein, the final weighted score is calculated for each alternative by summing up the weighted scores across all criteria.

Table 6. Final results of each security method.

Security Methods	Final Weight (Rank)
Secure Boot (S1)	0.508
TPM (S2)	0.144
Physical Lock (S3)	0.463
Hardware encryption (S4)	0.555

Final Weighted Score for "Secure Boot" (S1)

Final Weighted Score of Secure Boot = Sum of Weighted Scores of Secure Boot across all Criteria

$\approx$ 0.203 (Confidentiality) + 0.121(Integrity) +0.063 (Access Control) + 0.121 (Authentication) = 0.508

- **Calculation:** The final weighted score is obtained by summing up the weighted scores of Secure Boot across all criteria (Confidentiality, Integrity, Access Control, and Authentication).
- **Interpretation:** Secure Boot has a final weighted score of 0.508, indicating that it has the highest overall performance among the evaluated security methods.

Final Weighted Score of TPM (S2): 0.144

Final Weighted Score of TPM Boot = Sum of Weighted Scores of TPM across all Criteria

= 0.057+0.035+0.018+0.034= 0.144

- **Calculation:** The final weighted score is obtained by summing up the weighted scores of TPM across all criteria.
- **Interpretation:** TPM has a final weighted score of 0.144, suggesting a lower overall performance compared to Secure Boot but still contributing positively to the security objectives.

Final Weighted Score of Physical Lock (S3): 0.463

Final Weighted Score of Physical Lock = Sum of Weighted Scores of Access Control across all Criteria

=0.058+0.035+0.018+0. 350= .463

- **Calculation:** The final weighted score is obtained by summing up the weighted scores of physical lock across all criteria.
- **Interpretation:** Physical Lock has a final weighted score of 0.463, positioning it as the second-highest in overall performance, after Secure Boot.

Final Weighted Score of Hardware Encryption (S4): 0.555

Final Weighted Score of Hardware encryption = Sum of Weighted Scores of Hardware encryption across all Criteria

= 0.228+0.136+0.072+0.119= 0.555

- **Calculation:** The final weighted score is obtained by summing up the weighted scores of Hardware Encryption across all criteria.
- **Interpretation:** Hardware Encryption has the highest final weighted score of 0.555, positioning it as the top-performing security method among the evaluated options.

The ranking is based on the final weighted scores, where higher scores indicate better overall performance. Hardware Encryption secured the top rank, followed by Secure Boot, Physical Lock, and TPM [28]. The final weighted scores assist in decision-making by providing a quantitative measure of each security method's effectiveness across multiple criteria. Stakeholders can use these scores to make informed decisions on which method aligns better with their security priorities and requirements. Based on this calculation with respect to each alternative, the author finds that Hardware encryption obtained the highest final weighted score (0.555), which would be the preferred choice according to the AHP method for improving the security of the hardware of WSN [29]. Based on the obtained weight, authors assign the ranks S1<S3<S2 <S4. The obtained weight of the techniques is shown in Table **6** and depicted in Fig. (**7**). These calculations are obtained by equation 10.

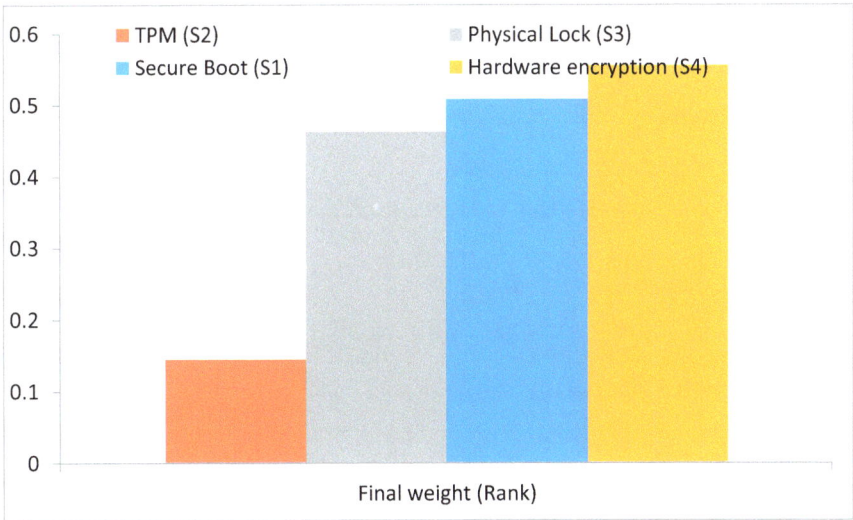

Fig. (7). Final rank of security methods.

CONCLUDING REMARKS

The application of AHP for hardware security assessment offers a valuable contribution to the field. Its structured and systematic nature empowers organizations to make informed decisions, ensuring the continuous improvement of hardware security in WSN systems. The study's success serves as a foundation for further exploration in different contexts, fostering a more resilient and adaptive approach to hardware security assessment in the ever-evolving landscape of cybersecurity. The proposed methodology for improving the security of hardware is assessed by using the AHP approach. The AHP provides a structured approach that can help organizations make informed decisions about hardware security. By identifying and prioritizing criteria, assigning weights, and evaluating techniques or systems against those criteria, organizations can make data-driven decisions to improve the hardware security of the WSN system. This study demonstrates the effectiveness of the proposed technique in identifying security methods and prioritizing actions to improve the security of the hardware of a wireless sensor network (WSN) system. Future research can explore the application of the proposed technique in other hardware security assessment contexts and the integration of other decision-making frameworks to support hardware security assessment.

REFERENCES

[1] W. Alhakami, A. Baz, H. Alhakami, M. Ahmad, and R. Ahmad Khan, "Healthcare Device Security: Insights and Implications", *Intelligent Automation & Soft Computing,* vol. 27, no. 2, pp. 409-424, 2021.
[http://dx.doi.org/10.32604/iasc.2021.015351]

[2] A. Kumar, A. Shelar, J. Etheredge, S. Prakash, S. Sharma, and M. Mp, "Analytical Hierarchical Process Based System for Image Fusion", *Signal Image Process.,* vol. 6, no. 5, pp. 01-14, 2015.
[http://dx.doi.org/10.5121/sipij.2015.6501]

[3] M. Ahmad, J. F. Al-Amri, F. Ahmad, S. Khatri, and A. H. Seh, *Comput. Syst. Sci. Eng.,* vol. 41, no. 2, pp. 811-828, 2021.
[http://dx.doi.org/10.32604/csse.2022.020097]

[4] A. Attaallah, M. Ahmad, M. Tarique Jamal Ansari, A. Kumar Pandey, R. Kumar, and R. Ahmad Khan, "Device Security Assessment of Internet of Healthcare Things", *Intelligent Automation & Soft Computing,* vol. 27, no. 2, pp. 593-603, 2021.
[http://dx.doi.org/10.32604/iasc.2021.015092]

[5] D. Arvind, and S. Guha, "Introduction to Hardware Security", In: *Hardware Security.* Springer: Cham, 2018, pp. 1-13.

[6] E. Luiijf, and R. Ottis, *Cyber security: protecting critical infrastructure.* Springer, 2015.

[7] S. Raza, and M.N. Malik, "Hardware Security Techniques: A Review", *J. Comput. Sci. Eng.,* vol. 5, no. 2, pp. 159-166, 2019.

[8] M. Ahmad, M. Nadeem, M. Islam, S. Ali, A. Agrawal, and R. Ahmad Khan, *Selection of Digital Watermarking Techniques for Medical Image Security by using the Fuzzy Analytical Hierarchy Process.* Recent Advances in Computer Science and Communications, 2023.
[http://dx.doi.org/10.2174/2666255816666230502100729]

[9] A. Algarni, M. Ahmad, A. Attaallah, A. Agrawal, R. Kumar, and R. Khan, "A Hybrid Fuzzy Rule-Based Multi-Criteria Framework for Security Assessment of Medical Device Software", *International Journal of Intelligent Engineering and Systems,* vol. 13, no. 5, pp. 51-62, 2020.
[http://dx.doi.org/10.22266/ijies2020.1031.06]

[10] A. Carranza, *Overview of Wireless Sensor Network (WSN).* Security, 2018.

[11] Y. Jin, K. Mohanram, and O. Sinanoglu, "Challenges and solutions for secure hardware design", *Proc.*

IEEE, vol. 104, no. 11, pp. 2196-2216, 2019.

[12]   J. Jiang, W. Liu, and C. Xu, "A secure boot mechanism for embedded systems using Intel SGX", *Journal of Information Security and Applications,* vol. 46, pp. 239-247, 2019.

[13]   S. Picek, A. Knezovic, and B. Skoric, "A framework for testing TPM security", *IEEE Trans. Inf. Forensics Security,* vol. 11, no. 5, pp. 941-953, 2016.

[14]   Q. Wang, X. Cheng, and X. Xu, "Hardware Security: A Survey of Hardware-Based Security Mechanisms and Applications", *Journal of Hardware and Systems Security,* vol. 2, no. 3, pp. 243-259, 2018.

[15]   Y. Makris, V. Karakostas, and N. Hatzimihail, "Hardware security verification: A framework and its effectiveness evaluation", *IEEE Trans. Depend. Secure Comput.,* vol. 15, no. 1, pp. 81-96, 2018.

[16]   Open Web Application Security Project (OWASP) Hardware Security Project. (n.d.). Retrieved from: https://owasp.org/www-project-hardware-security/

[17]   Common Vulnerability Scoring System (CVSS). (n.d.). Retrieved from: https://www.first.org/cvss/

[18]   National Institute of Standards and Technology (NIST) Cybersecurity Framework. (n.d.). Retrieved from: https://www.nist.gov/cyberframework

[19]   W. Hu, C.H. Chang, A. Sengupta, S. Bhunia, R. Kastner, and H. Li, "An Overview of Hardware Security and Trust: Threats, Countermeasures, and Design Tools", *IEEE Trans. Comput. Aided Des. Integrated Circ. Syst.,* vol. 40, no. 6, pp. 1010-1038, 2021.
[http://dx.doi.org/10.1109/TCAD.2020.3047976]

[20]   A.J. Cabrera-Gutierrez, E. Castillo, A. Escobar-Molero, J.A. Alvarez-Bermejo, D.P. Morales, and L. Parrilla, "Integration of Hardware Security Modules and Permissioned Blockchain in Industrial IoT Networks", *IEEE Access,* vol. 10, pp. 114331-114345, 2022.
[http://dx.doi.org/10.1109/ACCESS.2022.3217815]

[21]   Kalai, Yael Tauman, Ben, Kettle and Nickolai Zeldovich. Hardware Security. 2022.

[22]   B. Li, Y. Zou, J. Zhu, and W. Cao, "Impact of Hardware Impairment and Co-Channel Interference on Security-Reliability Trade-Off for Wireless Sensor Networks", *IEEE Trans. Wirel. Commun.,* vol. 20, no. 11, pp. 7011-7025, 2021.
[http://dx.doi.org/10.1109/TWC.2021.3079902]

[23]   V. Verma, and V.K. Jha, "An Efficient Wormhole Detection and Optimal Path Selection for Secure Data Transmission in WSN Environment", *Wirel. Pers. Commun.,* vol. 121, no. 4, pp. 2927-2945, 2021.
[http://dx.doi.org/10.1007/s11277-021-08856-8]

[24]   Gruss, D., Lipp, M., Schwarz, M., & Haas, W. Meltdown: Reading kernel memory from user space, In 27th USENIX Security Symposium (USENIX Security 18), pp. 973-990, 2018.

[25]   Hassayoun, Salem, Samer Lahouar and Kamel Besbes. SDR Bridge for a Secure Wireless Sensor Network (WSN). 2020 IEEE International Conference on Design & Test of Integrated Micro & Nano-Systems (DTS), pp. 1-5, 2021.

[26]   I. Butun, A. Sari, and P. Österberg, "Hardware Security of Fog End-Devices for the Internet of Things", *Sensors (Basel),* vol. 20, no. 20, p. 5729, 2020.
[http://dx.doi.org/10.3390/s20205729] [PMID: 33050165]

[27]   I. Askoxylakis, D. Gritzalis, and S. Katsikas, "Vulnerability analysis of hardware-based security mechanisms: A survey", *Comput. Secur.,* vol. 86, pp. 34-51, 201, •••.

CHAPTER 10

Unveiling the Sky: Exploring Synergies in Drone Robotics and Automation through Artificial Intelligence and Machine learning

Md Akhtar Khan[1,*], **Kiran Kumar**[2] and **Ahmed F. EI Sayed**[3]

[1] *Department of Aerospace Engineering, GITAM School of Technology, Hyderabad, India*

[2] *Department of Mechanical Engineering, GITAM School of Technology, Hyderabad, India*

[3] *Department of Mechanical Power Engineering, Zagazig University, Zagazig 2, Egypt*

Abstract: In the rapidly evolving landscape of unmanned aerial vehicles (UAVs) and automation technologies, this research delves into the synergistic potential of integrating artificial intelligence (AI) and machine learning (ML) into drone robotics systems. This paper examines the current state of drone technology, focusing on the challenges faced in optimizing their performance for complex tasks. By leveraging AI and ML algorithms, drones can evolve beyond traditional pre-programmed routes and manual control, unlocking the ability to learn from data, adapt to dynamic environments, and make intelligent decisions in real time. As drones continue to play an increasingly pivotal role across diverse industries, from agriculture and surveillance to logistics and emergency response, the fusion of advanced AI and ML promises transformative advancements in efficiency, adaptability, and autonomy. Internet of Drones (IoD) is evidently a promising and versatile application of Unmanned Aerial Vehicles (UAVs) across various domains. The adaptability of drones to unpredictable circumstances and their diverse range of applications make them valuable tools in numerous scenarios. Drones' outstanding mobility and dexterity allow them to identify areas that are dangerous or difficult for people to access.This is especially valuable in scenarios such as inspecting infrastructure, monitoring environmental conditions, or assessing the aftermath of natural disasters.

Keywords: Artificial intelligence, Dynamic environments, Drone robotics, Efficiency, Internet of Drones, Machine learning, Surveillance, Unmanned aerial vehicles.

* **Corresponding author Md Akhtar Khan:** Department of Aerospace Engineering, GITAM School of Technology, Hyderabad, India; E-mail: khan.akhtar24@gmail.com

Asif Khan, Mohammad Kamrul Hasan, Naushad Varish & Mohammed Aslam Husain (Eds.)

INTRODUCTION

The integration of AI and ML into drone systems has the potential to address various challenges, such as navigation, obstacle avoidance, and decision-making processes. This paper delves into the current state of drone technology, identifying areas where AI and ML can significantly contribute to advancing capabilities and overcoming limitations.

Autonomous vehicles (AVs) aim to achieve a high level of automation and safety, reducing the reliance on human drivers. Ongoing research and advancements in these fields continue to enhance the capabilities of autonomous vehicles, bringing us closer to a future where they can be seamlessly integrated into everyday transportation systems [1, 2]. Drones are a type of technology that can fly without the assistance of a pilot, and they can also be ground-based; they are becoming more prevalent in people's lives [3]. As drones' commercial use continues to expand, scientific researcher's attention has been drawn to their core technology. In order to provide services or send up-to-date information to users who are located far away and connected to specialized application servers, drones engage in simultaneous communication with a reference ground structure [4].

By utilizing machine learning approaches, research is done to try and identify UAVs, categorize them, and potentially even identify their flying path. Drones also improve network topology efficiency in terms of latency, performance, interdependence, and reliability [5]. However, there are a number of issues with drone deployment, including the high degrees of mobility, the erratic behaviour of the wireless medium, and the potential for quick topological changes due to battery life. Intelligent approaches and technologies are being employed to enhance decision-making skills in light of autonomous vehicle development, as Khayyam *et al.* noted [6].

Fig. (**1**) illustrates the security and safety features of A.V. In AV's safety system, mechanical and electrical safety systems as well as electrical and electronic safety systems are regarded as safety concerns.

The ability of the drone to make independent decisions in the event that humans cannot operate it or communicate with one another highlights the novelty of this proof of concept. The outcomes are used to give the "pilot" visual information so that it can plan the flight path based on the locations of the objects in its path. This makes employing the drone for rescue operations during natural disasters possible.

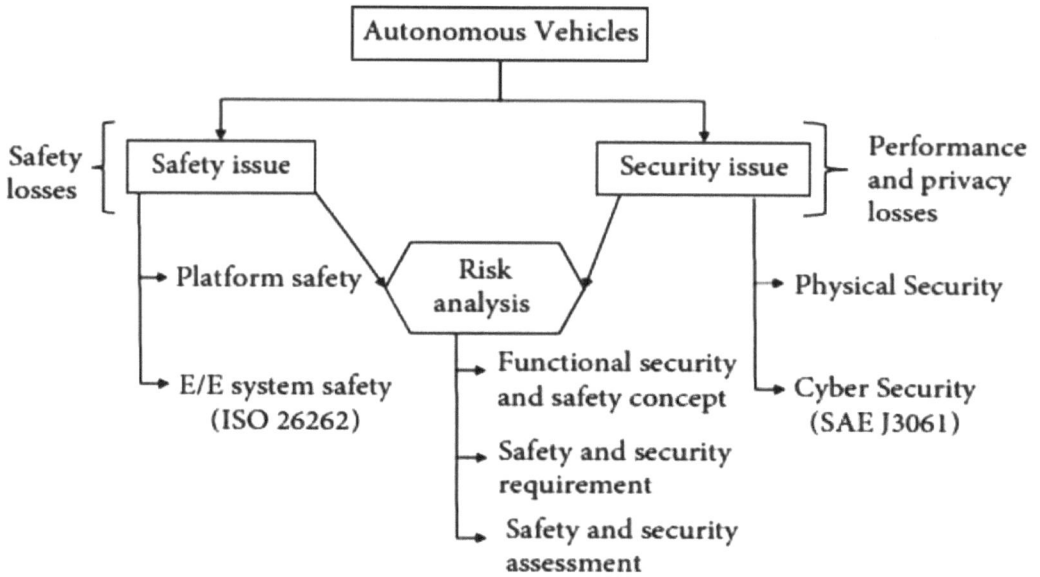

Fig. (1). Security and Safety Features of Autonomous Vehicles.

Integrating AI and machine learning with UAV technology has revolutionized various industries and expanded the capabilities of drones. This synergy has led to advancements in object recognition, autonomous navigation, obstacle avoidance, real-time decision-making, and collaborative operations. It is exciting to see how these technologies continue to evolve and drive innovation across multiple domains.

UAV-based advanced wildfire identification and warning systems are indeed gaining traction due to their ability to incorporate multiple remote smart sensors. Deep learning-based computer vision methods have emerged as effective tools for monitoring wildfires using UAVs. These methods leverage the power of AI and ML to analyze aerial imagery and detect signs of wildfires with high accuracy and speed.

UAVs outfitted with graphical remote sensing technologies have several benefits over more conventional approaches, such as dispatching maintenance teams into dangerous regions or depending solely on ground-based surveillance. They can access hazardous or inaccessible areas that are hard for people to enter, are affordable, and offer real-time data [7].

UAVs may also be swiftly deployed to monitor wide areas and issue early warnings, facilitating quicker reaction times and more efficient tracking and suppression of wildfires. This combination of UAV technology and deep learning-based computer vision holds great promise for improving wildfire management and reducing the impact of wildfires on ecosystems and communities [8]. As illustrated in Fig. (**2a**), UAVs are currently employed in a variety of sectors and Fig. (**2b**) depicts the general architecture of UAVs, which use communication links to connect to a satellite or ground control system (GCS) like a laptop or smartphone for connectivity.

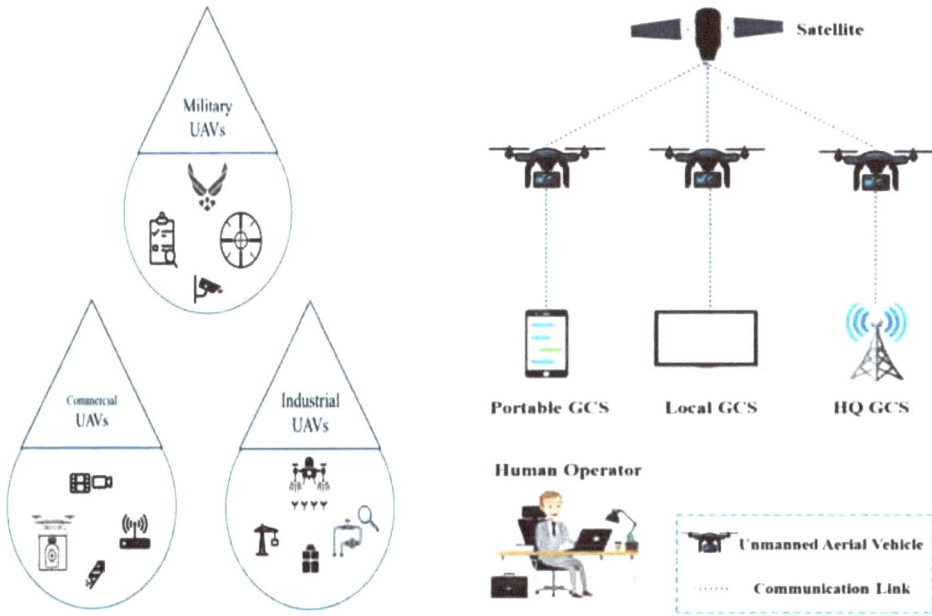

Fig. (2). (a) Application of UAVs [3] (b) Architecture of UAV [4].

ARTIFICIAL INTELLIGENCE IN DRONE SYSTEM FOR VARIOUS APPLICATION

Growing usage of drones for military, industrial surveillance, and agricultural purposes has led to significant technological advances in integrating unmanned aerial systems (UAS) into new enterprises and industries, particularly in urban areas [9]. The drone is adaptable, deployable, and fixable; it can examine a broad range of numbers at any time, from any location [10]. This is an inexpensive way to gather and send data to intelligent systems that can analyze critical data, such as real-time video or picture analysis.

Drones for Military Purposes

In several ways, drones have enhanced military capabilities globally. The enemy's movements, locations, and placements of strategic objectives can be vitally communicated using drones. Military experts swiftly combined artificial intelligence and drone technology to produce a drone that could, in some situations, outperform human reconnaissance teams. Drones and modern computer vision and image recognition technologies are being combined with military defence technology to tackle military challenges without putting human lives in danger. Numerous unmanned aerial vehicles and drones equipped with artificial intelligence capabilities employ a range of AI application cases concerning drone technology. AI appears to be widely used by the military to enable autonomous drone flight, which necessitates machine vision. The model of geo-reconnaissance and commanding (GRC) of the UAV system is illustrated in Fig. (3). Drones using artificial intelligence require a combination of computer vision, guidance equipment, and mechanical components [11].

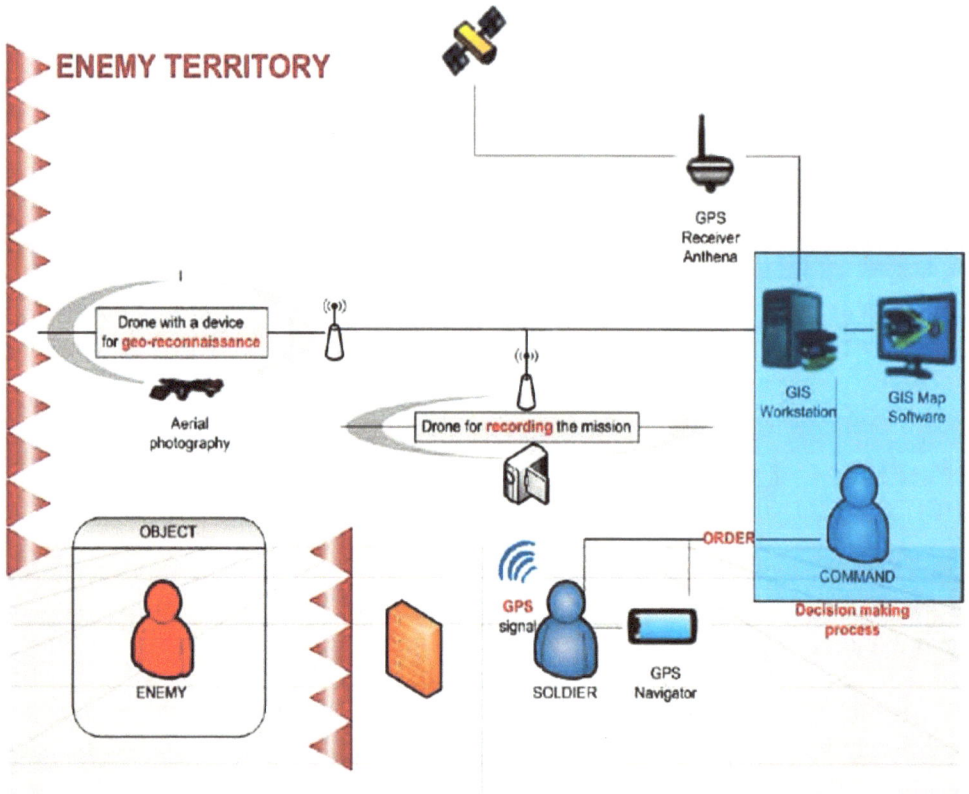

Fig. (3). GRC information system in UAV supported with C4IRS systems and AI [11].

The proposed framework aims to detect objects of critical military importance based on the images received from the video stream of military surveillance drones. The decisions will be based on the captured images or video results.

A significant problem with UAV operation is their short battery life. It is not recommended to increase the size or weight of the battery because doing so will ultimately increase payload and essential considerations. New wired or wireless power transmission (WPT) systems can be used to get charging for the drones [12].

Moreover, based on research, wireless power transmission (WPT) projected revenue for 2020 is approximately $2000 million [13]. The projected growing market for drones and WPT through 2025 is shown in Fig. (**4**). By 2025, overall sales are predicted to reach $43 billion with a Compound Annual Growth Rate (CARG) of 13.8% [14].

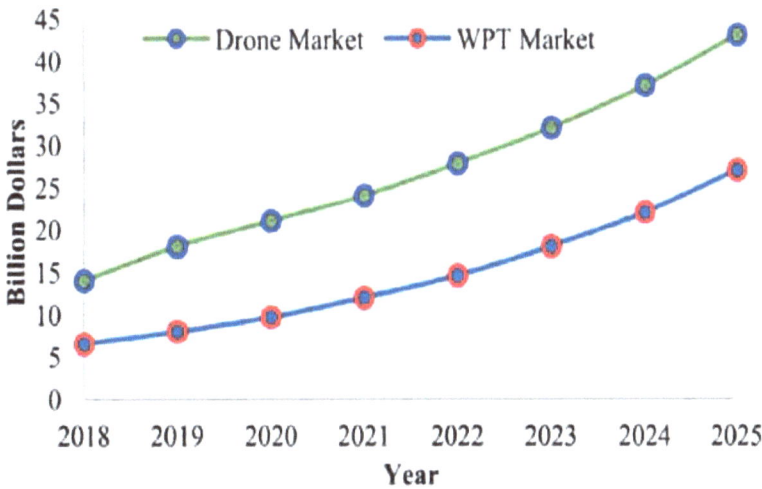

Fig. (4). Growth of the drone and WPT markets [15].

A significant advantage of adopting WPT techniques is the capacity to operate *in situa*tions where wired medium power transfer is risky or impossible. Radiative electromagnetic (EM) and non-EM WPT approaches are included together for the competent operation of drones [15]. Adopting WPT techniques is a significant advantage of operating in conditions where wired transmission power transfer is risky or unattainable. These techniques play an essential role in the drones used for military applications.

Drones for Disaster Management

Unmanned aerial vehicles (UAVs) can respond to disasters like terrorist attacks, tsunamis, and flooding that are too dangerous for human intervention. Natural disasters can impact power, telecommunications, water, and transportation infrastructure [16]. UAVs can help collect data, provide timely responses, and navigate debris. UAVs outfitted with sensors, radars, and high-resolution cameras can help rescue crews locate damage, initiate recovery activities, and deliver supplies like first-aid helicopters and medical packs. UAVs can provide real-time surveillance over large areas without compromising safety and security. Unmanned aerial vehicles (UAVs) can locate and rescue individuals and animals in peril [17].

Drones for Healthcare Delivery

Drones can potentially revolutionize healthcare delivery, especially in distant and underdeveloped locations. They allow for the quick and effective delivery of medical supplies, such as vaccines, drugs, and emergency equipment, to places with restricted access [18]. This is especially useful in emergencies, natural catastrophes, or isolated areas where traditional transportation options are inconvenient. In a few African nations, the successful implementation of aerial delivery of medical supplies to health institutions in rural populations is plagued by poor road infrastructure and undulating topography [19]. Research in the field of emergency healthcare has demonstrated that using drones to deliver automated external defibrillators (AEDs) in cases of out-of-hospital cardiac arrests (OHCA) within regions designated by the use of Geographic Information System (GIS) models is a safe and practical option [20].

Drones can serve as centres for mobile communication, monitoring, and medical assistance to improve telemedicine capabilities as illustrated in Fig. (**5**). Drones equipped with cutting-edge communication technologies can link wirelessly in isolated or disaster-affected locations, enabling patients and healthcare professionals to have real-time video consultations also when direct physical access is restricted, this allows remote diagnosis, medical guidance, and even remote-controlled medical treatments as illustrated in Fig. (**6**) [21].

Agricultural Drones

In modern agriculture, unmanned aerial vehicles (UAVs) could be deployed to gather precise data from ground-based sensors (water quality, type of soil, relative humidity, *etc.*), apply pesticides, identify and treat diseases, plan irrigation, identify weeds, and oversee crops [22]. Accurate 3D maps of fields can be produced using drones outfitted with GPS and mapping software, which enables farmers to evaluate the topography, drainage patterns, and soil heterogeneity of their fields. This information helps direct irrigation and drainage planning and the development of site-specific management methods. Drones can help with irrigation management decisions by utilising thermal and multispectral photography to determine crop water stress levels. Farmers can conserve water and increase the efficiency of their water use by recognising areas that are experiencing water stress and modifying irrigation schedules and techniques accordingly [23].

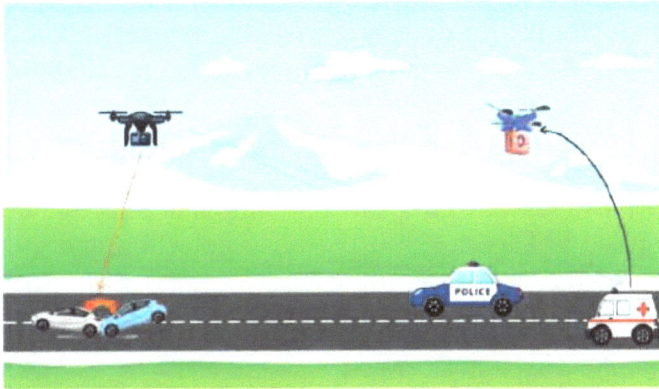

Fig. (5). UAV for monitoring and assistance.

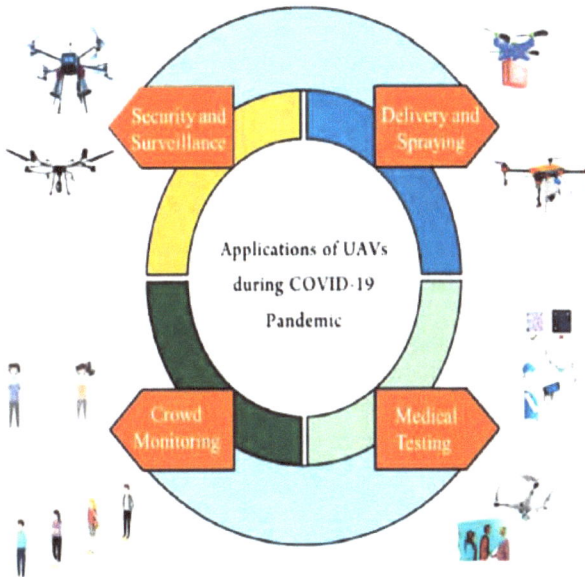

Fig. (6). Application of UAV in the medical field [16].

MACHINE LEARNING APPLICATIONS IN DRONE SYSTEMS

The term Internet of Drones (IoD) refers to a system architecture that enables communication between different networked devices situated on the ground and autonomous flying UAVs. Furthermore, various researchers have proven how to improve the practicality and efficacy of drone route planning by raising the convergence rate and robustness, resulting in a more appropriate flying path [24].

Machine learning techniques such as Hidden Markov Model (HMM) and Artificial Neural Network (ANN) play a significant role in reducing the False Rejection Rate (FRR) in fire detection systems in smart buildings. HMM is a probabilistic graphical model that is used to model temporal sequences of data. In the context of fire detection, HMM can analyze the time-series data collected from sensors to predict the likelihood of a fire outbreak based on patterns in the data. By training the HMM model on historical data, it can learn the normal behavior of sensor readings in a smart building and detect deviations that may indicate a fire hazard. This helps in the early detection and prevention of fire incidents [25].

HMM can capture the sequential dependencies in sensor data, allowing it to make more accurate predictions about fire outbreaks. This capability contributes to reducing the False Rejection Rate by improving the system's ability to identify potential fire incidents. ANN is a machine-learning model inspired by the structure and function of the human brain. In fire detection systems, ANN can be trained on sensor data to recognize patterns associated with fire hazards. By leveraging the learning capabilities of ANN, the system can adapt to new data and improve its accuracy in detecting fire incidents. This adaptability helps minimize false rejections by continuously updating the model based on new information. ANN can handle complex relationships in the sensor data and make decisions based on multiple input variables, leading to more robust fire detection capabilities in smart buildings [25, 26].

The Fully Connected Deep Neural Network (FC-DNN) algorithm plays a crucial role in enhancing the detection and identification of drones in sensitive areas by providing advanced capabilities for analyzing complex data from various sensors. The algorithms have shown excellent results in various applications such as image object detection, digital signal processing, radar detection, speech recognition, and more. By leveraging the power of DL, drone detection systems can achieve higher accuracy in identifying drones amidst background noise and clutter. It enables the fusion of data from multiple heterogeneous sensors, allowing for a more comprehensive analysis of drone-related signals. By combining data from different sensors, the algorithms can provide a more holistic view of the environment, leading to improved detection and identification capabilities. FC-DNN can efficiently process large amounts of data, including raw RF signals, to extract relevant features for drone detection and identification. By automating the feature extraction process, DL algorithms can handle complex data sets and identify patterns that may not be apparent through traditional methods. The ability to adapt and learn from new data, makes them well-suited for dynamic environments where drone threats may evolve over time. Fig. (**7**) depicts the workflow graphic flow chart of FC-DNN [26].

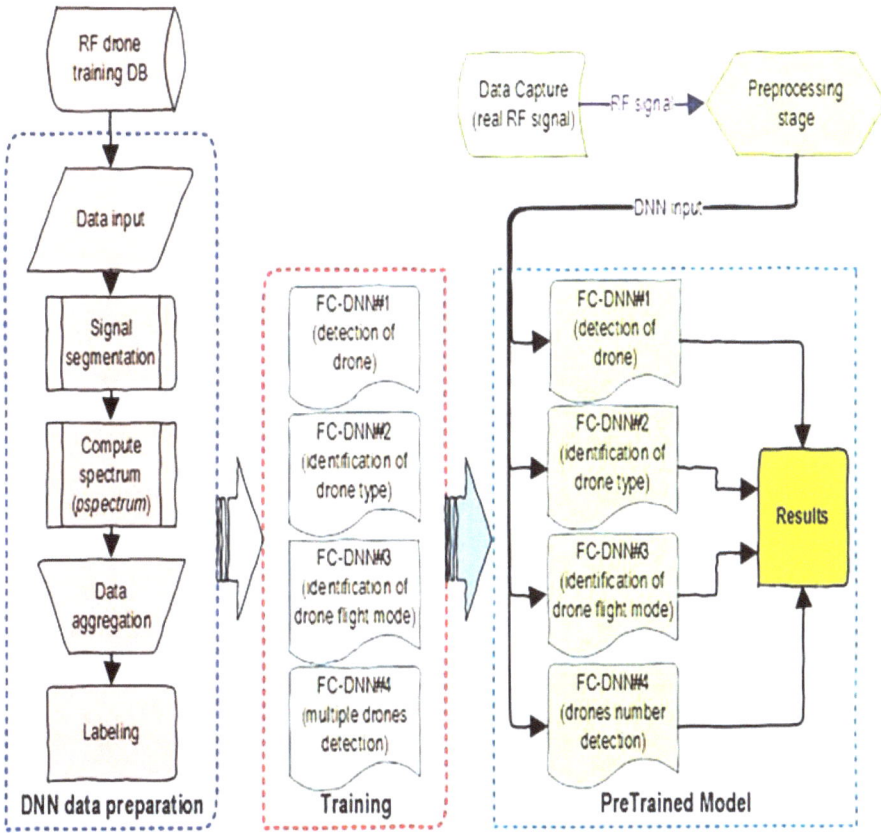

Fig. (7). Workflow graphical flow chart.

This adaptability allows drone detection systems to continuously improve their performance and stay ahead of emerging threats. By utilizing DL algorithms, drone detection systems can achieve better performance in terms of detection range, detection probability, and overall system efficiency. The algorithms can optimize the tradeoff between various system parameters to enhance the overall performance of the anti-drone system [27].

Machine learning (ML) techniques are used particularly in the context of predicting and detecting abnormal activities in living environments, such as daycares and crèches, using IoT technologies. The proposed method employs a combination of supervised learning techniques, including random forest (RF) differential evolution and kernel density algorithms, for activity detection shown in Fig. (7). The model also utilizes a deep neural network for training and predicting data. Additionally, the use of multi-classification techniques for input classifications from video frames is presented [28].

The proposed method aims to remotely monitor both static and dynamic activities and send notifications of abnormal activities to IoT notification devices. It emphasizes the significance of recognizing different kinds of human activities and differentiating between normal and abnormal activities in private spaces like daycares and creches.

The application of ML techniques helps particularly in the context of predicting and detecting abnormal activities in living environments and aims to address the critical need for constant monitoring and protection of vulnerable individuals in various living environments (Fig. **8**).

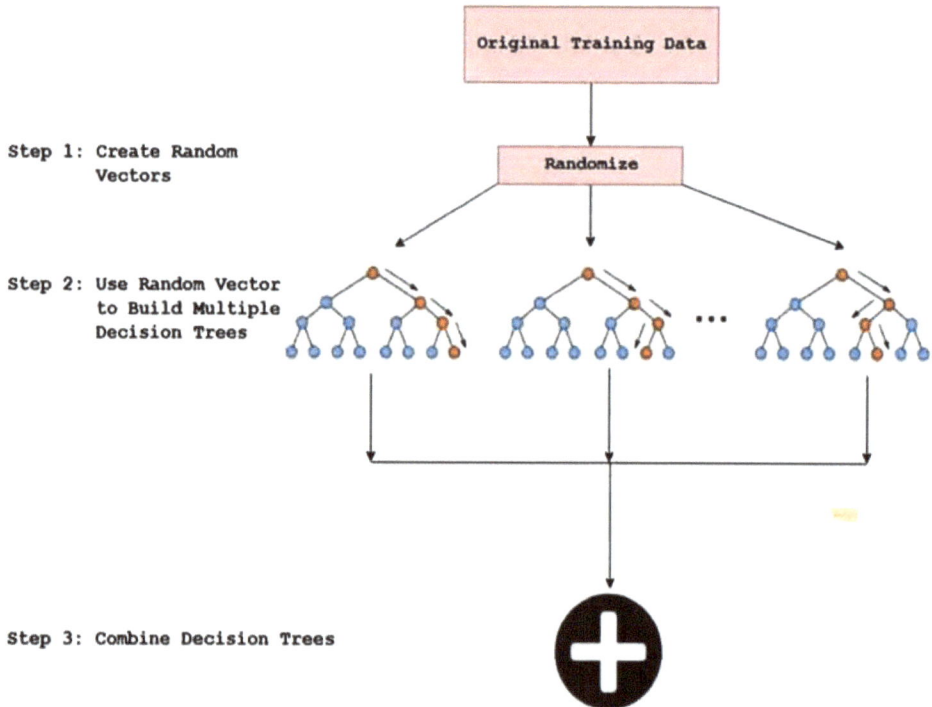

Fig. (8). Random Forest method.

INTEGRATION OF AI ML AND DRONE AUTOMATION

The convergence of Artificial Intelligence (AI) and Machine Learning (ML) with drone automation represents a significant advancement in unmanned aerial vehicle (UAV) technology. This integration unlocks a vast potential for various applications across diverse sectors.

CV algorithms enable drones to perceive their surroundings through image and video data. This allows for tasks like object detection, recognition, and tracking, crucial for autonomous navigation and obstacle avoidance [29]. Machine learning algorithms can be trained on vast datasets to enable drones to perform complex tasks like path planning, anomaly detection, and decision-making in dynamic environments [30]. Deep learning techniques, a subfield of ML, utilize artificial neural networks to extract high-level features from data. This empowers drones with advanced capabilities like object classification, image segmentation, and real-time object recognition [31]. Drones equipped with AI/ML can monitor crop health, identify pests and diseases, and optimize resource management by analyzing field data [32]. AI-powered drones can autonomously inspect bridges, pipelines, and other infrastructure for damage detection, improving safety and efficiency. Drones with AI-based object detection can assist in search and rescue operations by locating missing individuals in disaster zones or difficult terrains. AI/ML integration holds immense potential for autonomous drone delivery services, revolutionizing logistics and supply chains [33]. AI/ML algorithms enable drones to operate with greater autonomy, reducing human intervention and improving efficiency. Machine learning empowers drones to make real-time decisions based on sensor data and environmental conditions, leading to safer and more effective operations. AI/ML facilitates the collection and analysis of aerial data, providing valuable insights for various applications. The challenges and considerations for ensuring the safe operation of autonomous drones in airspace require robust regulations and safety protocols. Data security and privacy concerns arise with the collection and transmission of aerial data by drones. The ethical implications of AI-powered drone technology, such as potential misuse for surveillance, need careful consideration.

The field of AI/ML-powered drone automation is rapidly evolving. Future research directions include developing frameworks for seamless collaboration between human operators and AI-powered drones. Implementing explainable AI techniques to understand how drones make decisions, fostering trust and transparency. Establishing standards for AI/ML integration and data exchange between different drone platforms.

The proposed model comprises four modules: an online path planning algorithm, clustering-based network topology construction, reinforcement learning-based cluster management, and a data routing mechanism [34]. The dynamic path planning approach aims to cover all waypoints in a polynomial amount of time, while the topology construction module includes cluster head election and cluster formation based on various parameters such as the degree of centrality, surplus energy, link stability time, connectivity with the backbone UAV, and velocity. The cluster management process is determined using reinforcement learning called State Action Reward State Action (SARSA) in the ground control station. The proposed routing scheme shown in Fig. (9) enhances the packet delivery ratio and reduces delay, outperforming existing results in terms of path planning and routing metrics [35].

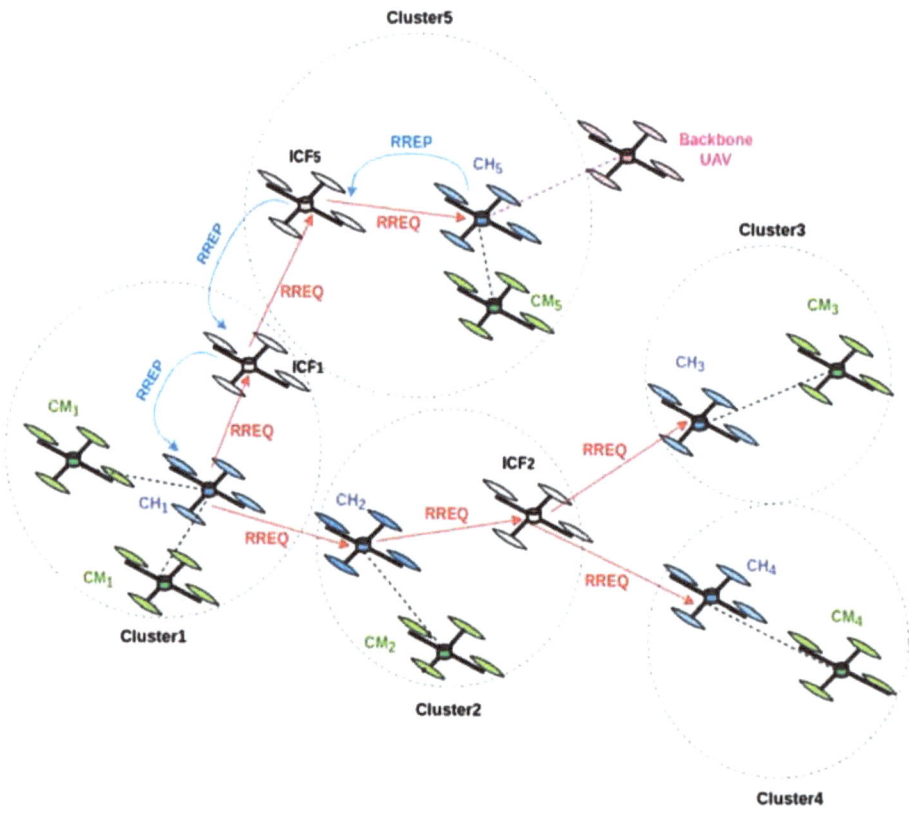

Fig. (9). Route discovery [33].

It emphasizes the advantages of using a swarm of miniature UAVs to execute tasks in a collective and ad hoc manner, emphasizing the unique characteristics of Flying Ad- hoc Networks (FANET). The limitations of existing path planning and routing mechanisms in UAV networks, lead to the proposal of a cluster-based routing approach that incorporates reinforcement learning for cluster management and dynamic path planning for UAV movement [36]. The proposed work aims to maximize ground area coverage by focusing on modeling, path planning, and routing approaches, offering significant contributions to the field of UAV-based applications. While deploying UAVs, it is critical to be familiar with their numerous types, categorization, and legal requirements. UAVs for surveillance purposes could be classified into two types: fixed-wing and rotary-wing UAVs.

Challenges and Future Directions

The challenges in UAVs are vulnerability to hijacking, denial-of-service (DoS), and distributed DoS assaults because of a lack of effective DoS/DDoS mitigation measures. Signal hoaxing and hijacking can negatively impact the behaviour of various UAVs [37]. GPS signal spoofing assaults occur when miscreants insert incorrect information into GPS channels, as shown in Fig. (**10**).

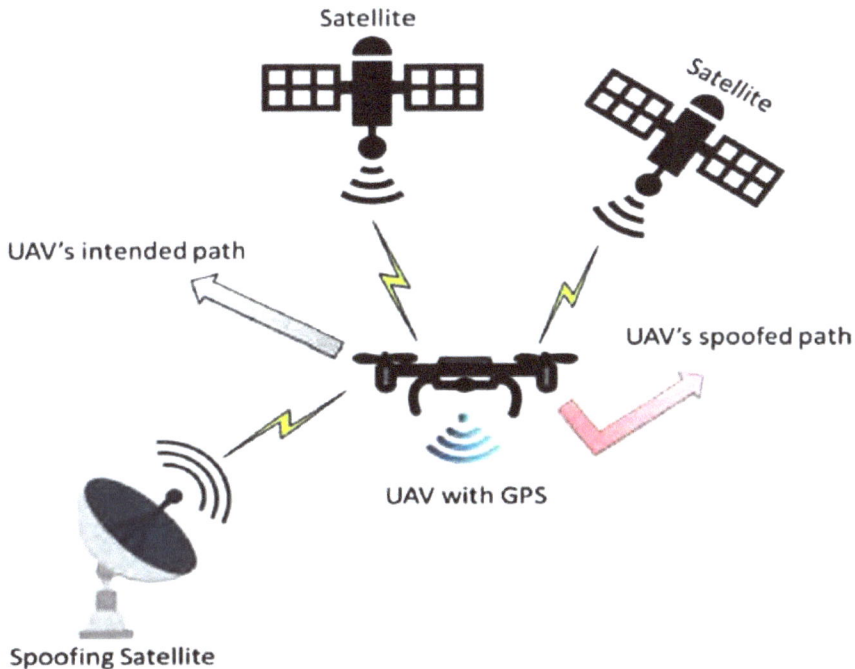

Fig. (10). GPS hoaxing and hijacking system [16].

DoS attacks occur due to an overflow of data in communication links to cause interruptions, putting extra load on processing units and depleting the batteries. In DDos, the attacker overwhelms the UAV by sending traffic to several sources to introduce inaccessibility issues. These attacks can be mitigated by sensing, tracing signal distortion, and high authentication. DoS attacks disrupt communication networks, overload processing devices, and drain batteries. DDoS attacks UAVs by distributing traffic from several sources, causing unreachability concerns. To avoid these attacks, we adopt signal tracing and strong authentication [36 - 38].

Currently, preventative measures methods are only available for single UAV networks. To accommodate multi-UAVs, existing algorithms must be modified or developed. Although UAVs have employed machine learning and neural network techniques, deep learning and reinforcement learning techniques have not yet been extensively applied. It is because of computational utilities and confined power. Researchers ought to come up with innovative deep-learning-based tactics for UAVs, especially for SAR missions [37]. Based on trajectory data, these methods can facilitate learning and contextual decision-making. The collected data can be used to guarantee practical autonomous UAV piloting. UAVs have limited storage and energy; therefore, lightweight and portable machine learning (ML), Deep Learning (DL), and Reinforcement Learning (RL) techniques can help overcome these limits [38].

The IoT ecosystem comprises a variety of sensors and devices, as shown in Fig. (11). A connected and shared architecture is necessary for real-time communication of information. Device information should be provided in real-time and processed quickly to facilitate decision-making.

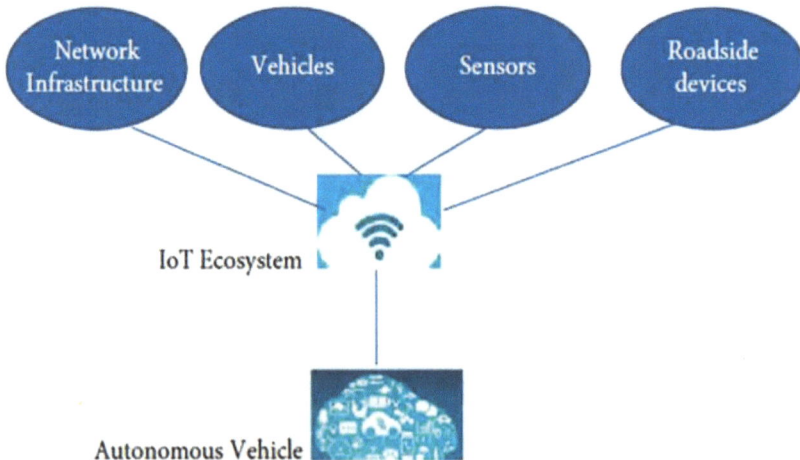

Fig. (11). The Internet of Things enabled an autonomous ecosystem [34].

The advanced technologies that can be used for the autonomous system where artificial intelligence combined with technologies including cloud computing, constraint programming, autonomous drones, knowledge representation, and the Internet of Things (IoT) can improve the functionality and networking of drones and autonomous vehicles are depicted in Fig. (**12**).

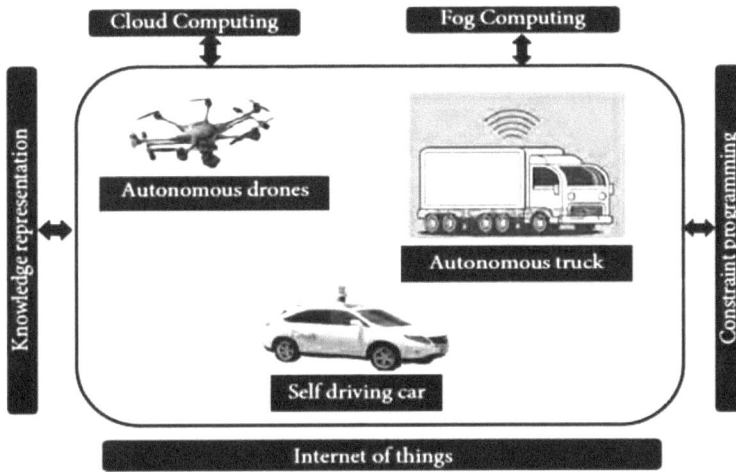

Fig. (12). Advanced technology for autonomous systems [36].

CONCLUSION

Drones have developed as invaluable instruments for gathering real-time pictures and sensor data for the military, agriculture, disaster relief, and healthcare sectors. Furthermore, they serve as an efficient means of getting medical supplies to remote places, mainly when the road system is hampered by rugged topography, leaving conventional transportation routes unfeasible. Applied AI is popular due to its transformational impact on numerous fields. It enhances processes, improves efficiency, and fosters creativity to address difficult real-world situations, demonstrating versatility and efficiency. UAVs' increased mobility, autonomy, and range necessitated the development of new battery swapping, docking, and precision landing systems. Finally we concluded that the use of unmanned aerial vehicles or drones with AI enabled in military operations and calamities improves efficiency and effectiveness, while also providing protection and reducing risk to humans. Further investigation must be conducted to integrate drones into current transportation systems and supply chains. This includes extending payload and flight lengths, as well as addressing cultural barriers to drone adoption in underdeveloped nations.

ACKNOWLEDGEMENTS

We would like to express our deepest gratitude to the GITAM School of Technology, Hyderabad for providing us with the necessary resources and facilities to conduct our study.

REFERENCES

[1]   A. Mukhtar, L. Xia, and T.B. Tang, "Vehicle detection techniques for collision avoidance systems: a review", *IEEE Transactions on Intelligent Transportation Systems,* vol. 16, no. 5, pp. 2318-2338, 2015.

[2]   S. Pendleton, H. Andersen, X. Du, X. Shen, M. Meghjani, Y. Eng, D. Rus, and M. Ang, "Perception, planning, control, and coordination for autonomous vehicles", *Machines,* vol. 5, no. 1, p. 6, 2017. [http://dx.doi.org/10.3390/machines5010006]

[3]   L.M. Clements, and K.M. Kockelman, "Economic effects of automated vehicles, Transportation Research Record", *Transp. Res. Rec.,* vol. 2606, no. 1, pp. 106-114, 2017. [http://dx.doi.org/10.3141/2606-14]

[4]   B. Bera, A.K. Das, and A.K. Sutrala, "Private blockchain-based access control mechanism for unauthorized UAV detection and mitigation in Internet of Drones environment", *Comput. Commun.,* vol. 166, pp. 91-109, 2021. [http://dx.doi.org/10.1016/j.comcom.2020.12.005]

[5]   Aleksandar petrovski, Marko Radovanovic, Aner Behlic, Application of drones with artificial intelligence for military purposes,International scientific conference on defence technology, pp. 92-100, 2022.

[6]   S. Lee, and Y. Choi, "Reviews of unmanned aerial vehicle (drone) technology trends and its applications in the mining industry", *Geosystem Engineering,* vol. 19, no. 4, pp. 197-204, 2016. [http://dx.doi.org/10.1080/12269328.2016.1162115]

[7]   S.D. Hogan, M. Kelly, B. Stark, and Y. Chen, "Unmanned aerial systems for agriculture and natural resources", *Calif. Agric.,* vol. 71, no. 1, pp. 5-14, 2017. [http://dx.doi.org/10.3733/ca.2017a0002]

[8]   D. Meng, Y. Xiao, Z. Guo, A. Jolfaei, L. Qin, X. Lu, and Q. Xiang, "A data-driven intelligent planning model for UAVs routing networks in mobile Internet of Things", *Comput. Commun.,* vol. 179, pp. 231-241, 2021. [http://dx.doi.org/10.1016/j.comcom.2021.08.014]

[9]   S. Singha, and B. Aydin, "Automated drone detection using YOLOv4", *Drones (Basel),* vol. 5, no. 3, p. 95, 2021. [http://dx.doi.org/10.3390/drones5030095]

[10]   R. Gupta, D. Reebadiya, and S. Tanwar, "6G-enabled edge intelligence for ultra-reliable low latency applications: Vision and mission", *Comput. Stand. Interfaces,* vol. 77, p. 103521, 2021. [http://dx.doi.org/10.1016/j.csi.2021.103521]

[11]   B. Vergouw, H. Nagel, G. Bondt, and B. Custers, *"Drone technology: Types, payloads, applications, frequency spectrum issues and future developments,"* in *Information Technology and Law Series.* T.M.C. Asser Press: The Hague, 2016, pp. 21-45.

[12]   T. Campi, S. Cruciani, and M. Feliziani, "Wireless power transfer technology applied to an autonomous electric UAV with a small secondary coil", *Energies,* vol. 11, no. 2, p. 352, 2018. [http://dx.doi.org/10.3390/en11020352]

[13]   Wireless power transmission: patent landscape analysis, 2020.

[14]　AirMed & Rescue. Available from: https://www.airmedandrescue.com

[15]　Drone Market Report, 2024, Drone Ind. Insights UG, Germany.

[16]　S.A.H. Mohsan, N.Q.H. Othman, Y. Li, M.H. Alsharif, and M.A. Khan, "Unmanned aerial vehicles (UAVs): practical aspects, applications, open challenges, security issues, and future trends", *Intell. Serv. Robot.*, vol. 16, no. 1, pp. 109-137, 2023.
[http://dx.doi.org/10.1007/s11370-022-00452-4] [PMID: 36687780]

[17]　M. S. Rauch, Drones in Military Warfare: The moral and emotional implications of an emerging technology, Acad. Manag. Proc., vol. no. 1, p. 10599. 2021.

[18]　B. Purahong, T. Anuwongpinit, A. Juhong, I. Kanjanasurat, and C. Pintaviooj, "Medical drone managing system for automated external defibrillator delivery service", *Drones (Basel),* vol. 6, no. 4, p. 93, 2022.
[http://dx.doi.org/10.3390/drones6040093]

[19]　I. Quintanilla García, N. Vera Vélez, P. Alcaraz Martínez, J. Vidal Ull, and B. Fernández Gallo, "A quickly deployed and UAS-based logistics network for delivery of critical medical goods during healthcare system stress periods: A real use case in Valencia (Spain)", *Drones (Basel),* vol. 5, no. 1, p. 13, 2021.
[http://dx.doi.org/10.3390/drones5010013]

[20]　S. Truog, L. Maxim, C. Matemba, C. Blauvelt, H. Ngwira, A. Makaya, S. Moreira, E. Lawrence, G. Ailstock, A. Weitz, M. West, and O. Defawe, "Insights before flights: How community perceptions can make or break medical drone deliveries", *Drones (Basel),* vol. 4, no. 3, p. 51, 2020.
[http://dx.doi.org/10.3390/drones4030051]

[21]　K.D. Bradley, "The good, the bad, and the future of drones in tactical/operational medicine", *J. Spec. Oper. Med.,* vol. 19, no. 4, pp. 91-93, 2019.
[http://dx.doi.org/10.55460/0U9U-GD66] [PMID: 31910479]

[22]　J. Li, B. Long, H. Wu, X. Hu, X. Wei, Z. Zhang, L. Chai, J. Xie, and H. Mei, "Rapid evaluation model of endurance performance and its application for agricultural UAVs", *Drones (Basel),* vol. 6, no. 8, p. 186, 2022.
[http://dx.doi.org/10.3390/drones6080186]

[23]　D. Keshet, A. Brook, D. Malkinson, I. Izhaki, and M. Charter, "The use of drones to determine rodent location and damage in agricultural crops", *Drones (Basel),* vol. 6, no. 12, p. 396, 2022.
[http://dx.doi.org/10.3390/drones6120396]

[24]　Sandhya Tarar and Namisha Bhasin, 2021, Fire Hazard Detection and Prediction by Machine Learning Techniques in Smart Buildings (SBs) Using Sensors and Unmanned Aerial Vehicles (UAVs), Digital Cities Roadmap:IoT-Based Architecture and Sustainable Buildings, (63–96) , 2021 Scrivener Publishing LLC.

[25]　B. Sazdić-Jotić, I. Pokrajac, J. Bajčetić, B. Bondžulić, and D. Obradović, "Single and multiple drones detection and identification using RF based deep learning algorithm", *Expert Syst. Appl.,* vol. 187, p. 115928, 2022.
[http://dx.doi.org/10.1016/j.eswa.2021.115928]

[26]　G. Vallathan, A. John, C. Thirumalai, S.K. Mohan, G. Srivastava, and J.C-W. Lin, "Suspicious activity detection using deep learning in secure assisted living IoT environments", *J. Supercomput.,* vol. 77, no. 4, pp. 3242-3260, 2021.
[http://dx.doi.org/10.1007/s11227-020-03387-8]

[27]　Luo, "Luo, F., Zhang, S., & Liu, M. Deep learning for object detection in aerial imagery", *Remote Sens.,* vol. 10, no. 4, p. 615, 2018.

[28]　Giattino, P., Savino, G., & Conte, D. , Machine learning for path planning of UAVs in disaster scenarios. IEEE Transactions on Intelligent Transportation Systems,2019, 20(10), 3824-3834.Liu et al., Liu, S., Zeng, X., Sun, Y., & Liu, Y., 2020, A survey of deep learning for remote sensing imagery.

Remote Sensing, 12(20), 3206.

[29] D. Andras, Z. Zsiborovszky, and I. Szalay, "Application of drone systems in precision agriculture", *Proceedings of the 13th International Conference on Precision Agriculture,* pp. 1006-1015, 2016.

[30] S. Hayek, H. Larijani, and B. Alavi, "Utilizing unmanned aerial vehicles (UAVs) for infrastructure inspection", *Autom. Construct.,* vol. 107, pp. 232-2, 2019.

[31] S. Swain, *Pabitra Mohan Khilar, Biswa Ranjan Senapati., A reinforcement learning-based cluster routing scheme with dynamic path planning for mutli-UAV network.* Elsevier, 2023, pp. 2214-2096.

[32] N.R. Kumar, "Use of next-gen technologies in rainfed agriculture Artificial Intelligence, Machine Learning and Drones", *Indian Farming,* vol. 75, no. 1, pp. 82-85, 2025.

[33] B. Singh, "Revolutionizing Supply Chains for Optimized Demand Planning, Inventory Management, and Logistics: An In-Depth Analysis of AI and ML Solutions in the Modern Era", *Supply Chain Transformation Through Generative AI and Machine Learning.* IGI Global Scientific Publishing, pp. 103-128, 2025.

[34] U. Ahmad, H. Song, A. Bilal, S. Mahmood, M. Alazab, A. Jolfaei , et al. 2021. A novel deep learning model to secure Internet of Things in healthcare. In Machine Intelligence and Big Data Analytics for Cybersecurity Applications (ed.). Springer, 2021, 341–353.
[http://dx.doi.org/10.1007/978-3-030-57024-8_15]

[35] G. Bathla, *Kishor Bhadane et al, Autonomous Vehicles and Intelligent Automation: Applications.* Challenges, and Opportunities, Hindawi Mobile Information Systems, 2022, pp. 1-31.

[36] S. Kaya, "Institute of Aeronautics and Applied Mechanics - Warsaw University of Technology, Z. Goraj, and Institute of Aeronautics and Applied Mechanics, "The use of drones in agricultural production,""", *Int. J. Innov. Approaches Agric. Res.,* vol. 4, no. 2, pp. 166-176, 2020.

[37] J. Fang, Y. Li, P.N. Ji, and T. Wang, "Drone detection and localization using enhanced fiber-optic acoustic sensor and distributed acoustic sensing technology", *J. Lightwave Technol.,* vol. 41, no. 3, pp. 822-831, 2023.
[http://dx.doi.org/10.1109/JLT.2022.3208451]

[38] M. Javaid, A. Haleem, I. H. Khan, R. P. Singh, R. Suman, and S. Mohan, "Significant features and applications of drones for healthcare: An overview," J. Ind. Integr. Manag., 2022.
[http://dx.doi.org/10.1142/S2424862222500245]

CHAPTER 11

An Expert System-Assisted AI Approach for Awareness and Prevention of Crimes against Women in India

Niranjan Panigrahi[1,*]

[1] *Parala Maharaja Engineering College, Berhampur, Odisha, India*

Abstract: The incorporation of Artificial Intelligence (AI) and its sub-domains for women's safety and security is a major requirement in the present technology-driven world. Most of the works in this context focus on leveraging Machine Learning (ML) technologies to predict harassment, violence, and other women-related crimes. However, ML approaches are mostly data-driven. In many poor and developing countries like India, where criminals' data are not well-documented and publicly unavailable, other alternative ways must be planned to prevent crimes against women. One feasible way is to spread awareness about laws and punishments related to women's crime using AI assistive technology. This will not only help to spread awareness about laws related to crimes against women but also help in preventing by creating fear of consequences for women-related crimes. In this context, a sub-domain of AI, known as a rule-based expert system, is proposed using a top-down inference method to help the user know about the penalty and legal action linked to the crime committed against women in India as per Indian legislative laws. Initially, a comprehensive set of 77 rules is collected from legal domain experts to design the knowledge base (KB) of the proposed expert system. For rapid prototyping, the proposed system is implemented in ES-Builder, an open-source, web-based expert system shell. To check the efficacy of the system, extensive testing of the system has been carried out by querying the expert system, which shows the desired results.

Keywords: Crimes against women, Expert system, Expert system shell, ES-builder, Indian penal code.

INTRODUCTION

A recent survey report by the World Health Organization (WHO) depicts that about one in three women globally suffer from violence directly or indirectly in their lifetime [1].

* **Corresponding author Niranjan Panigrahi:** Parala Maharaja Engineering College, Berhampur, Odisha, India; E-mail: niranjan.cse@pmec.ac.in

Asif Khan, Mohammad Kamrul Hasan, Naushad Varish & Mohammed Aslam Husain (Eds.)

This is an act of crime against women. This happens to the women who are close to their friends, relatives, and colleagues directly or by unknown persons indirectly in the society. India, though known for respecting women from ancient times, is in no way away from women-related crimes [2]. As per the recent report, India stood ninth among the world's most dangerous countries for women. It is fifth in case of violence by intimates and ranks first in the gender inequality index. So, preventing women's crime in the prevailing society is of foremost importance for their safety and healthy living in a society.

One feasible way to prevent women-related crimes is to spread awareness about laws and punishments related to women's crimes using AI assistive technology [3]. This will not only help to spread awareness about laws related to crimes against women but also help in preventing them by creating a fear of the consequences for women-related crimes. To automate the awareness and prevention of crime against women, AI approaches have shown significant contributions. Most of the works in this context focus on leveraging Machine Learning (ML) technologies to predict harassment, violence, and other women-related crimes [3, 4]. However, ML approaches are mostly data-driven. In many under-developed and developing countries like India, where criminals' data are not well-documented and publicly unavailable, other alternative ways must be planned to prevent crimes against women. One such field of AI is a rule-based expert system, which has been used successfully for various purposes [5 - 7].

In this paper, a rule-based expert system is proposed, based on a decision tree based top-down inference method, to help the user know about the penalty and legal action linked to the crime committed against women in India as per Indian legislative laws. The major contributions of this paper are as follows:

i. A novel rule-based expert system is proposed to spread awareness and thus prevent crimes against women in India
ii. A comprehensive set of 77 rules is collected from legal domain experts to design the proposed expert system and the rules are categorized as per age group to avoid noisy conclusions.
iii. A rapid prototyping of the system is carried out using ES-Builder, a web-based expert system shell, and the correctness of the system is tested with a series of questionnaires.

The rest of the paper is organized as follows. Section 2 presents a brief overview of IPC sections related to crimes against women and related work.

Section 3 gives the proposed system followed by implementation and testing in section 4. Section 5 concludes with future work.

BACKGROUND INVESTIGATION

This section briefly highlights the different IPCs on crimes against women in India and some important works in this field.

Crimes against Women and Indian Penal Code: A Brief

Indian Penal Code (IPC) is the official criminal code of India with a very clear and vivid objective. The objective of the Indian Penal Code is to provide a general solution and penalties to the citizens of India. These penalties are not subject to any privileges and shall treat people of all categories the very same. The IPC has several rules and regulations which have the whole penalty of crime pre-determined. These sets of rules are subject to change, and that is known to be the amendment acts. Every set of rules and regulations is subject to a lot of exceptions and is prone to be misused when used for the safeguard of women only. However, these rules establish the whole basis of the judicial system of this country. A summary of the crimes that occur against the women and the corresponding IPC is given in Table **1** [8].

Table 1. Penalty details of crime categories against women in India.

Crimes	Sections of IPC
For medical termination of pregnancy with or without consent.	Section 312 | Section 313
For committing rape in its various forms and cases.	Section 375 | Section 376
Kidnapping and Abduction cases of minor and major-aged women.	Section 363| Section 366A | Section 366B | Section 367 | Section 368 Section 369
Trafficking of one or more minor or major-aged women.	Section 370
Committing marital offense and torture to women.	Section 498A
Cases of molestation, stalking, voyeurism and sexual assault.	Section 354| Section 354A| Section 354B| Section 354C| Section 354D
Acid Attack	Section 326
Culpable homicide and Dowry Death	Section 304
Cases of Domestic Violence	Domestic Violence Prevention Act 2005
Child Labor	Child Labor Prohibition and Regulation Act
Child Marriage	Child Marriage Prevention Act

However, the common public and criminals are mostly unaware of IPC rules and penalties.

In this paper, an attempt has been made to collect and incorporate some important IPC rules and corresponding penalties for crimes against women in India in a rule-based expert system to spread awareness in public and fear among criminals, thus, preventing the crimes to some extent.

Related Works

In the last few decades, the rise in women-related crimes has been a topic of worry both for the victims, the administration and an area of concern for researchers of different domains. To prevent it, several AI-driven proposals are being developed by the research community in recent years. The authors [9] proposed an integrated expert system to establish security for working women and children. Similarly, the work in [10] is to establish quality decision making using expert system on crime against women in Indian judicial system.

In a study [11,12], the authors studied domestic violence on women in Liberia and compared a set of machine learning algorithms to predict vulnerability of domestic violence. The authors in another study [13, 14, 18] focused on analyzing textual content on social media for Iranian women and proposed a machine learning approach to predict the risk of domestic violence.

A hybrid approach using machine learning and sentiment analysis is proposed [15, 16] to analyze women harassment in Middle Eastern literature. A novel approach using machine learning techniques, based on EEG and blink signals of eye has also been proposed [17, 18, 19] for women safety. Some authors [19-21] proposed a method to detect harassment on women, based on Twitter data during period of pandemic by incorporating machine learning approach.

In summary, the recent state-of-the-art methods related to women's crimes are based on data-oriented machine learning approaches to predict violence or harassment but fail to spread awareness or prevent crimes against women. Keeping this as the motivation for this work, the present work focuses on spreading laws and punishments related to women's crime using AI assistive technology. This will not only help to spread awareness about laws related to crimes against women but also helps in preventing it by creating the fear of consequences on women-related crimes. In this context, a sub-domain of AI, known as rule-based expert system, is proposed using top-down inference method, to help the user know about the penalty and legal action linked to the crime committed against women in India as per Indian legislative laws.

PROPOSED APPROACH

This section presents briefly about preliminaries of expert system, the problem description and proposed architecture, rule set, Knowledge base (KB), and inference mechanism used in designing the proposed system.

Preliminaries

Expert system is a sub-domain of AI which has a very strong utilization in early timeline of AI. It is mostly suitable for decision-making process in a data-restricted environment by using a set of well-defined rules extracted from human expert in a particular domain. It is developed using three major components; the user interface (UI), inference engine (IE), and the knowledge-base (KB) [11]. The UI is used by the end-user for interacting with the expert system through a set of questionnaires to obtain the support and possible decisions. The IE uses either forward reasoning, also known as top-down approach or backward reasoning,

also known as bottom-up approach, to make a decision using the set of rules embedded in the background KB. The KB is created by knowledge engineer by interacting with a human domain expert and representing the acquired knowledge from human expert using suitable knowledge representation methods. Some well-known knowledge representation methods used for KB creation are frame-based, rule-based, and semantic net-based [12].

The overall expert system development can be possible by selecting suitable development tools. It may be a general-purpose software development tool or using expert system shell. An expert system shell is an existing prototype with built-in UI and IE and an empty KB. The only part to be created in this process is to design the KB depending on the domain of the problem. Hence, the development time and cost are normally reduced in case of using a shell for expert system development. Some well-known expert system shells are: CLIPS, JESS, ES-Builder, and Vidwan [13].

Using the above preliminaries as base for developing the required expert system-assisted AI framework for awareness and prevention of crimes against women in India, the following section presents the problem description in a formal way and proposes the system architecture to be followed.

The problem of designing a rule-based expert system for awareness and prevention of crimes against women can be formally represented as follows.

Given the input set, I= {I1, I2,…,In}, it is required to design an expert system that can infer and suggest the output set, O= {O1, O2, …, On}.

where I= set of possible women-related crimes, O= set of penalties and actions as per IPC of India.

The overall design of the proposed system is based on the architectural framework as given in Fig. (**1**). The system is proposed to be developed using expert system shell for rapid prototyping. The major phase involves creating a knowledgebase (KB) by consulting legal domain experts and other reliable sources. The knowledge thus acquired is represented using rule-based knowledge representation technique.

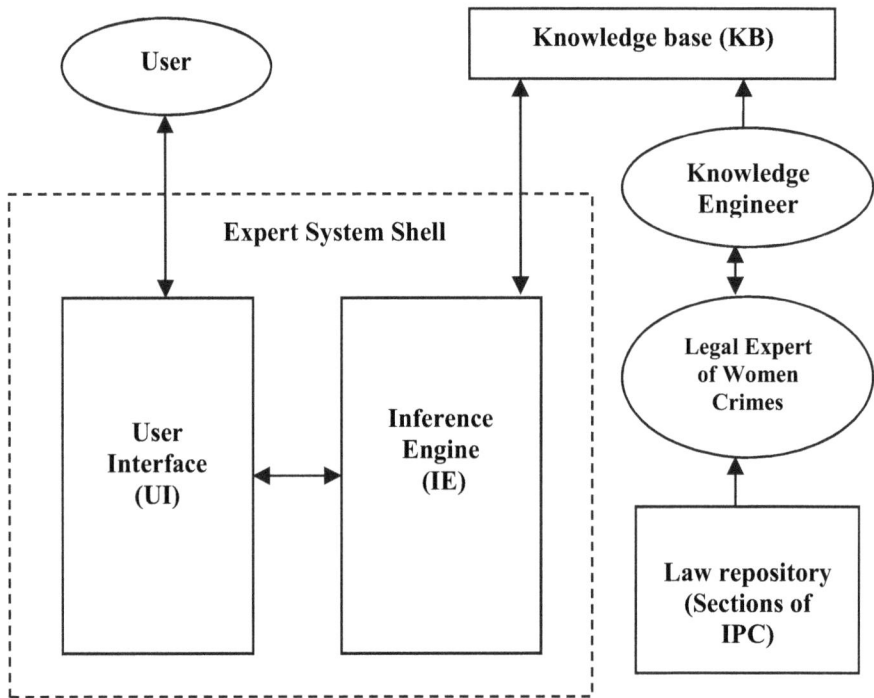

Fig. (1). Proposed architecture of expert system for awareness & prevention of women crimes.

Rule-set and KB

The knowledge-base (KB) contains the rule set derived from various reliable sources like consulting legal experts and IPC documents [8]. A rule set is created by collecting 77 rules. The rules are represented using production rules knowledge representation technique, based on IF-THEN structure. A sample set of 20 rules is presented in Table **2**.

Table 2. Sample set of 20 rules.

IF attribute pre-Birth **AND** crime committed? Abortion/Miscarriage? **AND** status of consent? With consent? **AND** type of Abortion? spontaneous/Natural **THEN** the most liable punishment is **The Miscarriage was legitimate!**	**IF** attribute pre-Birth **AND** crime committed? Abortion/Miscarriage? **AND** status of consent? With consent? **AND** type of Abortion? therapeutic **THEN** the most liable punishment is **Carried to safeguard lives of mother and unborn child.**
IF attribute pre-Birth **AND** crime committed? Abortion/Miscarriage?	**IF** attribute pre-Birth **AND** crime committed? Abortion/Miscarriage?
AND status of consent? Without consent? **AND** type of Abortion? therapeutic **THEN** the most liable punishment is **Carried to safeguard lives of mother and** **unborn child.**	**AND** status of consent? Without consent? **AND** type of Abortion? induced **THEN** the most liable punishment is **Section 313, Imprisonment for Life or 10** **Years + Fine.**
IF attribute pre-Birth **AND** crime committed? Abortion/Miscarriage? **AND** status of consent? With consent? **AND** type of Abortion? induced **AND** phase of gestation? Early Miscarriage? **THEN** the most liable punishment is **Section 312, 3 Years or Fine or Both.**	**IF** attribute pre-Birth **AND** crime committed? Abortion/Miscarriage? **AND** status of consent? With consent? **AND** type of Abortion? induced **AND** phase of gestation? Was the woman was quick with the child? **THEN** the most liable punishment is **Section 312, 7 Years + Fine.**
IF attribute formative **AND** crime committed? rape **THEN** the most liable punishment is **Rigorous Imprisonment for 20 years to** **life-Imprisonment+fine**	**IF** attribute formative **AND** crime committed? Physical and mental torture **THEN** the most liable punishment is **POSCO laws!**
IF attribute formative **AND** crime committed? murder **THEN** the most liable punishment is **Lifetime imprisonment to hang till** **death.**	**IF** attribute formative **AND** crime committed? kidnap and Abduction **AND** specificity? From India/unlawful guardianship? **THEN** the most liable punishment is **Section 363,7 Years + Fine**
IF attribute formative **AND** crime committed? Kidnap and abduction **AND** specificity? Procuration of a minor **THEN** the most liable punishment is **Section 366A,10 Years + Fine**	**IF** attribute formative **AND** crime committed? Kidnap and Abduction **AND** specificity? importation from foreign land, **THEN** the most liable punishment is **Section 366B 10 Years + Fine.**

IF attribute formative **AND** crime committed? kidnap and Abduction **AND** specificity? girls of <10 years with intent to steal **THEN** the most liable punishment is **Section 369 7 Years + Fine.**	**IF** attribute formative **AND** crime committed? Kidnap and Abduction **AND** specificity? Wrongfully confine **THEN** the most liable punishment is **Section 368, 7 Years + fine.**
IF attribute formative **AND** crime committed? Kidnap and abduction **AND** specificity? girls of <10 years with intent to steal **THEN** the most liable punishment is **Section 369 7 Years + Fine.**	**IF** attribute formative **AND** crime committed? kKidnap and abduction **AND** specificity? Wrongfully confine **THEN** the most liable punishment is **Section 368, 7 Years + fine.**
IF attribute youth years **AND** which are the crime they face in youth? child labor **THEN** the most liable punishment is **Child labor prevention, regulation act, 2 month-3yr+ 20k-50kfine.**	**IF** attribute youth years **AND** which are the crime they face in youth? Rape **AND** rape is committed to the victim by? people except them in Section-2 **AND** specificity of this Section yes **THEN** the most liable punishment is **Section 376 and attempt to murder with Imprisonment not <20 yrs.**
IF attribute youth years **AND** what are the crimes they face in youth? Rape **AND** rape is committed to the victim by? people except them in Section-2 **AND the** specificity of this Section no **THEN** the most liable punishment is **Only section 376, imprisonment not <10 Year's fine.**	**IF** attribute youth years **AND** what are the crimes they face in youth? Rape **AND** rape is committed to the victim by? Others **AND** what Kind? by any kind of person in authority, **THEN** the most liable punishment is **Section 376C, 6-10 yrs. imprisonment +fine.**
IF attribute youth years **AND** what are the crimes they face in youth? Rape **AND** rape is committed to the victim by? Others **AND** what Kind? gang Rape **THEN** the most liable punishment is **Section 376D, not <20yrs imprisonment+fine.**	**IF** attribute youth years **AND** what are the crimes they face in youth? Rape **AND** rape is committed to the victim by? Others **AND** what Kind? repeat offender **THEN** the most liable punishment is **Section 376E, Lifetime Imprisonment fine.**

Inference Engine

The decision tree based top-down approach is used to infer the conclusions where the conclusions are the penalties against particular crime under IPC. The decision tree was made after filling its nodes (attributes) with age group, crimes and conclusions with corresponding sections of IPC, which deals with that particular crime at the leaf level as shown in Fig. (**2**). The conclusions are reached based on forward chaining mechanism on the proposed decision tree.

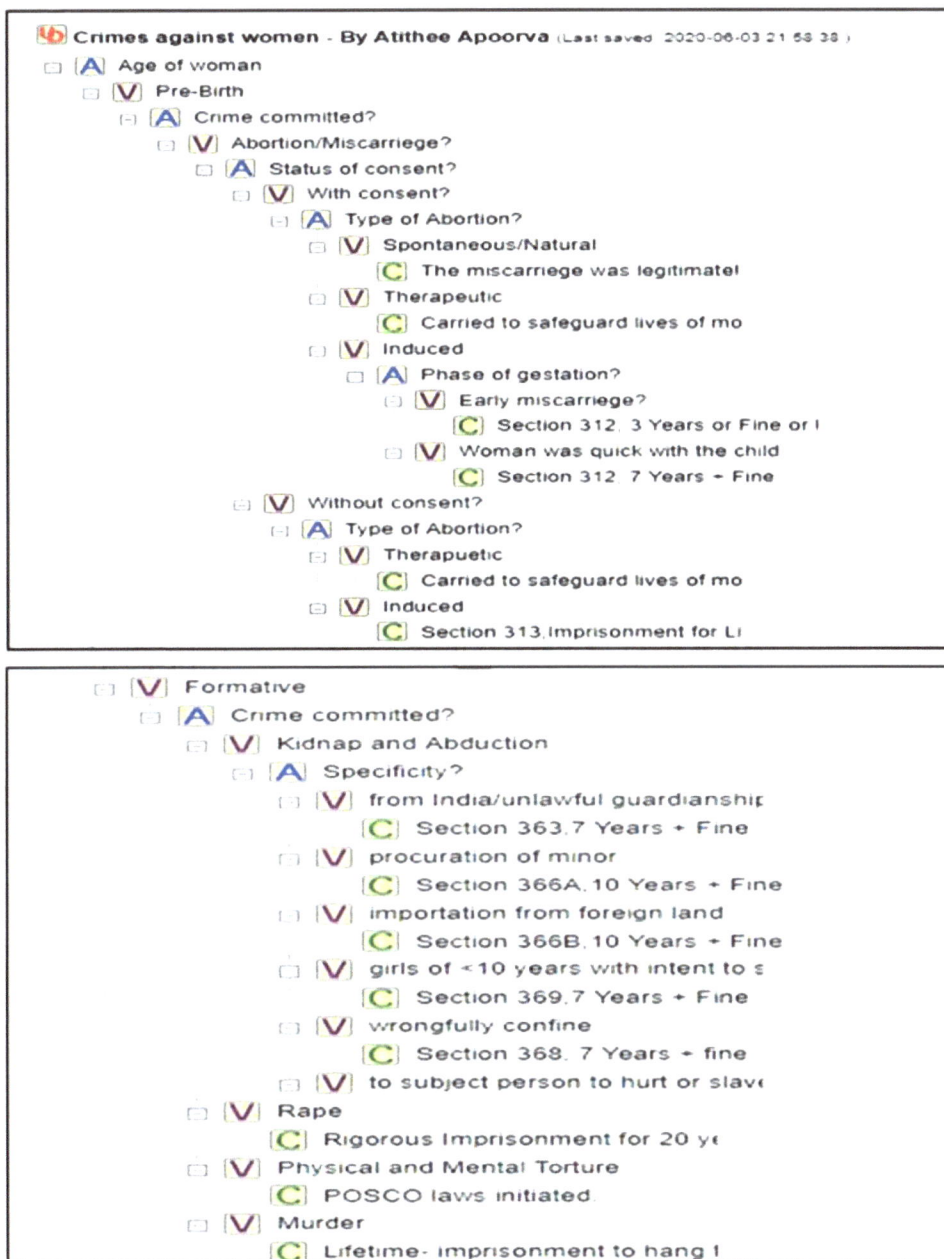

Fig. (2). A part of the proposed decision tree based top down approach for inference in the proposed system.

IMPLEMENTATION AND TESTING

Implementation

The proposed system is implemented in ES-builder [14], a web-based expert system shell. Fig. (**3**) shows the snapshots of testing the proposed system in ES-builder. The snapshots show one of the crime types, *i.e.*, abortion/miscarriage and its decision history as an explanation generated for the crime.

Testing

To test the efficacy and acceptance of the proposed system, technology acceptance testing is performed, which is mostly followed to evaluate expert system [22]. According to the chosen domain, a set of questionnaires is prepared to assess the user's satisfaction level. The questionnaires are based on some usage-related factors and domain-specific factors, which will decide the user's acceptability of the system. The user satisfaction level is decided following the standard Likert scale, varying from 0-5. The set of questionnaires is given below.

Q1: User-friendliness of the interface for interaction with the system

Q2: Satisfaction of explanations generated by the system

Q3: Language of interaction is easy to comprehend

Q4: Coverage of different age group of female

Q5: Coverage of potential crimes related to women

Q6: Coverage of feasible IPC sections related to women

Q7: Punishments related to different IPC are clearly mentioned

A survey was conducted online by distributing the web link of the developed expert system and the questionnaires to law students and law-practitioners who have knowledge about women-related crimes. A total of 38 responses are received, which are summarized in Table **3**.

Table 3. Count and percentage of responses on technology acceptance testing.

Q/Likert scale	0-NA		1-Totally disagree		2-Disagree		3-Neither agree/disagree		4-Agree		5-Totally agree		Total	
Freq.(F) & %	F	%	F	%	F	%	F	%	F	%	F	%	F	%
Q1	-	-	-	-	-	-	04	10.5	13	34.21	21	55.26	38	100
Q2	-	-	-	-	-	-	03	7.89	14	36.84	21	55.26	38	100
Q3	-	-	-	-	-	-	03	7.89	14	36.84	21	55.26	38	100
Q4	-	-	01	2.63	02	5.26	01	2.63	11	28.94	23	60.52	38	100
Q5	05	13.15	06	15.78	10	26.31	02	5.26	10	26.31	05	13.15	38	100
Q6	-	-	-	-	07	18.42	01	2.63	15	39.47	15	39.47	38	100
Q7	-	-	-	-	-	-	-	-	17	44.73	21	55.26	38	100

It can be observed from Table **3** that around 89.47% of responses agreed or totally agreed on the user-friendliness of the designed system, and approximately 92.1% are satisfied with the explanation generated by the system and the language of explanation. Similarly, 89.46% are agreed on the coverage of all age group of female. There are some responses of disagree or NA on query Q5, which is related to coverage of potential crimes related to women. This

is because all crimes are presently not recorded as rules in the KB of the proposed expert system which will be taken care in future work.

CONCLUSION AND FUTURE WORK

Awareness leads to prevention. Based on this philosophy, an attempt has been made in this paper to automate the awareness and prevention of crime against women in India using one sub-domain of AI, which is called expert system. A rule-based expert system is proposed, based on decision tree-based top-down inference method, to help the user know about the penalty and legal action linked to the crime committed against women in India as per IPC. The present work is restricted to a limited set of rules as per the Indian Penal Code. In future work, it can be extended by enhancing the rule-set and considering case-based reasoning for better inference.

ACKNOWLEDGEMENT

I would like to thank my B. Tech student, Atithee Apoorva, for carrying out the implementation of this work, using ES-Builder, a web based expert system shell.

REFERENCES

[1]   https://www.who.int/news-room/fact-sheets/detail/violence-against-women

[2]   U. Gupta, and R. Sharma, "Analysis of criminal spatial events in India using exploratory data analysis and regression", *Computers and Electrical Engineering,* vol. 109, p. 108761, 2023.

[3]   F. Dakalbab, M. Abu Talib, O. Abu Waraga, A. Bou Nassif, S. Abbas, and Q. Nasir, "Artificial intelligence & crime prediction: A systematic literature review", *Social Sciences & Humanities Open,* vol. 6, no. 2022, p. 100342, 2022.
        [http://dx.doi.org/10.1016/j.ssaho.2022.100342]

[4]   T.C. King, N. Aggarwal, M. Taddeo, and L. Floridi, "Artificial Intelligence Crime: An Interdisciplinary Analysis of Foreseeable Threats and Solutions", *Sci. Eng. Ethics,* vol. 26, no. 1, pp. 89-120, 2020.
        [http://dx.doi.org/10.1007/s11948-018-00081-0] [PMID: 30767109]

[5]   H.K. Jabbar, and R.Z. Khan, "Survey on development of expert system in the areas of Medical, Education, Automobile and Agriculture", *2nd International Conference on Computing for Sustainable Global Development (INDIACom), New Delhi, India,* pp. 776-780, 2015.

[6]   Mohammad Farajollahi, "Expert System Application in law: A review of research and applications", *International Journal of Nonlinear Analysis and Applications,* 2023.
        [http://dx.doi.org/10.22075/ijnaa.2023.31260.4596]

[7]   S.V. Menon, and N.E. Allen, "The Formal Systems Response to Violence Against Women in India: A Cultural Lens", *Am. J. Community Psychol.,* vol. 62, no. 1-2, pp. 51-61, 2018.
        [http://dx.doi.org/10.1002/ajcp.12249] [PMID: 29693250]

[8]   https://loksabhadocs.nic.in/Refinput/New_Reference_Notes/English/Crimeagainstwomen

[9]   "Dr. Nishamol M S, Drisya A, Noor Muhammad S, Renuka M, Anish S M, Jithin Prasad, 2019, Expert System based Women and Child Security System", *Int. J. Eng. Res. Technol. (Ahmedabad),* vol. 08, no. 11, 2019. [IJERT].

[10]   J.S. Jadhav, K.M. Nalawade, and M.M. Bapat, "Rule based expert system application for crime against women law in Indian judicial system", *IOSR Journal Of Humanities And Social Science,* vol. 16, no. 6, pp. 19-22, 2013.
        [http://dx.doi.org/10.9790/0837-1661922]

[11]   R.S. Hingole, Fundamentals of Expert System.*Advances in Metal Forming. Springer Series in Materials Science.* vol. Vol. 206. Springer: Berlin, Heidelberg, 2015.
        [http://dx.doi.org/10.1007/978-3-662-44497-9_3]

[12]   S.Y. Choi, and S.H. Kim, "Knowledge Acquisition and Representation for High-Performance Building Design: A Review for Defining Requirements for Developing a Design Expert System", *Sustainability (Basel),* vol. 13, no. 9, p. 4640, 2021.
        [http://dx.doi.org/10.3390/su13094640]

[13]   H.K. Jabbar, and R.Z. Khan, "Tools of development of expert systems: A comparative study", *3rd International Conference on Computing for Sustainable Global Development (INDIACom), New Delhi, India,* pp. 3947-3952, 2016.

[14]   https://www.mcgoo.com.au/esbuilder/index.php'

[15]   H. Vyawahare, S. Khandelwal, and S. Rathod, Artificial Intelligence in Detecting and Preventing Online Harassment.*AI Tools and Applications for Women's Safety.,* S. Ponnusamy, V. Bora, P. Daigavane, S. Wazalwar, Eds., IGI Global, 2024, pp. 14-35.
        [http://dx.doi.org/10.4018/979-8-3693-1435-7.ch002]

[16]   *2022 Second International Conference on Advanced Technologies in Intelligent Control, Environment, Computing & Communication Engineering (ICATIECE),* 2022pp. 1-5 Bangalore, India.
        [http://dx.doi.org/10.1109/ICATIECE56365.2022.10047377]

[17] R. Rahman, M.N.A. Khan, S.S. Sara, M.A. Rahman, and Z.I. Khan, "A comparative study of machine learning algorithms for predicting domestic violence vulnerability in Liberian women", *BMC Womens Health,* vol. 23, no. 1, p. 542, 2023.
[http://dx.doi.org/10.1186/s12905-023-02701-9] [PMID: 37848839]

[18] M. Salehi, S. Ghahari, M. Hosseinzadeh, and L. Ghalichi, "Domestic violence risk prediction in Iran using a machine learning approach by analyzing Persian textual content in social media", *Heliyon,* vol. 9, no. 5, 2023.
[http://dx.doi.org/10.1016/j.heliyon.2023.e15667]

[19] H.Q. Low, P. Keikhosrokiani, and M. Pourya Asl, "Decoding violence against women: analysing harassment in middle eastern literature with machine learning and sentiment analysis", *Humanities and Social Sciences Communications,* vol. 11, no. 1, p. 497, 2024.
[http://dx.doi.org/10.1057/s41599-024-02908-7]

[20] K. Shanmuga Priya, S. Vasanthi, R. Nithyanandhan, G. Vinoth Chakkaravarthy, P. Golda Jeyasheeli, M. Karthiga, and C. Pandi, "Blink talk: A machine learning-based method for women safety using EEG and eye blink signals", *Measurement: Sensors,* vol. 28, p. 100810, 2023.
[http://dx.doi.org/10.1016/j.measen.2023.100810]

[21] W.N.A.W. Mustapha, N.M. Sabri, N.A.A.A. Bakar, N.M.N. Daud, and A. Azizan, "Detection of Harassment Toward Women in Twitter During Pandemic Based on Machine Learning", *Int. J. Adv. Comput. Sci. Appl.,* vol. 15, no. 3, 2024. [IJACSA].
[http://dx.doi.org/10.14569/IJACSA.2024.01503103]

[22] P. Miranda, P. Isaias, and M. Crisóstomo, Evaluation of Expert Systems: The Application of a Reference Model to the Usability Parameter.*Universal Access in Human-Computer Interaction. Design for All and eInclusion. UAHCI 2011.,* C. Stephanidis, Ed., vol. 6765. Springer: Berlin, Heidelberg, 2011.Lecture Notes in Computer Science
[http://dx.doi.org/10.1007/978-3-642-21672-5_12]

CHAPTER 12

EfficientNet B0 Model Architecture for Brain Tumor Detection and Classification Using CNN

Vendra Durga Ratna Kumar[1,*], Fadzai Ethel Muchina[1], Md Muzakkir Hussain[1] and **Priyanka Singh[1]**

[1] *Department of Computer Science and Engineering, SRM University, AP-Andhra Pradesh, India*

Abstract: Brain tumors are a life-threatening disease, and a lot of people are losing their lives. These brain tumors are abnormal cells that develop in and around the brain. This research explores the cutting edge of medical imaging processing, focusing on enhancing the detection and categorization of brain tumors. EfficientNetB0 is the most advanced deep learning architecture that has been thoroughly compared with other deep learning models in order to improve brain tumor classification accuracy using the Kaggle MRI image dataset with 7023 images. The drawbacks of manual tumor identification techniques are discussed, and precise classification using deep neural networks is proposed, with special attention to the transition from binary to multi-classification. This chapter's primary focus is on improving and optimizing the EfficientNetB0 model through the addition of trainable layers on top of its basic architecture. Several techniques are used like global average pooling for spatial and dimensionality reduction with reduced parameters, dropout to drop layers, and dense net with softmax for multiclass classification. Concurrently, strategic layer freezing is used to refine the deep learning models for foundation design. The results show that the finetuned EfficientNetB0 model with hyper-parameter optimization guarantees exceptional brain tumor accuracy. EfficientNetB0 has achieved a good accuracy of 99.7% and a precision of 99.5% compared to Resnet50, VGG16, InceptionV3 and Xception. This work presents a unique deep-learning method in accordance with a transfer learning strategy for assessing brain cancer categorization accuracy using the enhanced ResNet50 model. As we advance the state-of-the-art, this chapter offers researchers, medical professionals, and patients a solid foundation for accurate and timely brain tumor diagnoses, thus contributing to the research community.

Keywords: Brain tumor, Classification, Deep learning, EfficientNetB0, Hyper-parameter.

---

[*] **Corresponding author Vendra Durga Ratna Kumar:** Department of Computer Science and Engineering, SRM University, AP-Andhra Pradesh, India; E-mail: vendradurga_ratnakumar@srmap.edu.in

Asif Khan, Mohammad Kamrul Hasan, Naushad Varish & Mohammed Aslam Husain (Eds.)

INTRODUCTION

Medical image analysis is at the cutting edge of technological developments aimed at transforming healthcare diagnostics. Primary brain tumors begin development inside the brain, whereas secondary brain tumors spread outside. Brain tumors are classified into glioma, pituitary, and meningioma using deep learning frameworks [1] as shown in Fig. (**1**). Brain tumors are complex in nature and can have potentially fatal outcomes, so it is essential to classify them precisely and effectively to provide personalized treatment regimens and correct diagnoses. The Cancer Society of America estimates that in 2023, brain and CNS (central nervous system) cancers will take the lives of about 18,600 people and 3,460 youngsters under the age threshold of fifteen. The survival rate for patients with brain tumors is disheartening, with only 42% surviving for five years and 36% surviving for ten years [2]. Traditional manual tumor detection methods are inherently laborious, handcrafted [3], and prone to errors, underscoring the need for advanced computer methodologies. As a subset of deep learning, convolutional neural network models (CNNs) have become highly efficient models able to automate the complex process of classifying brain tumors [4]. To improve the precision of brain tumor identification, this chapter compares and contrasts cutting-edge deep learning architectures like EfficientNetB0. This chapter's primary concern is implementing the switch from traditional binary classification techniques to a multiclass framework. Brain tumors have complex tissue compositions, a range of developmental patterns, and numerous cell sources. It becomes essential to move to multiclass classification to provide precise diagnoses and guide the right medical interventions.

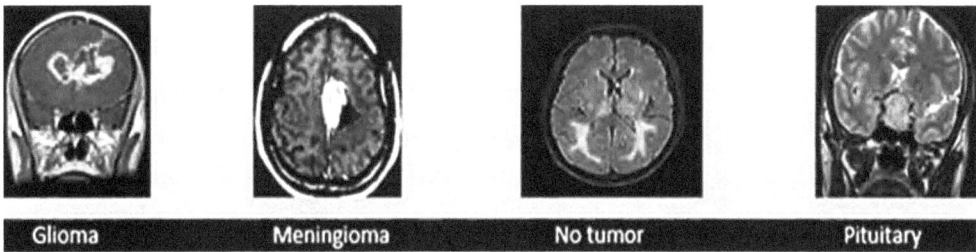

Fig. (1). Various types of brain tumors.

In our analysis, EfficientNetB0 assumes a central role and suggests optimizing its architecture, making every layer trainable, and adding new layers above the fundamental structure. Carefully adjusting hyper-parameters [5] further guarantees the best performance of EfficientNetB0 models, which helps reach the main goal of improving the accuracy of brain tumor classification [6]. Our research extends beyond methodological advancements. We utilize a comprehensive dataset comprising 7,023 images across four distinct tumor classes, providing a robust foundation for evaluating the EfficientNetB0 architecture. The Brain Tumor MRI dataset, sourced from Kaggle, facilitates a thorough comparative study. This chapter provides the scientific community with important insights as we push the boundaries of medical image analysis, providing a thorough understanding of EfficientNetB0's performance in the challenging job of neurological tumor classification. By combining methodological refinement with a diverse dataset, we aim to provide researchers, medical professionals, and ultimately patients with a reliable foundation for accurate and timely brain tumor diagnoses. But rather than focusing on segmentation, we are more interested in categorizing techniques in this chapter, which are grounded on the concept of transfer learning. The two main categories of these associations are approaches that are organized and those that are not. Using a mapping function to determine the input components in relation to their corresponding output labels, the methodology is applied in supervised techniques to evaluate new topic labels. Learning about trained data and its inherent tendencies through the use of techniques like artificial neural networks is the main objective [7]. Despite the numerous attempts made by researchers to identify cancers from MRI images, there are still several shortcomings (*i.e.*, poor accuracy, large, sluggish models, and expensive processing costs). Furthermore, the healthcare industry has long faced difficulties with larger data sets since patients' privacy concerns prevent researchers from disclosing medical information in an open manner. Moreover, the current methods' poor recall and accuracy levels lead to low efficiency and longer processing times for image classification, which may cause the patient's course of treatment to be delayed [8]. Recent research has employed deep learning to increase the efficacy of computer-assisted medical diagnostics in the study of brain cancer.

Problem Statement

Brain tumors present a critical challenge in medical image analysis due to their diverse cell sources, varied development patterns, and potentially life-threatening consequences. Traditional binary classification methods have proven insufficient in addressing the complexity and diversity of brain tumors, emphasizing the need for a robust multiclass classification framework. Convolutional neural network networks (CNNs), in particular, are automated methods based on deep learning and machine learning that have shown promise as solutions. This study specifically focuses on advancing brain tumor classification using the state-of-t-e-art deep learning architecture, EfficientNetB0 to enhance accuracy and provide valuable insights into their performance on a complex medical image classification task.

Challenges Associated with Traditional Approaches to Brain Tumor Classification

- Selection and Extraction of Features- Deep learning simplifies the process of manually extracting features, as it can recognize intricate patterns from unprocessed data, unlike traditional methods.
- Limited Generalization - CNNs and other deep learning models are very good at tolerating changes in imaging modalities and generalizing across a wide range of datasets.
- Inter-observer Variability - By training from consistent descriptions on huge data sets, deep learning mitigates the effects caused by human variability in medical image interpretation.
- Managing Complex Relationships- Medical images contain complex patterns and sophisticated spatial correlations that are well captured by deep learning models.
- Data-Intensive Nature -Given the high dimensionality of medical image issues related to classification, deep learning models are well-suited for processing large-scale datasets in an effective manner.

Literature Review

Advancements in medical image analysis, particularly the application of deep learning techniques [7], have significantly influenced the landscape of brain tumor classification. The complex nature of brain tumors, coupled with the critical need for accurate diagnosis and treatment planning, has driven researchers to explore innovative methodologies to enhance classification algorithms. Historically, binary classification methods have been the cornerstone of brain tumor detection, distinguishing between the presence or absence of tumors [8].

However, the limitations of these methods have become apparent as brain tumors encompass various tissue types and exhibit diverse characteristics. To address these complexities, a paradigm shift towards multiclass classification has gained prominence in recent research endeavors. The application of CNN in medical image analysis has emerged as a transformative approach. CNNs leverage deep learning to automatically extract intricate features from medical images, offering a more efficient and reliable alternative to traditional feature extraction methods [9]. This shift has significantly improved the accuracy of brain tumor classification, laying the foundation for advancements in the field of medical science.

Researchers have proposed automated techniques for brain tumor identification based on machine learning and deep learning models [10]. Researchers examined Xception, InceptionV3, InceptionResNetV2 MobileNetV2, EfficientNetB0, Generic CNN, and ResNet50. With an overall accuracy of 97.12%, InceptionV3 emerged as the top-performing CNN-based model in this comparison. In the study [11], optimized EfficientNet-B0 classification and detection accuracy was 98.87% outperforming InceptionV3, VGG16, Xception, ResNet50, and InceptionRes-NetV2. A novel hybrid approach is put forth in [12] for the classification of brain tumors, utilizing machine learning (ML) methods for classification and a special CNN framework for feature extraction. The hybrid model outperformed other hybrid models with an outstanding 97.15% mean accuracy and showed remarkable time simplicity over a 67-minute categorization process.

Excellent results were obtained by refined EfficientNetB2 [8], with test accuracy of 98.86%, precision of 98.65%, recall of 98.77%, and F1-score of 98.71%. Strong generalization is demonstrated by the model, which is lightweight and computationally efficient. The author's High accuracy was attained [12] with the fine-tuning and evaluation of a bespoke pre-trained. EfficientNetB7 model (CPEB7), with results for meningioma reaching 98.57%, pituitary 98.97%, and glioma 99.38%. With a misclassification rate of 1.02% and an MIOU of 95.73%, overall accuracy was 98.97%. With a 99.097% accuracy rate on fold-5 in cross-validation with k-folds, the model outperformed previous techniques. Among the 26 CNN models tested [13], EfficientNetB3 fared better, identifying brain tumor types with an accuracy of 98.98%. High accuracy was also attained by EfficientNetB2, DenseNet121, EfficientNetB5, and EfficientNetB4, all of which were above 97%.

The choice of architecture is critical to the performance of the EfficientNetB0 model, which has shown promise in the classification of brain tumors in medical image analysis. Unique in its scaling approach, EfficientNetB0 balances depth, width, and resolution for medical imaging tasks that are resource-constrained [13]. It is built for maximum efficiency. The goal of this work is to improve the efficiency and accuracy of brain tumor identification by fine-tuning and contrasting Efficient-NetB0.

Methodology

In the sections that follow, the suggested model with its many layers and pre-trained algorithms to improve brain tumor classification accuracy and efficiency will be covered. Fig. (1) illustrates how the proposed model goes through a preprocessing phase in which all of the layers are fine-tuned to parameters that can be trained, global average pooling, a dense layer with a RELU activation function and an average dropout rate of 0.5, and DenseNet using softmax for classification of multiple classes, training, and assessment. The suggested pre-tuning and transfer learning approach is based on DL algorithms that employ a large number of hyperparameters for both training and optimization. It also helps in reducing total loss and improving accuracy.

Dataset Description

A diverse brain tumor classification dataset comprising 7,023 images sourced from Kaggle encompasses four distinct brain tumor classes: meningioma, pituitary, glioma, and no tumor. This dataset provides a comprehensive foundation for evaluating the performance of EfficientNetB0 in a multiclass classification framework. The dataset was evenly split among the two categories, with 80% of the photos passing to be trained and 20% moving for validation, to prevent class dominance [14]. The evaluation of the suggested model is also tested using several images. Eliminating photos that could have deceived the model during training is essential to our subset selection. There is no predetermined size for the collection of photographs. For this reason, all input images are automatically scaled to 224 x 224 dimensions, and all image samples are normalized using an automated scaling algorithm from Keras. There is a freely available dataset for photos on Kaggle that was utilized during this research. The Brain Tumor Foundation provided fully anonymized photographs for the challenge database, an amended version of the authorized reference Brats2015 brain tumor dataset. Neural networks use the popular activated function of the softmax at the output layer for multiclass classification tasks, such as brain tumor classification. It is feasible to acquire interpretable probability ratings for each class by employing softmax at the neural network's output layer for brain tumor classification. This makes it easier to diagnose and classify brain cancers based on MRI data.

Preprocessing

MRI data preparation entails several procedures. Data collection, picture reconstruction, noise reduction, artifact correction, and contrast and resolution improvement are only a few of the phases that these approaches cover data preprocessing techniques that are essential for improving picture quality by using edge detection and data augmentation preprocessing methods. Researchers and medical professionals may keep pushing the limits of MRI imaging by utilizing cutting-edge algorithms and techniques. They increased the variance in the data samples using approaches for data preparation and augmentation to lessen the inaccurate predictions of the suggested models. This will provide novel insights into the composition and operation of the human body and enhance healthcare delivery around the globe.

Various preprocessing techniques include the following.

Data Acquisition

Image quality and diagnostic accuracy may be greatly improved by adjusting data acquisition, noise, artifacts, and signal-to-noise ratio (SNR) parameters in accordance with the particular use in medicine and target tissue characteristics.

Noise Reduction Techniques

MRI pictures naturally contain noise, which can deteriorate image quality and lower diagnostic precision. To suppress noise while maintaining image details, a variety of noise reduction techniques are used, such as statistical approaches, temporal and spatial filtering, and parallel imaging methods like compressed sensing, GRAPPA (Generalization Autocalibrating partial In parallel Acquisition), and SENSE (SENSitivity Encoding).

Correction of Artifacts

MRI images can be distorted and diagnostic accuracy compromised by a variety of aberrations, such as artifacts caused by motion, sensitivity artifacts, and aliasing artifacts. To reduce these distortions and enhance image integrity, sophisticated approaches including susceptibility artifact correction methods, gradient distortion correction, and motion correction algorithms are employed.

Enhancement of Contrast and Improvement of Resolution

For improved visibility of anatomy and disease characteristics in MRI scans, image contrast and spatial resolution must be improved. The extraction of fine anatomical features and improved diagnostic sensitivity are made possible by contrast enhancement techniques including equalization of histograms, brightness normalization, and image fusion approaches, which are combined with high-resolution imaging procedures and sophisticated reconstruction algorithms.

EfficientNetB0

The Google Intelligence Team created the CNN model EfficientNet [15]. Upon analyzing network scaling, these researchers discovered that performance may be increased by adjusting network depth, breadth, and resolution. They expanded a network of neurons to build more DL models, which produce results that are far more accurate and efficient than the CNNs that were previously used, to generate a new model. Accurate and reliable large-scale visual recognition was achieved using EfficientNet B0. The CNN designs in this series are about twelve times smaller as well as six times quicker to infer than the most exemplary existing techniques, such as VGGNets, GoogleNet, Xception all [16], ResNets, and InceptionResNet. EfficientNet-B0 uses a composite scaling strategy to generate various neural network and convolution family models. There is a correlation between a network's layer count and depth. The number of filters in a convolutional layer determines how wide that layer is. The resolution is determined by the height and breadth of the supplied picture. The most recent version of the EfficientNet-B0 baseline model, which takes a 224 x 224 x 3 channel input picture, is shown in Fig. (**2**). To gather attributes across layers, this method employs several convolutional layers *via* a 3 × 3 responsive area and an evolving inverted bottleneck Conv.

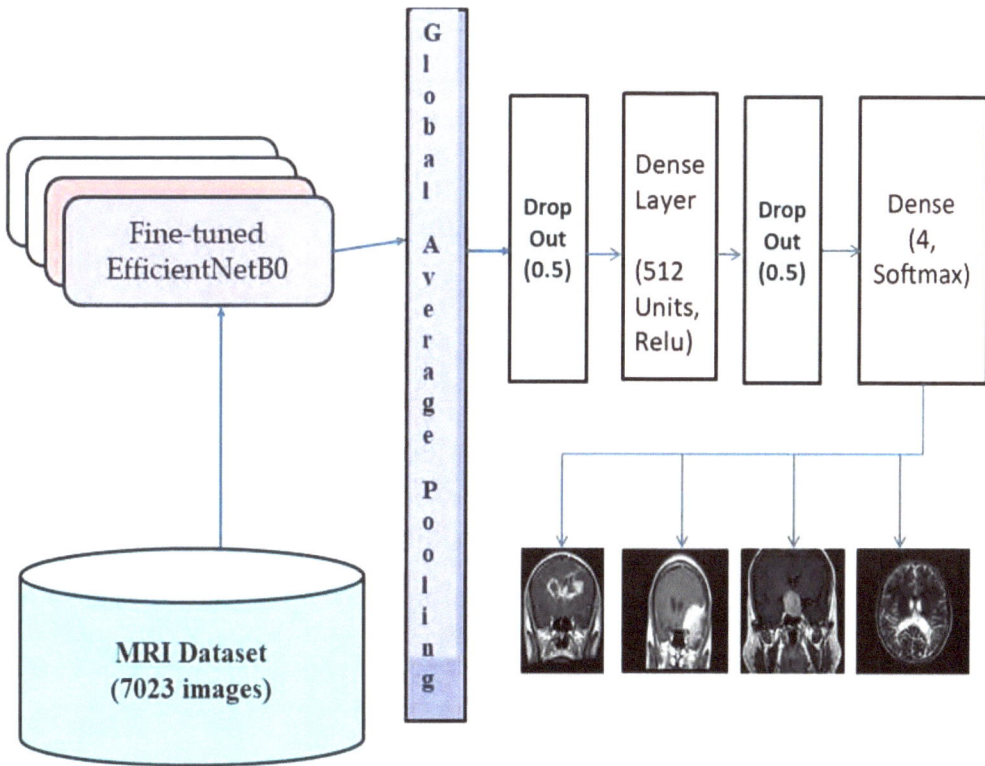

Fig. (2). Fine-tuned efficientnetb0 and proposed layers.

The authors suggest scaling the depth, breadth, and resolution with respect to §, as shown in equations (1–5).

$$\tilde{N} = \alpha \tag{1}$$

$$W = \text{ß}^{\S} \tag{2}$$

$$R = \gamma^\S \tag{3}$$

$$\text{s.t} \propto. \beta^2.\gamma^2 \approx 2, \tag{4}$$

$$\alpha >= 1, \beta >= 1, \gamma >= 1 \tag{5}$$

where Ñ, W, and R represent the network's depth, breadth, and resolution, respectively, and the grid-based hyperparameter tuning method was used to obtain the constant terms α, ß and γ. The entire model scaling resources are managed by the user-defined variable called the coefficient. Depending on the resources available, this method modifies the network's depth, breadth, and resolution to maximize accuracy and memory use. EffectiveNet-B0 outperformed other state-of-the-art models learned on the ImageNet dataset by adjusting every dimension using a predefined set of scaling coefficients, in contrast to other deep CNNs. Even using the transfer learning approach, EfficientNet established its usefulness outside of the ImageNet dataset and delivered excellent results. Developers and consumers may now take advantage of and offer enhanced ubiquitous connection equipped with DL capabilities in multiple platforms to satisfy a variety of purposes and the recent development of EfficientNet.

Proposed Layers

This study's primary goal is to utilize its EfficientNet-B0 commencing models with the updated final layers added by layer freezing through fine-tuning and training to handle the challenging issue of brain tumor identification and classification in MR images. The prepared EfficientNet-B0 model automatically retrieved the features from the photos after data improvement and augmentation were applied to images with the dimensions of 224 × 224 x 3. The rationale behind selecting EfficientNetB0 is centered on attaining maximum efficiency without sacrificing performance. Because of its innovative scaling technique, it is particularly well-suited for medical imaging tasks with limited resources and can be used in real-world applications where computing resources are a concern. The EfficientNetB0 architecture uses a scaling coefficient, which scales down the dimensions of the input image.

Fig. (2) shows the additional layers to the baseline architecture, EfficientNetB0's global average pooling layer is essential to feature collection and dimensionality reduction, which enhances the network's overall efficacy and efficiency for image classification tasks. To regularize the model, enhance generalization, decrease overfitting, improve robustness, and increase training efficiency, dropout layers that have a 0.5 dropout rate are added to EfficientNetB0. This results in a more effective and dependable deep learning algorithm for a variety of image classification tasks. In EfficientNetB0, the thick layer having 512 units and ReLU activation is essential for feature modification, irregular mapping process, dimensionality reduction, capacity management, and fine-tuning, which can enhance the model's effectiveness and efficiency across a variety of image-related activities. Lastly, it is possible to use the strength of deep learning to autonomously categorize MRI images of the brain into different tumor types, assisting in medical treatment and diagnosis planning. This is achieved by using EfficientNetB0 Neural networks that use the popular activated function the softmax at the output layer for multiclass classification tasks, such as brain tumor classification. It is feasible to acquire interpretable probability ratings for each class by employing softmax at the neural network's output layer for brain tumor classification. This makes it easier to diagnose and classify brain cancers based on MRI data.

Limitations

While EfficientNetB0 excels in efficiency

- It may face challenges in handling extremely large datasets with diverse variations.
- Its generic architecture may not capture specialized features inherent in complex medical images, potentially limiting its performance in certain scenarios.

Training

A systematic training procedure is used for EfficientNetB0 models, 80% of the total being used for training, and 20% for validation and testing. In order to maximize the framework for brain tumor classification, fine-tuning has been incorporated into the training process.

Evaluation Metrics

The model's performance is assessed using standard measures, such as recall, accuracy, precision, and F1 score. The models' capacity to categorize brain tumors into several categories is evaluated in-depth using these measures. Transparency, repeatability, and a solid basis for future studies in the field of brain tumor categorization are the goals we want to achieve by carefully outlining the technique. Sections that follow go into detail about our study's findings, interpretation, and original contributions, evaluating the performance of Efficient Net B0 and other advanced deep learning models.

Table **1** depicts the various accuracy scores of the EfficientNetB0 and other deep learning architectures. EfficienNetB0 demonstrates a remarkable accuracy score and F1 score in comparison to other cutting-edge models from earlier research.

Table 1. Comparing different Face detection methods.

Architecture Name	Recall%	F1-score%	Accuracy%	Precision%
VGG16 [1]	99.1	99.1	98.6	98.5
InceptionV3 [1]	97.6	96.4	97.5	97.7
Xception [1]	98.5	97.5	97.8	96.6
ResNet50 [1]	98.2	97.9	97.6	97.6
Pre-trained EfficientNetB0	**99.25**	**99.5**	**99.75**	**99.5**

Experimental setup

A machine with an Intel chipset G50-80 CPU with two cores, 12 Gigabytes of RAM, a 16 Gigabyte Graphics Processing Unit, and a 1TB hard drive is used to conduct the research. A Jupytor notebook has been used to aid with the experiment completed. The suggested method is implemented using Python and many popular libraries, including Scikit-learn, Keras, TensorFlow as tf, Seaborn as sb, Matplotlib as mpl, numpy as np, and Pandas as pd.

Metrics for Evaluating Performance

One popular technique for displaying the degree of accuracy with which a trained model can predict a given validation dataset is the confusion matrix (CM). In the CM, matched rows and columns represent the actual class and provide information about the classifications. On the other hand, the percentage of accurate and inaccurate predictions or classifications is displayed in the predicted values for every validation sample. True negatives show the number of accurately predicted negative samples as negative, while true positives show the number of effectively identified positive samples as positive. Predictions known as "false positives" occur when a picture is labeled as favorable when it is not. Negative results that seem positive are known as false negatives [16].

$$\text{Precision} = \frac{TP}{TP+FP} \qquad (6)$$

$$\text{Sensitivity} = \frac{TP}{TP+FN} \qquad (7)$$

$$\text{Specificity} = \frac{TN}{TN+FP} \qquad (8)$$

$$\text{Accuracy} = \frac{TN+FP}{TP+TN+FP+FN} \qquad (9)$$

$$\text{F1Score} = \frac{2(TP)}{2(TP+FP+FN)} \qquad (10)$$

Results and Analysis

This section covers the results of training and validating the proposed, improved EffectiveNet-B0 model. The model was trained utilizing MR images that were made available for free on Kaggle. To increase the quantity and caliber of this particular dataset, several cleaning techniques were applied. We trained our suggested model using a range of hyperparameters to enhance training. The CE loss function, the ReduceLROnPlateau callback uses a minimal learning rate of 10e-5, the Relu optimization algorithm with an initial rate of learning of 10e-3, and a batch size of 32 were used. A softmax classifier was the final one we decided to use. We used the Keras API along with the TensorFlow backend to train our improved EfficientNet architecture in the meantime. To train the proposed model, 20% of the information was utilized for validation and the remaining 80% for training. Fig. (**3a**) displays the instruction and validation outcomes. In Fig. (**3b**), the loss estimates with training phases are displayed. The recommended model's graph demonstrates that the given hyperparameters, both the training and validating datasets' accuracy increased gradually over a shorter period before stabilizing.

Epochs *vs.* Training and Validation Accuracy/Loss

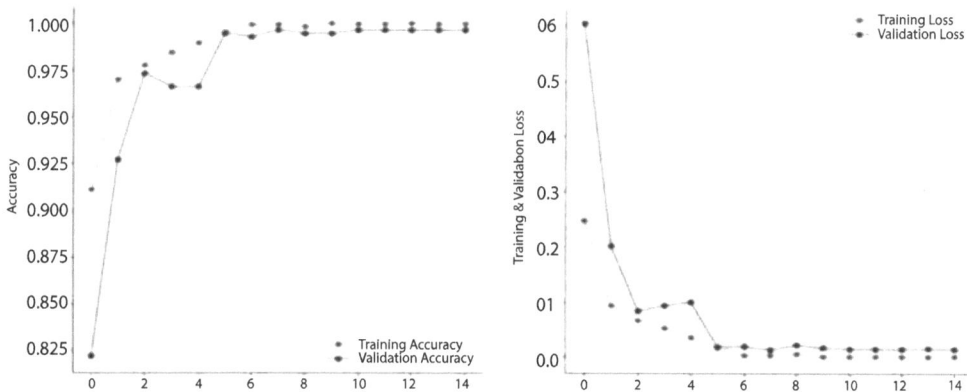

Fig. (3). (a): Training and validation accuracy Fig. (**3b**) Training and validation loss.

Heatmap of the Confusion Matrix

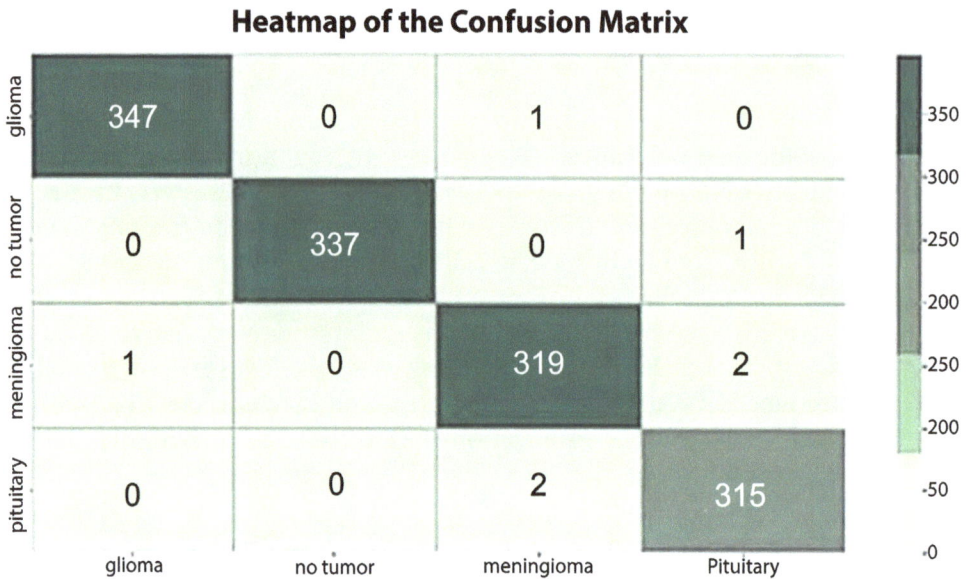

Fig. (4). The Confusion Matrix of EfficientNetB0.

According to the findings, EfficientNetB0 achieves 99.75% accuracy in brain tumor classification, outperforming ResNet50, VGG16, InceptionV3, and Xception. The variance in results highlights how crucial it is to choose the right deep-learning architecture.

The precise outcomes of EfficientNetB0 can be attributed to its effective architecture, scalability, and excellent transfer learning (Fig. **4**).

CONCLUSION AND FUTURE WORK

Our research demonstrates how well the Efficient-NetB0 model predicts brain cancers employing the MRI brain tumor picture dataset. At 99.75% accuracy, the model EffiecientNetB0 beats the current neural network frameworks in the multiclass classification of brain tumors. This finding opens up several fascinating possibilities for future brain tumor classification. It is worth looking at how EfficientNetB0 may be used in everyday scenarios for routine brain tumor identification and treatment scheduling. It is feasible to create a deep learning framework that is effective at differentiating between brain tumor stages.

REFERENCES

[1]   S.K. Zhou, H. Greenspan, and D. Shen, *Deep learning for medical image analysis.* Academic Press, 2023.

[2]   R. Fram, K.M. Fram, S. Saleh, N. Muhidat, F. Fram, Z. Khouri, B. Tarawneh, and N. Tarawneh,

"Cervical cancer screening in Jordan; a review of the past and an outlook to the future – facts and figures", *Przegl. Menopauz.,* vol. 22, no. 1, pp. 24-29, 2023.
[http://dx.doi.org/10.5114/pm.2023.126345]

[3]   A. Raza, H. Ayub, J. Khan, I. Ahmad, A. Salama, Y. Daradkeh, D. Javeed, A. Ur Rehman, and H. Hamam, *A hybrid deep learning-based approach for brain tumor classification. electronics 2022, 11, 1146,* 2022.

[4]   W. Ayadi, W. Elhamzi, I. Charfi, and M. Atri, "Deep cnn for brain tumor classification", *Neural Process. Lett.,* vol. 53, no. 1, pp. 671-700, 2021.
[http://dx.doi.org/10.1007/s11063-020-10398-2]

[5]   H. A. Shah, F. Saeed, S. Yun, J.-H. Park, A. Paul, and J.-M. Kang, *A robust approach for brain tumor detection in magnetic resonance images using finetuned efficientnet,* 2022.
[http://dx.doi.org/10.1109/ACCESS.2022.3184113]

[6]   H.J. Weerts, A.C. Mueller, and J. Vanschoren, "Importance of tun-ing hyperparameters of machine learning algorithms", arXiv:2007.07588v1, 2020.

[7]   V.R.K. Sajja, and H.K. Kalluri, *Classification of brain tumors using convolutional neural network over various svm methods.,* 2020.
[http://dx.doi.org/10.18280/isi.250412]

[8]   J.S. Paul, A.J. Plassard, B.A. Landman, and D. Fabbri, *"Deep learning for brain tumor classification,"* in *Medical Imaging 2017: Biomedical Applications in Molecular, Structural, and Functional Imaging.* vol. Vol. 10137. SPIE, 2017, pp. 253-268.

[9]   A. Verma, and V. P. Singh, *Design, analysis and implementation of efficient deep learning frameworks for brain tumor classification,* 2022.
[http://dx.doi.org/10.1007/s11042-022-13545-0]

[10] S. Gautam, S. Ahlawat, and P. Mittal, "Binary and multi-class classifi-cation of brain tumors using mri images", *International Journal of Experimental Research and Review,* vol. 29, pp. 1-9, 2022.
[http://dx.doi.org/10.52756/ijerr.2022.v29.001]

[11] M. Celik, and O. Inik, "Development of hybrid models based on deep learning and optimized machine learning algorithms for brain tumor Multi-Classification", *Expert Syst. Appl.,* vol. 238, p. 122159, 2024.
[http://dx.doi.org/10.1016/j.eswa.2023.122159]

[12] F. Zulfiqar, U. Ijaz Bajwa, and Y. Mehmood, "Multi-class classification of brain tumor types from MR images using EfficientNets", *Biomed. Signal Process. Control,* vol. 84, p. 104777, 2023.
[http://dx.doi.org/10.1016/j.bspc.2023.104777]

[13] M. Ofori, *Transfer-learned pruned deep convolutional neural networks for efficient plant classification in resource-constrained environments,* 2021.

[14] Q. Wei, and R.L. Dunbrack Jr, "The role of balanced training and testing data sets for binary classifiers in bioinformatics", *PLoS One,* vol. 8, no. 7, p. e67863, 2013.
[http://dx.doi.org/10.1371/journal.pone.0067863] [PMID: 23874456]

[15] K. Muhammad, S. Khan, J.D. Ser, and V.H.C. Albuquerque, "Deep learning for multigrade brain tumor classification in smart healthcare systems: A prospective survey", *IEEE Trans. Neural Netw. Learn. Syst.,* vol. 32, no. 2, pp. 507-522, 2021.
[http://dx.doi.org/10.1109/TNNLS.2020.2995800] [PMID: 32603291]

[16] C. Szegedy, S. Ioffe, V. Vanhoucke, and A. Alemi, "Inception-v4, inception-resnet and the impact of residual connections on learning", *Proc. Conf. AAAI Artif. Intell.,* vol. 31, no. 1, 2017.
[http://dx.doi.org/10.1609/aaai.v31i1.11231]

SUBJECT INDEX

A

Adaptive 48, 49, 54, 55, 58, 60, 62, 92, 122, 123
   fusion strategies, developing 92
   neuro-fuzzy inference system (ANFIS) 48, 49, 54, 55, 58, 60, 62
   tetrolet transform 122
   thresholding 123
Aging 16, 49, 50, 63
   accelerated thermal 49
   effects, mitigating 49
   process 50
Agricultural drones 188
AHP flow 176
AI 12, 14, 15, 16, 93, 193
   -based systems 93
   -mechatronics integration 12, 14, 15
   -mechatronics systems 16
   /ML-powered drone automation 193
AI-based human detection 92, 93
   systems 92
   technology 93
AI-powered 15, 38, 44, 193
   drone technology 193
   mechatronic devices 15
   risk assessment tools 38
   technology 44
Algorithms 5, 8, 9, 16, 19, 25, 32, 37, 42, 77, 84, 94, 101, 102, 115, 190, 219
   automated scaling 219
   machine-learning 9, 84
   motion-based 94
ANFIS method 62
Anomaly detection techniques 38
Anti-drone system 191
Artifacts 220
   aliasing 220
   sensitivity 220
Artificial 5, 13, 15, 39, 48, 54, 57, 58, 62, 63, 190, 193, 216
   general intelligence (AGI) 5

intelligence methods 39
intelligence systems 13, 15
neural network (ANN) 5, 48, 54, 57, 58, 62, 63, 190, 193, 216
Automated 188, 217
   external defibrillators (AEDs) 188
   techniques 217
Automation, industrial 6, 7, 17, 115
Automobiles 2, 32
   autonomous 32
Automotive industry 116
Autonomous vehicle development 183

B

Bayesian rough decision tree (BRDT) 103, 106
Brain cancers 216, 219, 223, 226
Building power systems 152
Bulk-generating systems 144
Business practices 79

C

Cardiovascular ailments 35
Chemical 49, 51, 54
   processes 49
   properties 51, 54
Cloud computing 197
Cluster 194
   head election 194
   management process 194
Clustering 38, 99, 124, 128, 194
   algorithms 124, 128
   -based network topology construction 194
   density-based 128
   methods 124
   techniques 124
CNN 32, 220
   architecture 32
   designs 220
Cognitive mechatronics 18, 19, 20

www.ingramcontent.com/pod-product-compliance
Lightning Source LLC
Chambersburg PA
CBHW050826220326
41598CB00006B/318